Reading
the Book of Jeremiah

Reading
the Book of Jeremiah
A Search for Coherence

Edited by

MARTIN KESSLER

EISENBRAUNS
WINONA LAKE, INDIANA
2004

Library of Congress Cataloging-in-Publication Data

Reading the book of Jeremiah : a search for coherence / edited by
  Martin Kessler.
      p.   cm.
Includes bibliographical references and index.
ISBN 1-57506-098-1 (hardback : alk. paper)
    1. Bible. O.T. Jeremiah—Criticism, interpretation, etc.   I. Kessler,
Martin, 1927–
BS1525.52.R43   2004
224′.206—dc22

                                                    2004017854

Contents

Thus says the LORD:
Let not the wise man glory in his wisdom,
let not the mighty man glory in his might,
let not the rich man glory in his riches.
But let him who glories
glory in this:
that he understands and knows me
that I am the LORD who practices
steadfast love, justice, and righteousness
in the earth;
for in these things I delight,
says the LORD.

—Jeremiah 9:23–24 (RSV)

Preface

Ferment is the correct word by which to characterize current Jeremiah studies, a deep and broad stirring that relies on previous scholarship but that seeks to move beyond that scholarship in bold and new ways. This collection of fine essays not only reflects that ferment but in important ways contributes to it and advances the discussion.

Most broadly, the current discussion seeks to move beyond the historical-critical categories of Sigmund Mowinckel and Bernhard Duhm and the classic formulation of three sources, A, B, and C. In Jeremiah as in other parts of biblical scholarship, the new questions concern the inadequacy of historical-critical readings of a positivistic kind and the prospect of synchronic readings, either through ideological analysis that seeks to show that ideology shapes the book, or through canonical readings that find a large theological intentionality to the whole of the book. It turns out, perforce, that ideological and canonical readings are closely twinned in their judgment about the literature.

This present collection, which includes both new voices and some of the established major players in the discussion, merits important attention. While the collection is rich and varied, the following accents in particular seem important to me:

• In ideological criticism and canonical reading, there is a great push beyond the "person" (persona?) of the prophet to the claims of the "book." While this is likely a move that will continue to be primary, it is interesting and suggestive that the "person" of the prophet still haunts the discussion. Indeed, it is not likely that scholarship will have done with the "person" for the sake of the "book," as has been widely proposed.

• The distinction between prose and poetry is an important one, and the linkage between them is more or less unsettled. It does seem apparent at the present time that the prose material with a Deuteronomic accent is a powerful shaping force for the final form of the text. This recognition means that the chapters that might seem ponderous and heavy-handed are to be taken with greater seriousness for our reading of the whole of the book.

• The pivotal role of chap. 25 and its drastic move toward apocalyptic discourse becomes increasingly evident. This development in the literature (handled differently in the LXX but with no less significance) may indicate the extremity to which the shapers of the final form were willing to go in order to have the "book" be a massive statement of hope.

• The cruciality of the "pro-Babylonian" material is handled suggestively in this collection, making clear that the "pro-Babylonian" accent is provisional and theological and not merely pragmatic and calculated. Thus the twinning of Nebuchadnezzar and YHWH as agents who pursue a common policy is a transitory twinning that finally must yield to the singular claims of YHWH, who relies upon and seeks no alliance among the rulers of this age. That is, chaps. 51–52 with the defeat of Babylon must be reckoned not as an addendum but as integral to the intent and structure of the final form.

As one reflects upon these several themes, it becomes evident that new ways of doing rhetorical and canonical analysis inescapably spin off toward theological interpretation, a linkage that was never possible with the questions of positivistic history. Martin Kessler has performed an uncommon service to us by gathering this collection, and we shall remain greatly in his debt.

Walter Brueggemann
Columbia Theological Seminary

Editor's Introduction

This book was written for those who do not claim to be biblical experts but who may appreciate some guidance as they read the book of Jeremiah. Though composed by a group of biblical scholars who are all highly knowledgeable in Jeremiah studies, this work is primarily intended for students and nonspecialists. Its format may betray this by the virtual absence of footnotes and by the concise bibliography, which is limited to English titles. Technical expressions or Hebrew words have been kept to a bare minimum and have usually been explained immediately.

However, these essays do not represent some kind of watered-down scholarship or popularizing venture. They are intended to be "state of the art," with an identifiable methodological thrust; these articles demonstrate a sustained search for literary coherence in the book of Jeremiah. There are good reasons for choosing Jeremiah. This book, the longest in the prophetic collection, offers more information about the nature of the prophetic office than any other. Moreover, the book spans a most critical era of Judah's history: the time leading up to the ruin of Jerusalem and its temple and the subsequent Babylonian exile.

The growing interest in the prophets of the Old Testament has also affected the study of the book of Jeremiah. What is this book, which takes us to great heights as well as abysmal depths, but that appears so difficult to grasp in its confusing arrangement—what is this book really trying to do? The authors have grappled intensively with this fundamental question. Their grappling has given us a mosaic of views, offering both variety and unity of endeavor. Some of the articles here in print deal with the book as a whole; others focus on a segment of the book, but even they have a broader literary context in view, in fact, the entire canonical book.

A further word needs to be said about the method that inspires these studies. For a century and more, Jeremiah scholarship has been inordinately concerned with the search for the "historical Jeremiah" and what exactly this prophet might have written himself. The result was that the text was evaluated for its reputed historical merit, which necessitated that the "genuine" and the "spurious" words, considered to be rather badly mixed in this book, needed to be distinguished. Such a procedure left the common reader understandably baffled and wondering whether biblical scholars could be of any help in their attempts to interpret the text.

What if we would provisionally set aside the common assumption that this book is fairly characterized as "mass confusion" and instead hope that a diligent "close reading" might actually turn up the contours of an overall plan and a theology that keeps the canonical book together, so that those who listen carefully will hear its message, perhaps in bits and pieces or in its totality? This is essentially what this book tries to accomplish.

The writers of this collection have, each in his own way, taken up the challenge of making sense of the text they have chosen to study. The approach is therefore fundamentally literary, for the simple reason that the book of Jeremiah is not so much a historical source in its intention as it is a literary work. However, while dressed in literary garments, its heart and spirit is theological. This turn is important and deliberate. There is minimal interest here in mining or "excavating" this literature for historical nuggets or in discovering what might lie behind the text. However, when the text deals with theological ramifications, these studies are not fearful of identifying and describing them.

This does not mean that the voice heard in the book of Jeremiah is singular. Professor Carroll's essay suggests that there are a variety of "voices" to be heard in the text. But, overall, the writers of these essays have also tried to show that, in spite of paradoxes created by multiple voices, the work demonstrates a unity of purpose and coherence that should be taken seriously. This conclusion could not have been arrived at if we did not take all of the book into account—including chaps. 50 and 51, which have all too often been ignored. In fact, these two chapters receive major attention, in the articles by Smelik, Amesz, Brueggemann, and Kessler.

Readers will discover that this work is both innovative and traditional, containing both "ferment" (in Brueggemann's words) and illumination. It is assumed that the meaning is to be found in the text itself and not in novel ideologies, no matter how popular they may be at present. Because Jeremiah is an important book that is accepted as Holy Scripture by two significant faith communities, when they open this book to read, these communities listen for what it may say and expect to hear its message. This message was originally intended for ancient Israel and particularly for the people of Judah living at the time of the exile. But as long as the Bible is honored as divine word by faith communities and remains a best seller, in the Western world at any rate, there still seem to be many readers who are interested in hearing its message.

Here we touch upon the oral aspect of the biblical literature. Martin Buber expressed something crucial about reading the Bible by saying that our concern is not a "book" but a "voice." The New Testament puts it even stronger because it affirms through Paul the Apostle that "the letter kills, but the spirit makes alive" (2 Cor 3:6). In the book of Jeremiah it is prophesied that God will put his Torah within his people, "and I will write it upon their hearts" (Jer 31:31).

This most likely should be heard as a word for a future age. Meanwhile, we need to cope with a cacophony of voices and interpretations. Will we ever reach the "definitive meaning"? We will not, of course, for this is literature for pilgrims, who, whatever critics and scholars may say, keep turning to this book so that they may hear a voice, which is always heard in the context of their lives and therefore not always perceived alike at different times and in different places.

Many typical critical questions are deliberately sidestepped in this book. Perhaps enough adrenaline has been used in sustained attempts to unravel the type of critical questions that never seem to find answers. Since authorship bears minimal relationship to exegesis, that subject is left on the backburner. The discussions on the *persona* of the prophet may well offer us a reasonable way out of that question.

We would rather proceed with more certainty (namely, with the text we have!) and with less speculation. Thus, we are more concerned with the form that the last "editing" or "writing" of the book has assumed. The final editors or authors have put their (kerygmatic) stamp on the book as a whole. A prominent member of the Jewish community has gone so far as to claim that the "final redactor" [R] is *Rabbenu*, that is "our teacher." Christians might be a bit more cautious, in part because they read this book (and all of the Old Testament) in the light of the New Testament. Nevertheless, the claim at least takes the final form of the text as seriously as it merits being taken.

The genesis of this book of essays was a conversation with Prof. Seitz (while he was still at Yale University) about the possibility of developing such a volume as this. The international nature of this work was not intentional but "just happened." We regard it as a bonus. It necessitated that several essays be translated from Dutch by the editor (van der Wal, Dubbink, Amesz, Smelik, Becking, and Mazurel). Three essays were published elsewhere and are here used by the kind permission of the respective copyright holders. Smelik's article "The Function of Jeremiah 50 and 51" was first published in *Nederlands Theologisch Tijdschrift*

41 (1987) in Dutch; the article by Brueggemann was adapted from *Journal of Biblical Literature* 110 (1991); and Stulman's article was first published in *Troubling Jeremiah* (Sheffield: Sheffield Academic Press, 1999).

The first seven essays deal with the book of Jeremiah as a whole. The other essays focus on various segments of the book. The final essay, on the employment of Jeremian texts in the New Testament, serves to illustrate the procedures followed in the New Testament, when the Old Testament is quoted.

The divine name is here written YHWH, the tetragrammaton ("four letters"), which represents the sacred, unpronounced name of the God of Israel, in deference to those who are offended by the use of *Yahweh*.

Since the thirteen authors of these articles submitted their work to be published in this book, one of us, Prof. Robert Carroll of Glasgow, was taken from us, on May 12, 2000. We miss him, his friendship, and his superb scholarship. R.I.P.

The editor is grateful for the admirable partnership of each of the authors, for their enthusiasm for the project, and to Eisenbrauns for accepting this book for publication. We hope and pray that all readers will draw benefit from our work.

M.K.

An Approach to the Book of Jeremiah

KLAAS A. D. SMELIK

Protestant Theological Faculty, Brussels

The story line of a book like Genesis is not difficult to follow. After chapter 11, it may be read as a family narrative. The accessibility of the book is related to its division into generations (*toledot*), for this is how Genesis is structured. The reader is led from generation to generation in a more or less chronological sequence.

The book of Jeremiah is very different, however. After the first chapter, where Jeremiah's prophecies are dated and his call is described, the reader is overwhelmed by a barrage of texts: prophecy follows prophecy, prose alternates with poetry. There is no chronological sequence; the same events are dealt with in different places in the book. For example, the capture of Jerusalem is described in chap. 39, but also in chap. 52. In chap. 7 we learn of the contents of a speech that Jeremiah does not give until chap. 26. Dates are sometimes out of place, as in 27:1, although the problem is often disposed of in translations. In short, the book seems to be in complete chaos.

Supporter of the Pro-Babylon Party?

Jeremiah speaks about Nebuchadnezzar, the Babylonian king, as the servant of the Lord to whom obedience is due. The reader may well conclude that the prophet supported the pro-Babylonian faction in Judah. To clarify: during the time of Jeremiah, a fierce battle raged between those who strongly relied on support from Egypt to withstand Babylon's onslaught and those who opposed a covenant with Egypt and who would rather have befriended Babylon, Egypt's enemy. The pro-Egyptian party was apparently more influential than the pro-Babylonian party: twice Judah had rebelled against Babylon, although both times with fatal results for the land. Thus, Jeremiah appears to have belonged to the unpopular pro-Babylon party.

Translated from Dutch by the editor.

Thus, it does not appear as a surprise when we read in chap. 27 how Jeremiah proclaimed during the fourth year of King Zedekiah (594/3 B.C.E.) that the king of Babylon must be served, since YHWH himself had granted world dominion to Nebuchadnezzar. Indeed, rebellion against Babylon would in fact be rebellion against God. How remarkable, therefore, to read at the end of chap. 51 that, in that same year, Jeremiah commissioned a trustee to curse Babylon by a symbolic act, so that it would be destroyed forever. On whose side was Jeremiah, exactly?

One might easily continue detailing surprises and inconsistencies in the book of Jeremiah, but in spite of this apparent chaos, the reader needs to be encouraged to take up this fascinating book. Two keys will be offered to make the book more accessible.

The First Key

The first key is given by the authors of the book of Jeremiah themselves in chap. 36, which is dated in the fourth year of Jehoiakim (605 B.C.E.). This was an important year in the history of the ancient Near East, the year in which Nebuchadnezzar defeated the Egyptian Pharaoh Necho II near Carchemish (cf. 46:2). By this conquest Nebuchadnezzar gained dominion over the entire Near East as far as the borders of Egypt. Even the pro-Egyptian Judahite King Jehoiakim had to subject himself to Nebuchadnezzar.

In that ominous year, Jeremiah was commanded by YHWH to write down all of his prophecies, in the hope that the people of Judah might repent when they heard the word of God. All the words that YHWH spoke to him, the prophet dictated to Baruch, the scribe. Baruch was then commissioned to read this scroll aloud in the temple. He did so and read it twice more in the royal palace, all on the same day. But it was all in vain, for King Jehoiakim personally destroyed the book and proved himself unwilling to give up his evil ways. He even wanted to imprison Jeremiah and Baruch, but as the author declared in v. 26, God kept them hidden.

The scroll was burned by the king, but YHWH once more commanded Jeremiah to dictate his prophecies to Baruch, to be written on another scroll. Again, Jeremiah complied, and Baruch wrote on a new scroll all the words that were originally in the document that Jehoiakim had burned. The chapter concludes with the comment that "additional words" were added to the scroll (v. 32): words that had not been spoken before 605 B.C.E.

The Original Scroll

In this manner the authors of the book of Jeremiah have indicated how they understood the origin of the collection of texts concerning Jeremiah, or rather, how they wished the reader to imagine the course of events. In this way they have provided later investigators with an occasion to speculate about what might have been written in the original scroll. First, one might attempt to reconstruct the size of the scroll. Since Baruch read it three times in one day, as suggested in chap. 36, with the necessary delays between each reading, the scroll could not have been extensive. Caution is demanded here, however; was it indeed the intention of the authors to give a historical account of the event, by definition, as accurately as possible? Or were they led by their feeling for the dramatic?

Even more interesting are the comments in chap. 36 concerning the contents of the scroll. Verse 2 speaks about

> all the words
> that I have spoken to you
> against Israel and Judah and all the nations
> from the day I spoke to you,
> from the days of Josiah
> until today.

The scroll consisted, therefore, not only of prophecies against Judah but also of prophecies against the former Northern Kingdom of Israel, which was destroyed ca. 720 B.C.E., as well as prophecies against foreign nations. Indeed, examples of all three kinds of prophecies are found in the present book of Jeremiah. The dating "from the days of Josiah" directs the reader to the second verse of the book, where we read that the word of YHWH came to Jeremiah "in the days of Josiah, the son of Amon, king of Judah, in the thirteenth year of his kingship" (1:2). Therefore, the scroll also contained earlier prophecies of Jeremiah, from the time prior to Jehoiakim.

In v. 7 we read:

> for great is the anger and wrath
> that the LORD has pronounced against this people.

Clearly these prophecies deal with judgment, by means of which YHWH revealed to what extent his people had excited his wrath by their evil works. Because the possibilty of repentance by the people is also mentioned, preaching of judgment must have been accompanied by calls to repentance, such as we regularly meet in the book of Jeremiah.

The most concrete example is found in 36:29, in which it is suggested that the following verse must have been in the scroll:

> Coming, yes coming, will be the king of Babylon
> and he will destroy this land,
> and will cut off from it man and beast.

Something remarkable is happening here. This is clearly a prophecy in accordance with the general tenor of Jeremiah's preaching, but this verse as such is not found elsewhere in the book of Jeremiah. The scroll of chap. 36 was therefore clearly not copied in its entirety in the final book of Jeremiah, or the authors were less careful in their report than one might think, based on the many names and eyewitnesses that they mention.

In addition we note that two genres of texts that occur frequently in the present book of Jeremiah are not mentioned at all in the report about the scroll. They are the biographical narratives in which events in the life of the prophet are detailed (e.g., Jer 38:1–13) and the so-called "Confessions," poetic parts in which Jeremiah complains about his sad fate and the enmity of his opponents (see 20:7–18; resp. 18:19–23). Were these lacking in the first scroll?

Reconstruction of the History of the Origin

Various hypotheses have attempted to answer the question of how the different biblical books originated. In the case of Jeremiah, chap. 36 has played an important role. One assumes that there must have been an original writing that formed the basis of the present book: the original scroll (*Urrolle*). This would be the document that Baruch read to King Jehoiakim and that later was supplemented.

This original scroll, supplemented by other authentic prophecies and the Confessions of Jeremiah, is called, following the Scandinavian scholar Mowinckel, "source A." A second source ("B") contained stories about Jeremiah that were supposed to go back to an eyewitness report of Jeremiah's life, possibly written by Baruch. Thirdly, an assumed redactional layer is labeled "C." This redaction was to have combined the original scroll with Baruch's memories, then was supplemented by a large number of further additions, mainly speeches put in the mouth of Jeremiah, not spoken verbatim by the prophet but reflecting the views of the redactors. Finally, at a still later stage, certain elements were added to the book of Jeremiah, such as chap. 52 (likely to have been copied from Kings) and the long judgment prophecy against Babylon (chaps. 50 and 51).

One might ask why the existence of a separate source C has been posited. For example, why is it supposed that chap. 6 is from Jeremiah's hand, while chap. 7 is not? Scholars have pointed to the differences in style between these chapters. Moreover, there is a close relationship between concepts that we find in the book of Deuteronomy, in the so-called Deuteronomistic History (Joshua–Kings), and in certain parts of the book of Jeremiah. This relationship is explained as follows: redactors who worked in the spirit of Deuteronomy not only concerned themselves with the books of Joshua–Kings but also edited and supplemented the text of the book of Jeremiah so that the prophet Jeremiah posthumously proclaimed their "deuteronomistic" ideas. The C source may also be colored by such Deuteronomistic editing.

Another Approach

We will not attempt to evaluate the correctness of the common hypothesis sketched above, though we will add a few notes. First, we might question whether the book of Jeremiah was indeed subjected to a Deuteronomistic redaction. Possibly, the authors of the book of Jeremiah inspired the Deuteronomistic History, instead of the other way around. In other words, the authors of Jeremiah may have been trendsetters instead of trendfollowers.

In addition, one might ask whether it is meaningful to distinguish between the "authentic" passages of Jeremiah (source A) and the "nonauthentic" (source C), whereby greater weight is given to the "genuine" prophecies of Jeremiah than to the "spurious." Are we ultimately concerned with the historical prophet or with the prophetic book? We must not forget that it was not the historical Jeremiah who was canonized but the biblical book named after him. Moreover, how can we determine with certainty what is "authentic" and what is not, as long as we do not have any material other than the biblical book itself?

Similarly, one might ask whether the enormous attention scholarship has paid to the differences between the Hebrew (Masoretic) text and the Old Greek translation of the book of Jeremiah, the Septuagint (which is approximately one-eighth shorter), is meaningful. Might we not simply accept the fact that we know the book of Jeremiah in two forms, each of which demands a separate exegesis, instead of searching for an "original text" (*Urtext*), which may never have existed?

Additionally, we may well question whether we are doing justice to the intention of the biblical writers when we read their accounts about Jeremiah as eyewitness accounts. Closer analysis of the chapters assigned to source B suggests that the events reported in these texts may not always have happened as described. For example, in chap. 26, which narrates a reaction to a prophecy of Jeremiah, a comparison is made with the reaction to the preaching of two other Judahite prophets. When this narrative is read as a kind of newspaper report, we meet with unsolvable logical and historical problems. However, if we interpret the chapter as the author's conscious composition, wherein everything is ordered so that the theological message is optimally communicated, such problems largely disappear.

It seems legitimate therefore to approach the problem of the origin of the book of Jeremiah in another manner, one that is more consistent with the final verse of chap. 36, which says that many similar words were added to the text of the scroll. We may then suppose that the biblical writers have brought together and joined texts of varying provenance. Texts that originated from different authors were put in order in a large unit by final editors because of their mutual relationship. This resulted in two versions circulating separately at an early stage— namely, the version used by the Septuagint translators, and the other, on which the MT is based. The ultimate goal of these biblical writers was to communicate a theological message that was based on the career of a historical prophet named Jeremiah. It was not their intention to write a historically accurate biography of this prophet (it may be questioned whether something like that even existed at that time), and they therefore did not hesitate to include in their book other texts under his name if they deemed this to serve their goal, namely, to call the readers to repair their broken relationship with YHWH.

If one reads the book in this manner, the difference between putative authentic and nonauthentic passages and the need for solving unsolvable historical problems disappears, and the dispute whether the Septuagint is more original than the MT becomes irrelevant. Instead, each text retains its own value within the whole, while the freedom of the narrators to tell their story as suited them best is recognized. Thus, contradictions and doublets may become meaningful. They may be explained as the technique of biblical writers to clarify complex ideas to their readers. We shall return to this point as we turn now to the second key to the book of Jeremiah.

The Second Key

Generally, the book of Jeremiah may be divided into five parts:

1. 1–25   mostly prophecies of judgment
2. 26–35   both prophecies of judgment and of deliverance
3. 36–45   narratives of Jeremiah's sufferings
4. 46–51   prophecies against the nations
5. 52   general conclusion.

This is a general division; it would be easy for the reader to point to passages that do not fit well in this division.

Yet, this division may be useful because it points to the key position of a number of chapters within the entire book. We are referring to chaps. 1, 25, 26, 36, 46, and 50–51. The position of these chapters is the second key that I wish to offer to the reader. In the cited chapters we can make a division between four essential parts: chaps. 1, 25, 36, and 50–51, and in addition: chaps. 26 and 46. Chapter 26, which describes negative reactions to YHWH's word in the time of King Jehoiakim, forms the prelude to chap. 36, discussed above, in which the same king destroys Jeremiah's scroll. Chapter 46 is a prophecy against Egypt, Babylon's opponent, and therefore serves as a counterweight to chaps. 50 and 51 (prophecies against Babylon). The name of the Babylonian king Nebuchadrezzar (an alternate spelling of Nebuchadnezzar in the book of Jeremiah) occurs no less than three times in this prophecy against Egypt. We shall, however, concentrate on chaps. 1, 25, and 50–51, since they form the central axis around which the book of Jeremiah revolves.

Jeremiah's Call

The first dating of the word of YHWH that came to Jeremiah is found in chap. 1. It is a conspicuous fact that the words are dated, not the prophet. This fact underscores my previous remark that the book of Jeremiah is concerned with the word of God, not with the biography of his servant.

The dating is from the thirteenth year of King Josiah to the eleventh year of his son Zedekiah (the exile of Jerusalem was in the fifth month of this year). Indeed, the book of Jeremiah ends (52:28–30) with the summation of the total number of exiles, though earlier in the book mention is made of events that took place after the exile in the fifth month of Zedekiah's eleventh year (chaps. 40–44). The very last part of Jeremiah (52:31–34) concerning the favoring of Jehoiachin was, in my opinion, borrowed from the book of Kings at a later stage and added to the book of Jeremiah. This means that the book originally ended with 52:30. Thus, an inclusio was formed by the Babylonian exile mentioned both at the beginning and at the end of the book, emphasizing the central place of the deportations of Judahites in the book.

After the dating of Jeremiah's words in 1:1–3, his call as prophet is described. An important sentence in this report is v. 10, in which YHWH says:

> See, today I appoint you
> over nations and kingdoms,
> to pluck up and to pull down,
> to destroy and to overthrow,
> to build and to plant.

Thus, the task of the prophet is not limited to Judah; his authority extends also to foreign nations. Viewed thus, it is fitting that the book of Jeremiah ends in the Masoretic Text with a series of prophecies against these nations (leaving chap. 52 out of the account).

In the Septuagint we find these prophecies in the middle of the book, connected with chap. 25, the chapter that we shall discuss below, in which God's judgment of the nations is central. It is understandable that some scribes and translators of the biblical text in antiquity chose to place the prophecies against the nations in chap. 25, which deals with God's judgment against the nations. The Masoretic placement of the judgment prophecies (at the back of the book) is preferable, however, since it provides a connecting thread that runs through the entire book—with the judgment against the nations in the beginning, in the middle, and at the end. After all, the preaching in the book of Jeremiah relates to all peoples of the earth, not only to the people of Judah (chap. 1). Accordingly, the book of Jeremiah presents the God of Israel as the Creator and Governor of the whole world (cf. chap. 27).

The sequence of the acts that the prophet will perform, according to 1:10, is also noteworthy; first, four verbs of destruction, then two verbs of building. Thus, the book first deals with the destruction of Jerusalem, thereafter with the construction of a new community of exiles in Babylon, and later still resettlement in the land of Israel. However, some prophecies against the nations also speak of the turn of their fate for good after they have suffered judgment. On the other hand, in the case of Babylon a reverse sequence appears: Babylonian world dominion is followed by the ruin of Babylon and its gods. This scenario as it relates to Babylon is attested in the book of Jeremiah as the second main part of the axis that runs through the book, to wit, chap. 25.

The Image of the Cup

Chapter 25, in the middle of the book of Jeremiah, is the central axis around which the entire book revolves. Two lines converge here: the prophecies of judgment against Judah and the oracles against foreign nations. The reader is first reminded of Jeremiah's proclamation as directed against Judah and Jerusalem; subsequently, the prophet announces Babylon's fate. From chap. 25 on, Nebuchadnezzar and Babylon play an important role in the book. The background of that role is expounded particularly in chaps. 27–29.

Chapter 25 is divided into five parts. The first part (25:1–7) contains a summary of Jeremiah's prophetic career up to this point in the book, and refers, by the dating in v. 3, back to the first chapter. Because the Judahites had not listened to Jeremiah, an announcement of judgment follows (25:8–11a). This judgment would be executed by the Babylonian king Nebuchadrezzar, here notably indicated with the biblical honorary title "servant of YHWH." After 70 years there would be a reversal, however, for Babylon must pay for its unrighteousness (25:11b–14). Then follows a long part about the drinking of the cup of God's wrath (25:15–29), after which the chapter is closed by a rather general judgment oracle against the nations (25:30–38).

Entirely in agreement with Jeremiah's call as prophet to the nations is the command in v. 15 for him to share the cup of the wine of God's wrath with the nations to which YHWH sends him. The drinking of the cup will ruin them. A long list of nations follows (25:18–26a). Surprisingly, the name of Babylon is lacking. However, at the conclusion of v. 26 it is said that the king of Sheshak (a code name for Babylon) will be the last one to drink. Babylon therefore occupies a totally unique place within YHWH's plan for his people and for the whole world. After all, not only Jerusalem and Judah are to be visited by God; the nations will not escape punishment in this great judgment (25:29; cf. 49:12).

The Prophecy against Babylon

The unique place that Babylon occupies within the divine plan is also affirmed in chaps. 50 and 51, a very long and complicated prophecy against this city, which stands as the climax to the series of prophecies against the nations (46–51). In 25:13 ("this book"), explicit reference is made to this prophecy (cf. 51:63). Moreover, in 51:7 we meet up again with the image of the cup, so that the reader is invited to relate chap. 25 to chaps. 50–51. In 51:7 it appears that Babylon herself was the cup that made the entire earth drunk. Babylon was the instrument of YHWH's

wrath. However, in 25:12, 14; 50:14, 24, 29; and 51:24 it is made clear
to the reader that this circumstance did not free Babylon of guilt. Even
if Babylon was the cup (or the battle club, 51:20–23) in Yнwн's hand,
she remained responsible for the misdeeds she had committed.

Traitor or Faithful Prophet of *Yнwн*?

We now return to the question that we asked at the beginning,
where we signaled a paradox in Jeremiah's position. On one hand, he
is introduced as propagandist for the subjection of Judah to Babylon, a
recommendation that led to his arrest as a traitor (37:11–16; after the
fall of Jerusalem he was treated with the necessary respect by Babylon,
39:11–14). On the other hand, back in 594 B.C.E., he commissioned a
trusted person to ritually curse Babylon (51:59–64).

The common way to resolve this contradiction is to regard the
prophecy against Babylon as a later addition, so that it may be kept out
of consideration in our understanding of Jeremiah. In my opinion, we
need a different approach to this paradox. As remarked above, biblical
writers had their own way of submitting complex questions to the
reader. They did this not with a nuanced argument, but by putting texts
side by side so that different aspects of the problem were treated separately and in their own way. The intention was that the reader should
relate these texts to each other to appreciate the full complexity of the
problem. A reading of the book of Jeremiah without chaps. 50 and 51
is therefore incomplete and even misleading. This should become
quite clear if we follow the line that runs from chap. 1 via 25 to 50 and
51. Jeremiah called Nebuchadrezzar "servant of the Lord," not because
he was pro-Babylonian (as his opponents and the Babylonians themselves thought). Rather, Jeremiah viewed Babylon as a tool in Yнwн's
hand. He was also convinced, however, that Babylon would be repaid
for its misdeeds, even 70 years later. For, although the Babylonians fulfilled a role in God's intervention in world events, they remained
responsible for their deeds like all human beings. Thus, the prophet
proclaimed that Babylon's hegemony would also end. On the other
hand he affirmed that Yнwн's electing love for Israel and Judah will remain forever.

A Vision with a Future

Having come thus far, we need to pause briefly at the remarkable
message that the authors of Jeremiah have communicated in their
book. We read these texts from the present situation, in which the

three great monotheistic religions (Judaism, Christianity, and Islam) have come from the Old Testament tradition. The God of Israel is presently accepted as the only God by a large part of the world's population, no matter how his worshipers might disagree among themselves. At the time of the authors of Jeremiah, the God of Israel appeared to be no more than the insignificant God of a defeated people. It may have appeared as if these people were destined to be assimilated to other peoples, and therefore that the days for this God were numbered. Precisely in this situation the authors proclaimed that their God, YHWH, was the Creator of heaven and earth, who even after the fall of Jerusalem still dominated world history (27:5–7). Nebuchadnezzar did not owe his world dominion to his god Marduk (= Merodach or Bel) but to the national God of one of the states that he thought he had crushed. Only as long as it pleased YHWH would Babylon retain its dominion. After that it would be destroyed, and Marduk would be ashamed (50:2), facing the true God of heaven and earth, the God of Israel. The daring predictive force of this vision, which became a reality already in antiquity, is truly amazing.

When we consider all of this, it becomes clear to us why it would be a misjudgment of the authors' intention to view Jeremiah 50 and 51 as a secondary addition. Indeed, these chapters are indispensable for the general tenor of the book. The customary reconstruction of the history of the origin of the book of Jeremiah in three sources offers therefore no satisfactory access to this biblical book, because it assigns these chapters, as a late addition, to an inferior place. Even though Jeremiah 50 and 51 may have been written later than other parts of Jeremiah, they belong to the central passages that the authors have composed to set the tone of their book. I expect that if readers follow the connective thread between chaps. 1, 25, 26, 36, and 50–51, they will understand how fascinating this biblical book is as a witness to a theopolitical vision that is also definitive for our culture.

Toward a Synchronic Analysis of the Masoretic Text of the Book of Jeremiah

A. J. O. VAN DER WAL

Hoofddorp, The Netherlands

1. Introduction

No reader of the book of Jeremiah will disagree with the judgment that it is a complicated literary composition. This complexity is underscored by a number of unsolved questions pertaining to the book as a whole: first, the problem of the differences between the Masoretic Text (MT) and the Septuagint (LXX); second, the connection between poetry and prose; third, the relationship between speeches and narratives; and fourth, the putative Deuteronomistic redaction of the book.

Assuming that the book in its present form is a carefully considered, coherent composition, I offer a synchronic analysis in this essay. First, I describe some current explanatory models (§2) followed by my own comments (in §3). The discussion is summed up in a brief conclusion (§4).

2. Current Proposals

2.1. Sections That Are Based on a Division between Jeremiah 25 and 26

Many exegetes assume an important dividing line between chaps. 25 and 26. In their view, there is a break in chap. 25; the MT oracles against the nations (25:15ff.; chaps. 46–51) in the LXX follow 25:13 (14). Beyond that, different solutions have been proposed. A representative sampling follows.

In his commentary P. Volz (*Der Prophet Jeremia*) distinguishes the sections chaps. 1–36 (introduced by 1:1–3) and 37–45, with chap. 52 as an

---

Author's note: This English essay was translated by the editor. I thank Dr. K. Spronk (Culemborg) for his comments on an earlier version of it.

13

appendix. Volz ascribes 25:15–38 and chaps. 46–51 to a "Deutero-Jeremiah." He divides chaps. 1–36 into two parts: 1–25 and 26–36; he asserts that Jeremiah 25 and 36 correspond, for 25:1–14 forms the complementary speech to 36.

Another commentator, J. A. Thompson (*The Book of Jeremiah*), outlines as follows:

a. Superscription (1:1–3)
b. Call of Jeremiah and the two visions (1:4–19)
c. Divine judgment on Judah and Jerusalem (chaps. 2–25)
d. Jeremiah's controversy with false prophets (chaps. 26–29)
e. Book of consolation (chaps. 30–33)
f. Incidents from the days of Jehoiakim and Zedekiah (chaps. 34–39)
g. Jeremiah's experiences after the fall of Jerusalem (chaps. 40–45)
h. Oracles against the nations (chaps. 46–51)
i. Fall of Jerusalem (chap. 52).

A five-part structure of the book of Jeremiah is proposed by T. Miles Bennett (*Southwestern Journal of Theology*):

a. Introduction (chap. 1)
b. Divine judgment on Judah and Jerusalem (chaps. 2–25)
c. Events in the life of Jeremiah (chaps. 26–45)
d. Prophecies concerning the nations (chaps. 46–51)
d. Historical postscripts (chap. 52).

R. P. Carroll (*Jeremiah*) describes the book of Jeremiah as "a miscellaneous collection of discrete and disparate writings." His divisions are as follows:

a. Prologue, chap. 1
b. Part I (chaps. 2–25) is introduced by a preface, 2:1–3, followed by several books/collections: chaps. 2–6; 7–10; 11–13; 14–17; 18–20; while chaps. 21–24 function as appendix and 25:1–14 as closing summary
c. Part II (25:15–38 and chaps. 46–51)
d. Part III (chaps. 26–36) consists of the collections in chaps. 27–29 and 30–31, appendixes in chaps. 32–33, and a series of separate stories in chaps. 26, 34, 35, and 36
e. Part IV (chaps. 37–45) includes the collections in chaps. 37–38; 39:1–40:6; 40:7–41:18; chaps. 42–44; 45
f. Epilogue (chap. 52).

"These many 'books' melded into one large work and held together by a redactional framework explaining the individual parts as the work of Jeremiah constitute the Jeremiah tradition."

W. L. Holladay (*Jeremiah*) divides the book of Jeremiah into two parts: chaps. 1–25 and 26–52. In his *Architecture of Jeremiah 1–20*, he makes these distinctions:

The Call	1:4–14
The Seed Oracle	2:2–3
The Harlotry Cycle	2:5–37; 3:1, 5, 12b–14a, 19–25
The Foe Cycle	4:1–6:30; 8:4–10a, 13
The Temple Sermon and Further Prose	7:1–8:3
The Supplementary Foe Cycle and Related Material	8:14–10:25
Chaps. 10–11	

In Part II (chaps. 26–52), he offers the following divisions

A Separate, Hopeful Scroll	26–36
The Final Months of Jeremiah's Career	37–44
Yahweh's Word to Baruch	45
The Oracles against Foreign Nations	46–51
A Historical Appendix	

G. Wanke (*Jeremia*) represents the view that the structure of the Septuagint version of the book of Jeremiah is closer to an older version of the book than the Masoretic version. The Septuagint has a structure that is comparable to the books of Isaiah, Ezekiel, and Zephaniah:

a. Judgment on Israel and Judah (Jeremiah 1–24 MT)
b. Judgment on the nations (25:1–13; 46–51; 25:15–38 MT)
c. Promises for Israel (26–35 MT) and narratives (36–44[45] MT)
d. Historical appendix (52 MT).

2.2. Divisions That Do Not Assume a Hiatus between Chapters 25 and 26

According to J. Rosenberg (*The Literary Guide to the Bible*) the book of Jeremiah shows a "symmetrical pattern":

a. Historical superscription, 1:1–3
b. Commission, 1:4
c. "Prophet to the nations" theme introduced, 1:5–10

d. Doom for Israel; poetic oracles predominate, chaps. 1–10
e. Prophet cut off from Anathoth; focus on his trials and conflicts; prose predominates, chaps. 11–28
f. Optimistic prophecies; renewal of Israel; prose brackets poetic center, chaps. 29–31
e'. Prophet returns to Anathoth; focus on prophet's trials and conflicts; prose predominates, chaps. 32–45
d'. Doom for the nations; poetic oracles predominate, chaps. 46–51
c'. "Prophet to the nations" theme culminates in chaps. 50–51
b'. Prophet's concluding message, 51:59–64
a'. Historical appendix, chap. 52.

Rosenberg further describes what he calls a "striking symmetry" in chaps. 20–40.

R. D. Patterson (*Westminster Theological Journal*) offers the following schematic analysis. The two parts reflect the prophet's twofold commission:

a. Part I: chaps. 2–24
b. Part II: chaps. 25–51, which are composed of three parts: chaps. 26–35, 37–44, and 46–51. Chapters 25, 36, and 45 each offer a key to part II; all three chapters are dated in the fourth year of King Jehoiakim

Finally, A. Rofé (*Zeitschrift für die alttestamentliche Wissenschaft*) distinguishes four "collections":

a. chaps. 1–24 (visions, prophecies, laments, mostly undated)
b. chaps. 25–36 (separate episodes, all dated)
c. chaps. 37–45 (a running "biography" of Jeremiah)
d. chaps. 46–51 (sayings about foreign nations).

In his view the structure of the book is based on two principles: units were formed on the basis of similarity of subject or form, and each unit has a symmetrical structure. Thus, the first unit opens and closes with visions (1:11–14; chap. 24), the second and third units are framed by stories that play out in the fourth year of Jehoiakim (chaps. 25, 36, and 45), while the fourth unit is framed by the great powers, Egypt (chap. 46) and Babylon (chaps. 50–51). Later redactional activities in the book of Jeremiah, such as the formation of the book of comfort (chaps. 30–33), made the original plan of the book unclear.

2.3. Evaluation

The above overview of structuring proposals illustrates a number of current opinions relative to the composition of the book of Jeremiah. There is broad agreement on chap. 52, which is usually viewed as a (late) historical appendix. A difference of opinion relates to the position of chaps. 25, 36, and 45, however. Many scholars include (the first half of) chap. 25 with what precedes; others connect this chapter with what follows. Chapter 25 may also be viewed as part of a larger unit (chaps. 11–28); or, it is seen as related to chap. 35 or to chap. 36 (chap. 25:15–38); both passages mention the cup.

We have several options regarding chap. 36: it may be seen as the completion of a unit, or as a part of a larger collection, or as an introduction to the unit that follows. Chapter 45 is viewed by most authors as the completion of a "biographical" part of the book of Jeremiah; the extent of this part has been conceived differently, however; examples are chaps. 26–45, 32–45, 37–45, or 40–45. Alternately, chap. 45 may be viewed as a separate entity.

Following the above summarized proposals on structure, I offer my own suggestion. Contrary to Rosenberg, I think that no division should be made between chaps. 28 and 29; these chapters belong together; over against the "two years" of Hananiah (28:3, 11) are the "seventy years," concerning which Jeremiah must speak in God's name (25:11, 12; 29:10). Further, both chapters are connected by the pronouncement that God did not send prophets of the stripe of Hananiah (28:15; 29:9). The problem with Rofé's idea is that the mere date (the fourth year of Jehoiakim) bears no relationship to content. Regarding the proposal of R. D. Patterson, one might ask whether the two main parts are indeed a reflection of a twofold call of the prophet. In my proposal below I use the linguistic elements of the text as the starting point for a synchronic analysis.

3. Proposal for the Structuring of the Book of Jeremiah

3.1. Jeremiah 52 as Appendix

In Jer 1:1 the phrase "history of Jeremiah" appears. We meet it again in 51:64, so that we have an inclusio of the book. Since the book contains both the words and deeds of Jeremiah, we cannot translate the phrase "the words of Jeremiah." Because of this inclusio I regard chap. 52 as an appendix, possibly a later addition.

3.2. Two Parts: Chapters 1–23 and 24–51

Within chaps. 1–51 one may note the formal agreement of the visions described in 1:11–12, 1:13–14, and chap. 24. These descriptions of visions are sometimes compared with those in Amos 7:7–8, 8:1–2, and Zech 5:1–4. The common elements are:

a. The question "what are you seeing," Jer 1:11, 13; 24:3
b. The answer is the first-person singular "and I said," followed by the prophet's description of the object that God showed him: Jer 1:11, 13; 24:3
c. A saying from God relative to the object shown: Jer 1:12, 14; 24:4–10.

Likewise, the conclusions of chap. 23 (vv. 39, 40) and chap. 51 (vv. 63–64) are comparable. Both segments deal with casting (away) / plucking up, 23:39; "throwing down," 51:63; spoken over a land (Judah and Jerusalem, Jer 23:39) and over Babylon (51:64); which leads to eternal ruin (23:40; 51:62).

Because of these correspondences between chaps. 1 and 24 on the one hand, and between Jer 23:39–40 and 51:63–64 on the other hand, I propose that the corpus (1–51) consists of two parts: 1–23 and 24–51.

We may attempt to describe these two divisions further. In the first part of the book, we meet the expression "prophesying through Baal"; this expression occurs only in Jer 2:8 (*Niphal*) and 23:13 (*Hitpael*). In 2:8 this clause is used for the prophets of Judah, in 23:13 for the prophets of Samaria/Israel. From the sequel of chap. 23, it appears that the prophets of Judah exceeded the prophets of the Northern Kingdom in ungodliness. This inclusio might suggest that chap. 1 should be read as an introduction to chaps. 2–23.

When one regards chap. 24 as an introductory chapter, one discovers that the second part (chaps. 24–51) is surrounded by corresponding passages in chaps. 25 and 50–51, dealing respectively with the rise (chap. 25) and the ruin (chaps. 50–51) of Babylon, a theme that was introduced in 25:12–14. These passages (chaps. 25 and 50–51) share much vocabulary, as the following list illustrates:

a. Image of the cup, Jer 25:15, 17, 28; 51:7
b. The construction "Kings of Media," Jer 25:25; 51:11, 28. The name "Media" does not occur anywhere else in the book of Jeremiah
c. The expression "raise the shout of victory," Jer 25:30 and 51:14, is found nowhere else in the Hebrew Bible

   d. The term "escape," Jer 25:35; 50:29 (only here in the book of Jeremiah)

   e. The proper name "Sheshach," a pseudonym for Babylon, Jer 25:26 and 51:41, is found nowhere else in the Hebrew Bible.

Moreover, there is much similarity between the judgment oracles addressed to Judah/Jerusalem in chap. 25 and the judgment oracles against Babylon in chaps. 50–51. Both lands are "put in the ban," Jer 25:9; 50:21, 26; and 51:3 (this verb only occurs in these places in the book of Jeremiah). The sword will be taken up against them, Jer 25:16, 27, 31; 50:35–38 (six times!). They become an object of amazement / a desert, Jer 25:9, 11, 18, 38; 50:3, 23; 51:29, 37, 41, 43. Jer 25:9, 25:18, and 51:37 add that the land will become an object of hissing. Judah/Jerusalem and Babylon will be destroyed (with YHWH as the agent), 25:36 and 51:55. In 51:49 the fates of Israel and of Babylon are connected.

Having sketched both cases of inclusio, we may now offer a detailed description of the parts of the book. An inclusio normally mentions the main theme of the passage that it frames. The first part of the book of Jeremiah (chaps. 1–23) may be labeled a prophetic discourse concerning Judah's failure to repent and its resultant guilt, with a specific reference to the role of prophecy, which is viewed very critically (chap. 23!). Also, this first part contains Jeremiah's confessions, keenly illustrating how the prophet was victimized by his prophetic activity. At the end of the unit, other opponents are introduced: priests (20:1–6) and kings (21:1–23:8); in the series of "disputes," one may discover the design of the list of opponents (1:18; 2:8, et al.).

The second part (chaps. 24–51) describes Judah's downfall and rise in relation to Babylon's. Confessions are lacking in this part, and the prophetic "I" only occurs in 31:26 as a personal note with a promise of salvation. The rest of these chapters speak about Jeremiah in the third person.

3.3. Further Delineation

Chapters 46–51 are generally regarded as a separate collection. I remind the reader of the inclusio formed by Egypt (chap. 46) and Babylon (chaps. 50–51). Chapters 1–45 are enclosed by passages that are directed to one person: Jeremiah (chap. 1) and Baruch (chap. 45). These two chapters share personal promises of God's protection (Jer 1:8, 18–19; 45:5).

To illustrate the composition of the book of Jeremiah further, the chart below presents the series of verbs dealing with the motifs of "tearing down"and "building up" as they occur in Jer 1:10 (pluck up; break down; destroy; overthrow; build; plant).

	pluck up	break down	destroy	overthrow	build	plant
1:10	x	x	x	x	x	x
18:7–10	x	x	x		x	x
24:6	x			x	x	x
31:28	x	x	x	x	x	x
42:10	x			x	x	x
45:4	x			x	x	x

Clearly, these terms illustrate a major [leading] motif in the book of Jeremiah. Interestingly, the four-part combination build/break down/ plant/pluck up (Jer 24:6; 42:10; 45:4) is limited to the second division of the book of Jeremiah. In 18:7–10 and 42:10 the word series is used in conditional sayings. One might suppose that Jer 24:6 and 45:4 form an (antithetical) inclusio within the second part. The formulation in 1:10 and 45:4 may be viewed as summarizing the overall proclamation of Jeremiah. If this is correct, then we have an additional argument for the connection between chaps. 1 and 45.

3.4. Further Divisions in Chapters 1–23

Jer 1:18 mentions two metals, iron and copper. This twin also occurs in Jer 6:28 and 15:12. The confession Jer 15:10–21 has in common with chap. 1 the phrase "they will fight against you, but they will not prevail against you" (1:19; 15:20). On the basis of these considerations, two units may be distinguished in chaps. 1–23, namely, 1–15 and 16–23. Within 1–15, 1–6 and 7–15 might further be distinguished as distinct units. Jer 1:17–19 and 6:27–30 form an inclusio. Each one of these three units (chaps. 1–6, 7–15, and 16–23) begins with a prophetic narrative; in addition, the units chaps. 1–6 and 7–15 end with a personal section. Jeremiah 1–6 functions as a thematic cluster in which themes are introduced that are developed and expanded in subsequent chapters (7ff.).

3.5. Further Divisions in Chapters 24–51

The collection of nations in 46–51 is comparable to the list in Jer 25:19–26. The following are mentioned seriatim: Egypt (25:19; chap.

46); Philistines (25:20; chap. 47); Moab (25:21; chap. 48); Ammon (25:21; 49:1–6); Edom (25:21; 49:7–22); Arabia (25:24; 49:28–33); Elam (25:25; 49:34–39); Babylon (25:1–14, 26; chaps. 50–51). Damascus (49:23–27) is lacking in the list of chap. 25.

Chapters 32–44 also present themselves as a separate collection. Jeremiah's prophetic acts are placed here within a biographical frame. Chapter 33 fits into this because of the localizing of the prophet during the reception of the divine revelation (33:1). Based on arguments of content, the unit chaps. 32–44 may be divided into two parts: 32–39 and 40–44, with the capture of Judah and the destruction of Jerusalem as the dividing line.

Chapters 25–31 remain. As the first part of the book of Jeremiah is introduced by a thematic cluster, so the second part of the book is introduced by chaps. 24/25–31. Chapter 24 mentions removal from the land (24:9), return (24:5–6), building and planting (24:6), covenant (24:7), heart (24:7), and conversion (24:7). All of these themes return in chaps. 25–31. The "Book of Comfort" (chaps. 30–31) is not a freestanding part but a closure of the preceding thematic cluster.

Chapter 26, dated during the reign of Jehoiakim, refers once more to Jeremiah's efforts to move the people of Judah to repentance. This chapter, which has much in common with chap. 7, is one of the many connecting links between the two parts of the book of Jeremiah. The prophet's appeal in the temple was in vain, however, so that chaps. 27–29 ask that the unavoidable subjection to Babylon be accepted. In chap. 27, dated during the time of Zedekiah, Jeremiah proclaims this message of subjection to a threefold audience: foreign political leaders (27:2–3), King Zedekiah (27:12), and priests and people (27:16). In chap. 28 Jeremiah defends this message against a prophetic opponent, again in the temple. In this, the list of "adversaries" mentioned in 1:18 may be recognized. Thus, a link is forged between both parts of Jeremiah. In chap. 29 the prophet writes a message of subjection to the exiles who already live in Babylon. Jer 29:10–14 reiterates the themes of "heart" and "return" from chap. 24. Likewise, the image of figs (29:17) and the saying "I send the sword, hunger, and pestilence" (29:17) are quoted from chap. 24. The time span of 70 years, introduced in chap. 25, is mentioned again in Jer 29:10.

The themes we encounter in chaps. 27–29 are rounded off in chaps. 30–31:

- yoke (Jer 27:8, 11, 12; 28:2, 4, 11, 14; 30:8)
- hope (29:11; 31:17)

- to bring about a change (29:14; 30:3)
- heart (29:13; 31:33).

The following chapters (32–33) duplicate themes of 30–31. When Jeremiah purchased the land of a family member (chap. 32), he thereby underscored the promised return recorded in chaps. 30–31. Jer 33:15–17 mentions a Davidic king who will reign after the return, as in 30:9. Additionally, chap. 33 contains the expressions "to bring a change": 33:11 and 26, as in 30:3 and 30:18; "to have mercy": 33:26, as in 30:18 and 31:20; this chapter also speaks of the covenant (33:25, also 31:31–34); while the people of God are described as "Jacob" (33:26, as in 30:7, 10 [bis], 18; 31:7, 11). The form of 33:25–26 is very similar to 31:35–36 and 31:37.

Finally, chaps. 30–31 may also be fruitfully compared with chaps. 25 and 50–51. With this observation we touch the decisive axis of the interpretation of the second part of the book of Jeremiah. The following examples may support this contention.

a. *Jeremiah 25–Jeremiah 30–31*
    (1) The term "leave unpunished," 25:29 (three times); 30:11 (twice)
    (2) The image of the storm to portray God's wrath, 25:32; 30:23. This noun only occurs additionally in the book in 23:19
    (3) The theme of serving foreign powers, 25:11; 30:8
    (4) The theme of joy disappearing in 25:10, and returning in 31:7

b. *Jeremiah 30–31–Jeremiah 50–51*
    (1) The image of men becoming women, 30:6; 50:37. The term "like a woman in labor" relates to Judahite men in 30:6 but in 50:43 to the king of Babylon
    (2) The term "shame" expresses Judah being ashamed in 31:19, while it refers to Babylon in 50:2 (twice) and in 51:47
    (3) The people of God are called "Jacob" in 30:7, 10 (twice), and 18; 31:7, 11; 51:19
    (4) The image of pain, 30:15; 51:8
    (5) The idea that the people of Judah are "devoured," 30:16; 50:7, 17; 51:34
    (6) The description of God as redeemer of his people, 31:11; 50:34. These are the only two passages in Jeremiah where this term is found
    (7) The description of God as an "abode of righteousness," 31:23; 50:7
    (8) The people returning and weeping, 31:9; 50:4

(9) The theme of the covenant, 31:31–34; 50:5

(10) The theme of God's forgiveness, 31:34; 50:20

c. *Jeremiah 25–Jeremiah 30–31–Jeremiah 50–51*

Among the themes that these three passages have in common, the following may be mentioned:

(1) God visits and avenges the oppressors for their oppression of the Judahites, 25:12; 30:20; 50:18; etc.

(2) The burning wrath of God, 25:37, 38; 30:24; 51:45

(3) The restoration of Judah

4. Conclusion

The present proposal concerning the structure of the book of Jeremiah in its present form takes no account of the poetry-prose distinction in the book or of the source division (A, B, and C [D]) common since Mowinckel. The division between prose and poetry is insufficiently clear, as the investigations of W. L. Holladay have demonstrated. The question of which passages in the book are deuteronomistic, which has not been answered definitively thus far, relates to the redactional history of the book of Jeremiah, while I have attempted to unravel the structure of its current form.

Neither has the Septuagint version been taken into account. Because the oracles against the nations have been placed differently in the LXX and the MT, the Septuagint operates with a different structure. In my opinion, the material in this Masoretic book of Jeremiah is not arranged chronologically but thematically. I see chaps. 24–31 as the center of the book, for this is where Jeremiah's message of judgment and deliverance is concentrated.

I have also referred to some of the connections that exist between the two parts of the book of Jeremiah. The events in the town of Anathoth are representative of the themes of both parts of the book. In chap. 11 the opposition by the citizens of Anathoth is heightened to the point that they wish to kill Jeremiah, while in chap. 32 the purchase of land in the same city functions as a preliminary sign of the total restoration of Judah.

Getting Closer to Jeremiah:
The Word of YHWH and the
Literary-Theological Person of a Prophet

JOEP DUBBINK
University of Amsterdam

In this essay, I attempt to define the dominant role that Jeremiah plays in the book by his name. The focus will not be so much on the biography of the historical prophet or his religiopsychological development but rather on his literary-theological function. Particular attention will be directed to the relationship between Jeremiah and the word of YHWH, of which the prophet is both the first recipient and the proclaimer. I will also show that the so-called biographical portions (the biography by Baruch and the Confessions) are not extraneous additions but are essential to the book, since they are needed to underscore its central message.

Book or Sources? Questions of Introduction

Students of Jeremiah are quite aware of the complex questions of introduction such as date, authorship, historical reliability, and others. In the past, some commentators resorted to assigning verses to "layers" and distinguishing multiple phases of editing. However, such a fragmentizing approach precludes the possibility of writing a "theology of the book of Jeremiah." This is what we are searching for in this essay: a "red thread" running through the book with its central theological thoughts.

This is not to say that the book is a seamless unity. It offers a great variety of thoughts, styles, and genres. These add up to the remarkable paradox that is the book of Jeremiah. It may be correct to assign late

---

Author's note: This essay, translated by the editor, is a revision of the final chapter of my doctoral dissertation (University of Amsterdam, 1997): *Waar is de HEER? Dynamiek en actualiteit van het woord van JHWH bij Jeremia* [Where is the LORD? The Dynamics and Actuality of the Word of YHWH in Jeremiah] (Gorinchem: Narratio, 1997).

dates to large parts of the book. A crucial point in the discussion is the presupposition of an underlying historical figure named Jeremiah. Contrariwise, if we de facto remove the person from the book, we are left with a very different product.

Is it possible to combine the two; that is, to assign a central place in the book to the "person" of Jeremiah without insisting on "the historical Jeremiah" as the only or the chief author of the book? It is, by speaking about the "image" of Jeremiah that the text calls forth, the literary-theological Jeremiah, whom I shall call "Jeremiah" to avoid confusion. We have, of course, no other Jeremiah to work with; thus, we cannot postpone our reflection about the theology of the book until we are certain about the precise provenance of the texts—if this is indeed achievable. Therefore, I opt for a synchronic approach in this essay. In support I cite the familiar adage by Gerhard von Rad that working toward a kerygmatic maximum is more fruitful than searching for a historically demonstrable minimum. Childs writes: "a canonical approach . . . strives to understand the full dimension of the interpreted testimony" (*Introduction*, 353). Thus, we seek a theology of the book as a whole. It is my purpose to show that this theology cannot be formulated without taking into account the *person* of the prophet, as the book presents him.

The Message of Jeremiah

There is remarkable consistency between "the man" and "the message." The prophetic image portrays someone who stands *opposed* to the mainstream of contemporary thought, a "man of conflict" (15:10), for on every level, whether political, societal, or religious—he is in conflict with the dominant opinions of his time. In Jeremiah's time, two theological lines collide: the promise and the demands of the covenant (Bright, *Covenant and Promise*, 165).

An example is Jeremiah's attitude toward temple, worship, and sacrifice. His sharply critical judgment of these is based on a fundamental critique of all thinking based on fixed certainties. This remains true even when the texts concerning the unjustified expectation of deliverance did not originate in the time of the historical prophet. The first readers of the book lived after the exile. They would have heard these words with their own temple in mind, the Second Temple, even if the words were originally directed against Solomon's Temple, for both temples shared a comparable theological function: they formed a culmination point of unconditional trust in Yʜwʜ. While the First Temple was a tangible building from the time of Solomon, related to the dynasty of David and fixed Judahite theology, the second was an equally impressive, rebuilt temple and as such a sign of God's continuing support for Judah.

The critique of the temple in the book of Jeremiah is not to be reduced to sociological data. There may have been tensions and even rivalry between the returned exiles and those who had remained in the land, but the crucial element of the conflict is a *theological* difference of opinion on the basic question of faith in the God of Israel, a question about who he is and what his word means. Buber correctly avers that for Jeremiah "vain confidence is the enemy of faith" (Buber, *Prophetic Faith*, 169). For the same reason, overconfidence in self, and in the same manner the Davidic dynasty was also criticized (22:1–9). This critique, like the critique of the temple service, was not an absolute rejection; the book also expects a reconstituted Davidic kingship (23:5–6; 30:9–11).

The critical attitude of "Jeremiah" is not exhausted with this and continues in unusual ways:

> How can you say,
>   "We are wise,
>   and the Torah of YHWH is with us"?
> Indeed, the false pen of the scribes
> has made it into a lie! (Jer 8:8)

This is a most remarkable text. Even the Torah, here seen as the product of the "pen of the scribes," the written form of the word of YHWH, is not a sufficient guarantee of safety but falls under Jeremiah's unsparing critique. This is not about the contradiction between the spoken and the written word, for if necessary Jeremiah uses the latter as well (36:3, 32). Neither is the verse directed against copyists who would purposely falsify sacred texts: *šeqer* [lie] in Jeremiah does not usually mean "subjectively dishonest" but "factually untrue."

Our concern here is the *dynamic* nature of the word of YHWH, which comes again and again in its newness and freedom. Apparently, no "truth in solidified form," whether it be the stones of the temple, the gold of the royal crown, or even Holy Scripture, is adequate to express the truth of the word of YHWH. True wisdom is only to be gained in repeated questioning for an actual word of God in a given situation.

Quite possibly, Jer 8:8 is directly aimed at the lawbook that was found in the temple (2 Kings 22). This would do much to clarify the critical attitude of Jeremiah toward the Deuteronomistic reform. In any

case, this text is directed against a form of theologizing also found in
the book of Deuteronomy:

> 5   See, just as YHWH my God has charged me,
>   I now teach you statutes and ordinances
>   for you to observe in the land that you are about to enter and occupy.
> 6   You must observe them diligently,
>   for this will show your wisdom and discernment to the people,
>   who, when they hear all these statutes, will say:
>   Surely, this great nation is a wise and discerning people.
> 7   For what other great nation has a god so near to it
>   as YHWH our God is whenever we call to him? (Deut 4:6–8).

In v. 6 we find a motif that is replicated in Jer 8:8, "wisdom." Israel's wisdom is found in keeping the commandments, so that the surrounding
peoples will view it as wise and understanding, and as a "great" people.
No other people has a God who is so near!

This does not need to contradict the theology of Jeremiah. There
are points of contact such as the keeping of the covenant laws, though
it is notable that with Jeremiah we hardly hear the common Deuteronomic terms *mišpaṭ* [commandment] and *ḥoq* [prescription]. These concepts may be too static for the theology of Jeremiah.

But when the transition from v. 6 to v. 7 is seen as automatic, the
proximity of YHWH becomes a dogma and then there is a direct conflict with Jeremiah. Instead, Jeremiah speaks of a God who is "far off"
(23:23) who is *not* immediately available. He draws the critique of his
opponents into the heart of theology, to what is said about YHWH himself. His opponents have a domesticated faith and trust, and a fixed image of God. Their God is where he belongs: with his people, in the
temple, and wherever someone calls on his name. Jeremiah considers
this faith a lie.

The battle against the so-called "false prophets" deals with the same
concept of *šeqer* [lie], and precisely the same thing is involved there as
in Jeremiah 27 and 28. Since these chapters are dated after the first deportation (between 597 and 587 B.C.E.), they introduce a new situation.
A part of the judgment announced by Jeremiah has taken place and
therefore the prophet might be expected to gradually gain supporters.
But the opposite is the case; the theology of unconditional trust in
YHWH, the "thought of security," is rooted so deeply that even the appearance of Babylonian armies, the removal of the king, the carrying
off of a group of Judahites, and the looting of temple vessels do not
lead to a change of views. All of these ominous events might still be
placed within the context of the unconditional covenant, for the proph-

ets of promise (deliverance) do not exclude YHWH's critical position toward the people. However, this is about divine disapproval and purification, not a radical breach with YHWH.

What provokes anxiety, even when we realize that this narrative follows the events, is that Jeremiah finds himself opposed to *prophets*. Instead of serving a critical function in society, they were found to have fed empty trust. We may leave aside the question of how far this portrayal is historical; it is implied that there was a debate, during or perhaps after the exile. Clearly, religion, then as now, serves an ambiguous function: claims of serving God are not necessarily justified. The word of Deuteronomy that YHWH is near whenever he is called upon may become a lie if torn from its context.

As stated elsewhere in the book, Jeremiah's opponents particularly comprise religious professionals. In Jeremiah 2 YHWH wonders why his people do not inquire of him anymore:

> They do not say:
>   Where is YHWH,
>   who brought us up from the land of Egypt,
>   who led us in the wilderness,
>   in a land of drought and deep darkness,
>   in a land that no one passes through,
>   where no one lives? (Jer 2:6)

Where Is YHWH?

The question "Where Is YHWH?" deserves particular attention, even if it is quite rare; in addition to this chapter, it occurs only one more time. In Jeremiah 2, the same question returns, in a verse that complains about religious functionaries and other leaders:

> The priests did not say:
>   Where is YHWH?
> Those who handle the Torah did not know me.
> The rulers transgressed against me.
> The prophets prophesied by Baal
> and went after things that do not profit. (Jer 2:8)

It appears to deal with idol worship, leaving YHWH, and following other gods, but this is really not the main problem that the book assails. Certainly, serving other gods had been a problem before the exile as well, but the description of how groups of Judahites, disappointed with the catastrophe that broke loose over Jerusalem, turned away from the service of YHWH (see Jeremiah 44) appears to be an exceptional incident.

Jeremiah was chiefly occupied on another front. His opponents thought that they served YHWH also, even if in a totally different way. But in the vision of the book of Jeremiah, idols may be served, while people are still calling on the name of YHWH! Precisely the statement about the God who is near, who may be called upon at any time, is the one that may be a lie under certain circumstances. This is the reason that Jeremiah strongly emphasizes the God who is "afar off," unrestrained, one who may change, and one who must be *sought* again and again. Just as Elisha in 2 Kgs 2:15, after Elijah had left (assuming that the Spirit of God would be on him from then on), still asked: "Where is he, YHWH, the God of Elijah?"; just so, Jeremiah's contemporaries should have kept asking that question. However, priests, scribes, and prophets, as well as the shepherds (rulers, political leaders) occupied themselves with very different things. Possibly they gradually turned their backs on YHWH; but it was probably worse yet, because the people occupied themselves with "Baalized" worship of YHWH. No one asked for YHWH. His presence was presupposed and taken for granted, just as Baal was by his worshipers. That YHWH was different was not considered. The image that Jeremiah uses is exceptionally clear:

> My people have committed two evils:
> they have forsaken me,
> the fountain of living water,
> and dug out cisterns for themselves,
> cracked cisterns,
> that can hold no water. (Jer 2:13)

Opposed to the living water, symbolizing the living God, are the cisterns, whose stagnant water of dead tradition are expected to quench thirst. That will not work; water in cisterns becomes stale, and moreover, these cisterns cannot hold water because they are cracked. This is a powerful image counterposed with the dynamic word of YHWH, which cannot be caught and stored. Even if these verses were used originally in polemics against other gods, they would now be heard as a criticism of the people's own (YHWH) worship. These words might then have been heard, for example, against the background of Jer 12:2, where the prophet complains to YHWH about his opponents: "You are near in their mouths, yet far from their hearts."

The concept of the word of YHWH as dynamic and active was squarely opposed to the beliefs of the great majority of preexilic people. At least, this is the picture that the prophet evokes, and there is little reason to doubt it. More importantly, the detailed picture of the opposition against Jeremiah suggests that later on the authors of the book of Jeremiah also had difficulty with this message. Naturally they had the advantange of retrospect over the historical prophet; the crisis was past, and the facts had proved the false prophets wrong. Yet, the authors of the book deemed it necessary to spell out the conflicts in detail again; even after the somber prophecies of Jeremiah had been fulfilled, theological discussion had not yet been silenced. The question remained what kind of God YHWH was, and where he was to be found.

Jeremiah and the Word of YHWH

In the theology of the Old Testament as well as of the book of Jeremiah, the concept of "the word of YHWH" plays a very important role. The word of YHWH is more than one word or opinion among others, even if powerful. The translation 'word' for *dābār* is inadequate because it neglects its deed-character. The word of YHWH sets an event in motion; it makes history. It may be seen as God's revelation in history. His word seizes the prophet (1:5), sets his objections aside (1:6–7), and occupies him. It sets him over nations and kingdoms (1:10), with no other authority than his commission to speak the word of YHWH. It is the highest word with the highest authority but also the most despised word. Not only is this word in itself "like fire . . . like a hammer that breaks a rock in pieces" (23:29), it retains this power in the mouth of the prophet, where it is also described as being "like fire" (5:14).

However, this power is but one side of the story. The other side is that this word of YHWH is unverified; it lacks confirmation. Jeremiah is sent to the nations and to his own people with a royal commission (cf. 1:10: pluck up, pull down, build, plant), but his authority is of a totally different order than royal authority supported by physical power. To be sure, he is equipped like "a city fortified with a bronze wall" (1:18; 15:20–21), but this imagery cannot conceal that he remains a vulnerable man, mirroring in his person the vulnerability of the word.

Jeremiah's theology is different from that of his opponents; it is not based on certainties such as dynasty and temple but only on the word of YHWH. This certainty is of a different order: it is challenged, as the dialogues between true and false prophets illustrate. The prophet is drawn as a picture (in the Confessions, but not only there) of a man in a challenged position. He does not doubt that his version of the word of YHWH is right, but he suffers, afraid that he may not be shown to be convincing to others. Moreover, God does not support his words with acts—apart from the single instance in which Hananiah, the false prophet, died according to the word of Jeremiah (28:17). Because of the perceived lack of support, Jeremiah feared that his words might lose their efficacy (cf. 12:4; 15:15, 18; 17:15).

Thus, the word of YHWH could also be a joy for Jeremiah (15:16) but—and the book testifies to this with far more intensity—it could also be an almost unbearable burden (20:7). This fact was so contrary to common belief that it seemed unacceptable to virtually all of his contemporaries. In the Confessions it is the direct cause of the isolation the prophet experiences.

In addition to the Confessions, prose literature also witnesses to the upheaval that God's word caused in the prophet, even beyond despair. Chapters 37–44 narrate the fortunes of the prophet in the final months before the fall of Jerusalem. Here we see no hero of faith but a fearful messenger of God, who is only convinced to speak a word from God after being urged to do so (38:14–28; cf. 20:9!). Kremers comments about the secular vein in which this history runs its course: no signs occur anywhere, nowhere does one notice that YHWH supports his prophet by letting his words come true; we only see a prophet immersed in hopeless misery. While it would have been relatively easy to describe these events in retrospect from the standpoint of the exile as simply the acts of YHWH, the emphasis falls completely on the upheaval and desperation that the main persons experienced at this time of crisis. Without the closure of Jeremiah 45 (see below), the message of these chapters would be unambiguously comfortless.

Prophecy in a Time of Crisis

A comparison of the book of Jeremiah with other prophetic books brings to light great differences as well as expected agreements. The prophecy of Jeremiah clearly distinguishes itself in content and form from that of other prophets, a fact that seems to be related to the particular time in which the book plays out. The profound crisis that the exile signified in the life of Israel resulted in the inadequacy of traditional prophecy; it never resumed its former position after the exile. Von Rad remarks that the human questions of the prophet become increasingly urgent. The threatening chaos and destruction that finally materialized in an explosion led to increasing frustration about the futility of prophesying. According to von Rad, the tension between the prophet as a human being and his prophetic office became so high that this office was seriously endangered.

Often the solution to this problem is sought in the biographical-psychological development of the prophet: Jeremiah is regarded as a rather weak prophet who is not able to stand firm in his office (as should be clear from Jer 1:5, his shy attempt to refuse the office from the beginning). Von Rad is strongly opposed to this kind of psychologizing exegesis of Jeremiah and proposes an alternative explanation: "The fact that with Jeremiah, and not earlier, the earthen vessel was broken is related to the fact that [he] had taken up the prophetic office in a breadth and depth not seen before."

He relates the problems with the prophetic office not to the psyche of Jeremiah but to the weight of his burden. This is much better than reducing the tensions to psychology, but we are still looking for an explanation on the level of the historical prophet. It seems to me that the special place and content of the book of Jeremiah must be seen as the result of a number of factors. First of all *the situation*: the effect of the fall of Jerusalem can hardly be overestimated. Since God did not appear to protect the city unconditionally, entirely new answers to old questions needed to be formulated, and a new relationship to the word of YHWH was needed—answers that are being sought in the book of Jeremiah. Additionally, a *theological development* is to be noted that, even without the exile crisis, may have played a role. A movement may be discovered that pointed to change. The "Deuteronomists" were part of it but also the writers responsible for the book of Jeremiah. The problem of the diversity within that movement and the mutual influences on it is complex. It may suffice here to point out that the crisis situation in itself would not have meant anything, had not a group of people been ready to search for a new significance of temple, prophecy, covenant, and many other aspects of faith. Inside that movement, creative and renewing theological work took place. Thus the exile was interpreted as a result of the failure of the people; they had broken their fidelity to the covenant and had not lived in a befitting way in the land that was given them by YHWH. This interpretation, which may strike us strange, was *for them* the only possible way to interpret the crisis.

The crisis was of such a dimension that previous responses were insufficient. The prophetic word that commands "directly from above" and calls to conversion seemed no longer sufficient. Feelings of despair and forsakenness by God must be expressed in one way or another; the prophet's function therefore must go beyond that of a courier communicating messages from YHWH. The *person* of Jeremiah plays a very important role here. He—the literary-theological person—becomes the point of concentration for the theological development of this time. This requires further reflection.

The Person in the Play

We now turn to the question of why *in the given situation* a book in its present form should result. Is it by chance that the prophet who spoke so critically to his people at such a crucial moment in Israel's history should project so strongly as a person? Various "models" have been posited to describe this.

Example

The simplest answer is the concept that the prophet was an example for his readers, including encouragement. This is how Carroll sees the "Jeremiah of the Confessions": Jeremiah plays the exemplary role of a suffering righteous man (*Jeremiah*, 397). This aspect is irrefutably present. Jeremiah's role is different from that of Job, however: Jeremiah is not an empty name, filled only by unjust suffering, but a concrete historical personality: *this* prophet with *this* critical message is suffering, and his suffering is tightly connected with his message.

Paradigm

Carroll dates the Confessions late to very late, after 400. Unlike Carroll, Pohlmann sketches a clear picture of the authors: the group that follows Jeremiah is eschatologically oriented. It has no faith in the rebuilt temple and the cult but expects a new judgment from YHWH that will purify both the heathen and Israel. This group must struggle with the resistance of those who have invested themselves in the renewed institutions and, with that, are left stranded with their own uncertainty, as the judgment of YHWH is delayed. With the help of Jeremiah—the "figure" or role-player, in character, of course; not the historical prophet—this uncertainty may be conquered, since he stood firm in the tension between expectation and the delay of its fulfillment (Pohlmann, *Studien zum Jeremiabuch*, 33–41, 104–5).

This vision has its attractive points: it gives the *persona* of Jeremiah a more intelligible place, apart from the historical prophet. The notion of life in tension between promise and reality merits serious attention. But is it really possible to indicate the historical situation of the authors with such precision? What has happened in the centuries between the exile and the time where Pohlmann places the authors? Pohlmann has no answer to the question concerning the continuity between the first generations—the prophet and his first followers—and this much later group that uses him as figurehead.

Polk carefully describes and reflects on the paradigm concept. In his conclusion he approximates Pohlmann when he asks: "Is a model of obedient faith to be seen in the struggle itself, in the very tension between faith, praise and anguish?" (Polk, 160). This appears to be the case: the tension in which Jeremiah lives is an integral part of his prophetic existence.

"Jeremiology"

The concept of the prophet as paradigm remains close to that of the prophet as example to be followed. Yet, there is a certain arbitrariness in the choice of Jeremiah as paradigm: why Jeremiah? Polk has acknowledged this danger and calls attention to Jeremiah's unique place: "Even as he becomes an exemplar of trust, a wisdom-styled model of obedience in suffering, Jeremiah remains the prophetic figure of a definite time, place, and mission" (Polk, 150).

We may sharpen the identity of the prophet that Polk envisages. Though the prophet is a paradigm, might not also the narrative about this man, who remained steadfast in an exceptionally desperate situation, serve a purpose? Why might it not witness to the goodness and faithfulness of YHWH, that even in judgment he did not abandon his people, that at least *one* prophet kept proclaiming the word of YHWH? In Deut 18:15 Moses says: "YHWH your God will raise up for you a prophet like me from among your own people; you shall heed such a prophet." According to Rashi, this is not about the one-time sending of a prophet but about prophetic succession: the people will never be without a prophet and thus without the word of YHWH. Jeremiah is deliberately painted as one of them and not the least of them. It may be illustrative to compare the "Servant of YHWH" in Deutero-Isaiah. Clearly, the Servant is significant *in himself*, even if he above all is a figure lending itself for further development. Blank makes an interesting connection between the Servant and Jeremiah, when he describes the Servant of YHWH as "a personification / of the people of Israel / as a prophet / after the manner of Jeremiah" (Blank, "Paradigma," 31). Deutero-Isaiah took Jeremiah's life as a source of inspiration for his imaging of the Servant of YHWH and used both as "models" for Israel's prophetic mission.

The difference between Jeremiah and the Servant of YHWH is that the identity of the historical "Servant of YHWH" eludes us, while Jeremiah is on much firmer historical ground. Yet they are comparable in many respects. A comparison between Jer 1:4–10 and Isa 49:1–6 shows that both are called "to [prophesy to] the nations" and "from the mother's womb." This double agreement, both in form and content, says that these two men had their whole beings grasped by the word of Yhwh (cf. Polk, 169). Their commission knows no boundaries but includes all of their life in time and space. Their own existence is meaningless and unthinkable without the word of Yhwh. Negatively, this leads to a text such as 20:14–18, but in a positive sense, to the figure who indicates the presence of the word of Yhwh in a hopeless situation, thus guaranteeing the presence of God in a situation without prospect, such as the time preceding the fall of Jerusalem. More emphatically, might Jeremiah himself not be seen as a personification of the word? Polk claims: Jeremiah in his struggle is a type, a metaphor, for God's word. Welten claims precisely the same for the Jeremiah of the Baruch narrative: Jeremiah's experiences are those of the word of Yhwh; he was sent by Yhwh but was vulnerable, misunderstood, almost destroyed, yet delivered (Polk, 170). The figure of Jeremiah is therefore not only of interest insofar as the reader may be able to identify with him, but is also itself a paradigm for the word that he proclaims.

Jeremiah and Israel

The Servant of the Lord suggests a very different model. The Servant may also be interpreted collectively: in Deutero-Isaiah the people of Israel are called "my servant" by Yhwh (Isa 41:8; 44:1, 21). Buber and Heschel believed that this also pertained to Jeremiah: the prophet was pars pro toto for Israel; the great separation between Yhwh and Israel took place in his life (Buber, 180–83; Heschel, *Prophets*, 112–22). This does not mean that the prophet was an extension of Israel; there was often conflict, for Jeremiah did what Israel did not do: *he heard*, that is, he listened and obeyed. Polk writes: "As a paradigm who stands *over against* and *in contrast to* the people, Jeremiah also foreshadows, paradigmatically, the fulfillment of the divine purpose for the nation." Polk (137) relates this particularly to the judgment that touches the prophet before it does his fellow-citizens. The exegesis of 15:15–18 and 20:10 might confirm this. But might it be possible that his steadfastness and survival, his being rescued in the nick of time, reflect something of the salvific perspective for his people?

A Complaining Prophet

One of the most characteristic aspects of the book of Jeremiah is the Confessions, penetrating lament psalms handed down in the name of the prophet. Not all exegetes find the complaining prophet equally acceptable. Some have difficulty fitting the laments into their image of the prophet. Accordingly, in their exegesis, they try to neutralize the most pointed texts. Three texts may be considered. In 15:18 Jeremiah accuses YHWH of being a "deceitful brook." YHWH chides him for this (15:19–20; in 12:5 we also hear a reprimand; however, the answer in 15:11–14 must be seen as encouragement for the prophet). Second, in 20:7–9 we hear the complaint that he was "enticed, overpowered" by God's word. This complaint is at the same time his own answer (in v. 9), for he "cannot hold it in," which is followed by a strong declaration of trust, 20:11–13. Finally, in 20:14–18 he curses his birth. This lament is *not* answered, but the narrative continues with a new prophetic word in 21:1.

These texts give a varied picture. They are often seen psychologically as a learning process for the prophet, or theologically as a process of spiritual maturing. This is not impossible and not incorrect, certainly in the case of 15:18, but 20:14–18 does not fit. Might another solution be that the manner of speaking about YHWH is changing? While Amos and Micah do not protest and, while we hear nothing of the difficulty with their call, Jeremiah gives full space to this, as the reprimanding voice of YHWH recedes progressively: the prophet is *permitted* to complain, for he has good reason to do so. Indeed, his lamenting has a function within the proclamation. Where the prophetic word from above has lost its automatic authority, the only chance to communicate with man is by a man who not only communicates the message but *lives* it. Buber (182–83) indicates the contrast between the God of Jeremiah, who is far away—much farther than the false prophets think—yet, who is very near in the suffering of the prophet.

In sum: the image of the prophet converges; there are clear connections between the different "layers," though the picture is ambiguous. An analogy is suggested with Christology which needs many titles to express the mystery of Jesus of Nazareth. The image of "Jeremiah" as man, prophet, proclaimer of the word of YHWH and its personification, as well as model for the people of Israel remains a composite of many facets. The construction of this composite appears to be a deliberate process in the composition of the book. The book is hardly satisfied with a prophetic functionary who steps back from his task and mission, but it draws a picture of a man who lives in the tension of his calling, who stands beside and opposite the reader. In the words of Polk (173–74): the book speaks the "language of the heart." This is not because the psychology of the prophet needs independent attention but because only in this manner could there be a reaction to the crisis in which the people of Israel had landed and because, only thus, could the word of Yhwh get through to people.

Perspectives

The book of Jeremiah contains a very small number of promise oracles. A lamenting and accusing tone has so characterized the book that we have an English word, "jeremiad," which is defined as "a prolonged lamentation or complaint." The scant place for deliverance oracles is no surprise: the book played out in a period in which the people were heading toward catastrophe. Accordingly, prophecies of promise spoken in that period proved to be false prophecy. The emphasis on judgment prophecy stamps also the literary-theological person of Jeremiah: his own life of suffering foreshadows the suffering of his people.

We meet with the same theological milieu in Jeremiah 45, which is dealing with a lament by Baruch:

2. Thus says Yhwh the God of Israel, to you, Baruch:
3. You said:
   "Woe is me,
   for the Lord has added sorrow to my pain;
   I am weary with my groaning,
   and I find no rest."
4. Thus you shall say to him:
   "Thus says the Lord:
   See, what I have built I break down,
   and what I have planted I pluck up,
   and the whole land, it is mine.
5. And you, you seek great things for yourself?
   Do not seek them.
   For see, I bring disaster on all flesh
   —saying of the Lord—
   but I will give you your life as a prize of war
   in every place where you may go."

Like Jeremiah, Baruch complained about his present need, and he received an answer. "What *I* have built, I break down." In these words we taste God's sorrow concerning the future. Many scholars correctly interpret v. 4 as an expression of God's suffering because of the unfaithfulness of people and the measures he was forced to take. Baruch, and humankind with him, are called to share in the suffering of God. Compared with God's suffering, Baruch's own troubles appear small.

Yet, he receives a promise oracle: he will receive his life "as a prize of war." This expression only occurs in the book of Jeremiah and indicates survival for those who do not seek "great things" but do what is necessary in a given situation, namely, in 21:9 and 38:2: those who surrender to Babylon; in 39:18: Ebed-Melech, who saves Jeremiah from the pit into which he was thrown. May we call this deliverance in the form of "simple survival" or even salvation? Indeed we may. It may not seem much, but it is more than what Baruch and Jeremiah might have expected. It is a deliverance not *from* judgment but *through* judgment, as often stated in the book of Jeremiah.

This brief chapter forms the close of the so-called biography of Baruch. Chronologically it is misplaced by some twenty years (v. 1 is dated 604 B.C.E. whereas chap. 44 plays out after the fall of Jerusalem in 587 B.C.E.) The placement of this chapter is based on obvious content-theological grounds. This is not about the personal fate of Baruch; instead, he becomes a paradigm and his lament is almost identical with Jeremiah's: their functions are identical. The life of Baruch is like that of Jeremiah, an image of the fate of his people: as Baruch will survive, so the people will have a future through the depth of the exile. They will survive the crisis. Judah will lose city and temple and much more, but the "soul"—life and "essence"—will survive. Thus, Baruch portrays in this promise a glimmer of hope that remains in spite of impending gloom.

This was no time for celebration. The book of Jeremiah witnesses to the struggle to find new words of faith where old words proved invalid, a new certainty where the old was slipping away. This struggle consists largely in the demolition of beautiful-sounding but unreliable words of deliverance. What remains, however, no matter how scant, is far more encouraging than the empty sounds of lying prophecy, because these words are closely related to the situation at hand and at the same time carry the power of a true word from YHWH. In a similar vein, Dietrich Bonhoeffer, who was often encouraged by Jeremiah 45 while in a Nazi prison, wrote: "It is not the task of our generation 'to covet great things' again, but to save our soul from chaos and to keep it."

Jeremiah the Prophet:
Astride Two Worlds

LOUIS STULMAN
University of Findlay

One of the distinctive characteristics of the book of Jeremiah is that the persona of the prophet looms as large as or larger than the message itself. Ordinarily in the Hebrew Bible, prophets are eclipsed by the oracles they announce. This ought not be surprising given their role as messengers and spokespersons. As in the books of Amos, Micah, and even Isaiah, both the person and the persona of prophet are often obscured by the word of the Lord. Consequently, it is difficult at best to construct a character sketch for the majority of the so-called writing prophets. Jeremiah is an exception, however. Right from the start, the reader confronts a prophet whose life is clearly and inextricably interwoven with the words he proclaims. In particular, the book's biographical and autobiographical prose reflects a shift from the message to the messenger. Von Rad also observes this shift in the Confessions of Jeremiah when he claims that Isaiah and Micah were solely proclaimers of God's word but that in the case of Jeremiah we have something new in the prophetic assignment. Jeremiah served God not only with what he said but with his life, which was deeply involved in God's cause on earth. The prophet was equipped to be a witness to God not only by virtue of his charisma but by means of his very humanity. Therefore, the *life* of Jeremiah qua prophet takes on the authority of a witness (von Rad, "The Confessions of Jeremiah," 98).

One could even argue that the interpretive community of Jeremiah *transforms* the person of the prophet into the message itself, so that the two—the person and the message—coalesce to articulate together the poignant *dābār* ("word" or "event") of the Lord. In Jeremiah, therefore, the prophetic word and the prophetic persona converge to create

Author's note: This essay was adapted from my *Order Amid Chaos: Jeremiah As Symbolic Tapestry* (published by Sheffield Academic Press, 1998).

meanings and significance that are greater than either the word or the persona by itself.

In light of this union, I examine in this essay the persona of Jeremiah as presented in the book's two-part drama of the fall and rise of a nation (in the first and second scrolls, i.e., in chaps 1–25 and chaps. 26–52, respectively). The text presents the persona of Jeremiah as inextricably intertwined with the theme of dismantling and rebuilding. It draws a symbiotic relationship between the life and destiny of Jeremiah and that of the nation of Judah. Jeremiah is presented on a course that corresponds to, contrasts with, and at times intersects the course of the community. Both prophet and nation are called by God (chaps. 1 and 2); they suffer the shattering and death of a world (in Scroll One); and both emerge from the desolation as wounded survivors (in Scroll Two). Thus, the persona of Jeremiah acts as a mirror that reflects the nation's descent into utter hopelessness (in chaps. 1–25) as well as its emergence as an ill-treated yet enduring community (in chaps. 26–52).

Through the prophetic word and prophetic person, Jeremiah serves as Yhwh's iconoclastic voice that shatters and destabilizes certain world constructions in favor of new social and religious arrangements. He rejects conventional and hegemonic constraints of the state religion for fresh liturgical and ethical possibilities and moves from an ideology of certitude (in the first scroll) to an alternative order that is less defined and more ambiguous (in the second scroll). Ultimately he generates liberating counterclaims and authorizes an alternative social and symbolic world for a battered and bruised community of faith.

The Starting Point and Context for the Discussion

It is no coincidence that artists, poets, social critics, and playwrights have paid greater homage to the *person of Jeremiah* than to his words of judgment and consolation. Commentaries and Old Testament/Hebrew Bible introductions are likewise quick to point out that the life and personality of Jeremiah play a more prominent role than that of any other prophetic book.

The presentations of the Jeremiah's life are mediated through all three major types of literature in the book: the poetry (or the "A" material), the so-called "biographical" prose (or "B" tradition), and the autobiographical and/or sermonic material (the "C" block). In other words, portraits of Jeremiah are not restricted to any one genre but are constructed throughout much of the book. The poetry of Jeremiah comprises not only oracular material often set in a dirge meter but also the prophet's call and complaints or Confessions. His call (Jer 1:4–10) uses formulaic language to describe the prophet's authorization as well as his averse and ambivalent response to YHWH's claim upon his life. In his complaints Jeremiah continues to appear as a chosen yet conflicted man/prophet. Although there is no consensus regarding the function of the Confessions in the Jeremiah tradition, these poems on a surface level reflect the dissonant life of Jeremiah and his cries of outrage *on account of a vocation* that demands "plucking up and pulling down, destroying and overthrowing." Consequently, the prophet both speaks for God and also suffers on God's behalf as a result of his subversive activity. As such, Jeremiah is shown to be beyond a mouthpiece, a person; beyond an instrument, a partner with God.

While the story line of the so-called "B" materials (chaps. [36] 37–45) is also much disputed, these prose sections present a prophet who confers with kings, is imprisoned for alleged treason and eventually released, is deported to Egypt, and while there still refuses to be silenced. There are clearly a number of theological claims at work in the narrative. Nonetheless, Jeremiah is depicted here as one who endures the same destiny as the word of God that he proclaims: he is scorned and utterly rejected by the community, a rejection that brings to light Judah's culpability and YHWH's innocence.

The Jeremiah emerging in the prose sermons is part (and perhaps the last) of an institutional succession of inspired spokespersons of the Torah, of which Moses was first and preeminent. Like Moses, Jeremiah is portrayed as a Torah proponent who denounces Israel for Torah infractions (see, e.g., Jer 7:1–15; 11:1–13; 17:19–27). As a direct consequence of such actions, the prophet often evokes (Deuteronomic) curses for noncompliance (see especially Deuteronomy 28). However, even hopeful words are often governed by Torah ideals, as is most clearly the case in the promise of a new covenant for Judah and Israel (31:31–34). The prose sermons, therefore, employ memories of Moses, especially in his capacity as prophet and intermediary, in the formation of Jeremiah's character and message.

These and other representations of Jeremiah have been used for many years to reconstruct a *psychological profile* or *historical biography* of the prophet. At the beginning of this century, for example, Bernhard Duhm argued that the prophet was a sensitive, quiet, and profound person with the most tender sentiments and a gentle disposition. Duhm, however, could come to this understanding of Jeremiah only after excising all malevolent elements of the Confessions (e.g., 18:18–23; 11:21–23; 17:18) and labeling them non-Jeremianic. A few years later Sigmund

Mowinckel would contend that the poetry of Jeremiah reveals the prophet's complex and "multifaceted" personality. According to him, Jeremiah was rich in ideas, profound in insight, and predisposed to a wide range of moods. Mowinckel argued, however, that the prose sermons (the "C" material) transformed the prophet's dynamic character into a "shadowy figure" who proclaimed what he called a "dogmatic theology." In C nothing remained of the man Jeremiah who was introduced to us in sources A and B. Mowinckel judged the complex and varied Jeremiah of the poetry as historically more accurate; it was nothing less than the authentic representation of the prophet. In contrast, the dogmatic preacher of the prose sermons produced a later, inauthentic Deuteronomistic construction.

Not all engaged in the quest for the historical Jeremiah discerned disparities between the Jeremiah of history and the literary persona of the prophet. Unlike Duhm, Mowinckel, and their followers, many who championed a "biographical" reading of Jeremiah argued that the book affords us a literal rendering of the prophet's life and times. As a result, they perceived the "authentic voice" of Jeremiah in all the "sources." For these scholars, coherence and correspondence take precedence over the growth and development of the tradition. Like the approach of Mowinckel and Duhm, however, historical questions still very much governed their interpretation of the book, and reconstructing the "original" historical settings was understood as an integral component of the exegetical task. Consequently, it was assumed that the proper interpretive milieu was located in the networks of meaning presented in the original historical setting. Determining, for example, the proper date of Jeremiah's call, the prophet's response to the so-called Deuteronomic Reform of 622 B.C.E., and a suitable social setting for the work remain dominant concerns of a biographical-historical reading of the text.

Whether one is a "minimalist" (like Duhm) or a "maximalist" (like Holladay), the dominant paradigm of historical criticism has placed constraints on one's reading of the book of Jeremiah. Brueggemann asserts in this regard that a preoccupation with history and historical questions "holds the imagination of the text-creators hostage to historical experience, as though the writer-speaker could not imagine beyond concrete, identifiable experience. The logic of such a view is to require imagination to live within the limits of known historical experience, obviously an inadequate way of receiving such evocative literature" ("Jeremiah: Intense Criticism/Thin Interpretation," *Interpretation* 42 [1988] 270).

T. Polk is also doubtful about the advantages of a referential and diachronic approach and avers in his discussion of the Confessions of Jeremiah:

> it matters not whether the compositions are the product of the historical Jeremiah himself or later redactors. In my opinion, it violates the integrity of the text, *qua* poetry, to replace the given literary context with the conjectured historical occasion of the writing process and so to construe the text as referring to authorial circumstances rather than to the subject as it is literarily defined. (Polk, *The Prophetic Persona,* 165)

Both Brueggemann and Polk reflect a shift in recent scholarship that assigns greater importance to the literary character of the book and persona of Jeremiah than to historical criticism and the historical Jeremiah. While some scholars still show interest in reconstructing a psychological or biographical profile of Jeremiah, others have focused on the social world of the *text* and its metaphorical character. Accentuating the "Jeremiah of the text," however, is not necessarily done at the expense of the "Jeremiah of history." Underscoring the "Jeremiah of the text" simply acknowledges that the text's primary interests and focal concerns are not biographical or historical but theological and artistic— that is, a rendering of literary and symbolic art. "The theological intent is to articulate this person of Jeremiah as a *model* or *paradigm* [emphasis added] for what a prophet is, for what a believing person is, for what Israel might be" (Brueggemann, "The Book of Jeremiah: Portrait of a Prophet," 132). The *Tendenz* of the book is thus not to preserve biographical or autobiographical exactitude but to proclaim and instruct by employing historical memory and poetic imagination.

The Persona of Jeremiah as Presented in Scroll One

In light of the kerygmatic and didactic character of the text, I hold historical questions in abeyance in order to examine the literary and theological relationship of persona and message. When we move forward in this direction, the figure of Jeremiah surfaces in the text as diffuse and polyphonic as the oracles he proclaims. Jeremiah is represented in his book as a son of a priest, a messenger and spokesperson for God, an actor, a litigant, a gleaner, a sentry, a righteous sufferer, a covenant mediator, an iconoclast, a writer, a surrogate city, an impregnable wall of bronze, a confidant of kings, a prisoner and exile, a prophet to the nations, an assayer and tester of peoples' ways, and a proponent and opponent of God. Moreover, Jeremiah appears as a champion of Torah teaching, an intercessor forbidden to pray, a subversive poet, the voice of God and the voice of the poor, a madman, a survivor and witness, a symbol of destruction and hope, and a prophet like Moses. He is portrayed as compulsive, embittered and disillusioned, writhing in pain, vengeful, explosive, tormented and tormenting, conflicted, stern yet compassionate, volatile, penetrating, sanguine, sensitive yet detached, timorous, powerful and powerless.

As extensive as this list may be, it is by no means exhaustive but only indicative of the wide range of dissonant voices heard in the book (see the essay by Robert Carroll in this volume, pp. 77–85). Again, we find message and messenger interwoven. The discordant and diffuse character of Jeremiah appears to evolve out of the jumbled social and symbolic world of the text. The text does not afford Jeremiah the opportunity to abscond from a shattered world that is under siege from within and without. The prophet participates fully in the frantic and pathos-filled environment of Judah's crumbling milieu as well as in the wild and turbulent response of God to betrayal and unrequited love. Like Judah and YHWH, Jeremiah cannot stand at a distance, detached and with reticence. He too must share in the dreadful end of a world. As such, Jeremiah, a fractured and broken prophet, died with his countrymen. With Judah, however, he arose from utter despair as a wounded survivor. Because of the faithfulness of God, death and dismantling are the last words for neither Judah nor Jeremiah. Thus, although the persona of Jeremiah is diffuse and cannot be subsumed under any single heading, the text presents the life and destiny of the prophet on a course that parallels and intersects that of the nation.

In the first scroll (chaps. 1–25), Jeremiah's participation in the death of Judah's world comes to the fore most poignantly in the prophet's laments. We witness in these prayers a prophet in complete "solidarity with his people in their danger . . . such as we shall never meet again" (von Rad, *Old Testament Theology,* 2.196). In greater detail than any part of the first scroll, the complaints of Jeremiah reflect the marriage of persona and message, prophet and people, prophet and God. This convergence is evident when Jeremiah suffers with, on behalf of, and on account of the community that he was called to address. The convergence is stressed in the juxtaposition of the complaints of Jeremiah with the prose sermons. Although the relationship between the prose sermons and laments is somewhat fluid and probably not formally coherent (in chaps. 1–25), the two genres are generally located in the same literary environment. The correlation of prose discourses and laments may be clearer from the following outline:

Prose Sermon and Lament 1

Jer 7:1–8:3	The Dismantling of the Temple Ideology (prose)
Jer 8:4–17	Poetic Oracles Announcing Imminent Disaster
Jer 8:18–9:1[2]	Jeremiah Laments Judah's Response to His Denunciation of Temple Ideology

Prose Sermon and Lament 2

Jer 11:1–17	The Dismantling of Covenant Understandings (prose)
Jer 11:18–12:6	Jeremiah Laments the People's Violent Reaction to His Denunciation of Covenant Ideology

Prose Sermon and Lament 3

Jer 15:10–21	Jeremiah Laments the Rejection of His Prophetic Words: The Prophet's Declaration of Innocence and Cry for Divine Intervention
Jer 16:1–13 (15)	The Divine Response: A Call to Abandon All Expectations for Social and Cosmic Order (prose)

Prose Sermon and Lament 4

Jer 17:14–18	Jeremiah Laments the Community Taunts and Prays for the Restoration of Symmetry
Jer 17:19–27	Moral Symmetry of Torah or Covenant Observance (prose)

Prose Sermon and Lament 5

Jer 18:1–12	The Dismantling of Election Understandings (prose)
Jer 18:13–17	Poetic Oracles Condemning Judah for Forsaking God
Jer 18:18–23	Jeremiah Laments His Ill-Treatment and Uses Imprecatory Language against His Adversaries

Prose Sermon and Lament 6

Jer 20:1–6	Imprisoned by Pashhur—Whose Name Is Changed to "Terror-All-Around"
Jer 20:7–18	Jeremiah Cries Out in Rage against God and Utters His Own Death Wish
Jer 21:1–10	The Dismantling of Royal-Dynastic Ideology (prose)

The close proximity of Jeremianic complaints to the prose sermons of the first scroll is neither fortuitous nor incidental. In the extant form of the text, the prophet's screams of pain and his dangerous prose sermons participate in an intentional symbiotic relationship. This relationship seems to accent key facets of the multiplex persona of Jeremiah as it takes shape in the first scroll. As a suffering servant of God, Jeremiah is persecuted as a direct result of Judah's violent reaction to the prose sermons (see especially 11:18–12:4; 18:18–22). That is to say, when the complaints are read in conjunction with the prose sermons, Jeremiah's suffering appears to have been bound to, and a direct consequence of, his frontal attack on Judah's well-established conventional arrangements. As such, the text does not focus merely, or even primarily, on Jeremiah's personal suffering but on suffering that grows "out of his specific situation as a prophet" (von Rad, *Old Testament Theology*, 2.204). More precisely, a contextual reading suggests that the prophet's distress occurs as a result of his bold and subversive prose sermons. These prose discourses, which provide the literary artifice for the divine work of undoing the nation's inept and oppressive structures, provoke a response of rage and engender concerted efforts to silence the prophetic voice of judgment.

On the heels of the prophet's ominous sermon on covenant observance, for instance (Jer 11:1–17), he cries out to God that his life is under siege by community members who desire to destroy him (Jer 11:18–20). In the face of adversity and persecution, Jeremiah maintains his own innocence and places full blame on those who attack him. Furthermore, the prophet prays for both protection and the restoration of moral symmetry (see especially 12:1–4). However, in a world that is unraveling at the seams, even such modest expectations are met with stern and cryptic warnings (12:5–6). When this complaint is read as a response to Jeremiah's scathing sermon on covenant observance, his grave condition may be construed as a direct consequence of the community's onslaught against God's covenant mediator. In an effort to cut off the prophet "from the land of the living," Judah desperately attempts to nullify the terrifying prose indictment for breach of covenant observance. Such actions, however, are ineffectual and only expose the corruption of the nation.

A similar reaction of rage follows Jeremiah's assault on Judah's elect status (Jer 18:1–11). In the extant form of the text, the hearers of the prose sermon respond to the prophet's invitation to "return" to YHWH with a resounding "No!" (18:12). Moreover, following an intervening indictment in poetry (18:13–17), certain (unknown) people now plot against Jeremiah because they perceive in his words an attack on the very power structures that sustain community life (Jer 18:18).

Apparently privy to such schemes, Jeremiah defends his innocence and prays for the total destruction of his adversaries and their families (18:19–23).

The juxtaposition of this prophetic lament with a prose sermon not only draws a direct correlation between Jeremiah's suffering and the prose announcement of cosmic crumbling but it also functions as a theodicy. Jeremiah's innocent suffering at the hands of community members reveals Judah's unmitigated guilt, because the nation rejects both the covenant suzerain and the covenant mediator. All that the prophet endures and every beleaguered word he speaks highlight Judah's unjust and idolatrous posture. Even Jeremiah's ambivalent obedience brings to light Judah's unambiguous apostasy.

As one whose entire life and service to God heightens the community's wrongdoing, Jeremiah functions as a foil character in the book. This role is not confined to his laments, however. There are already hints that his life and destiny would parallel and counter that of Judah's in the call narrative. Here God embraces Jeremiah before birth and "predestines," "consecrates," and "appoints" him to be a prophet to the nations (1:4–5). Jeremiah responds to YHWH's summons with reluctance, identifying himself as only a "young man" who does not know quite how to speak. Although Jeremiah is uncertain about and even resistant to the word of YHWH, he nonetheless emerges from the chapter as one who is obedient, chosen, set apart, and empowered by God to face the fierce opposition that would be waged against him by the nation and its power brokers: by kings, princes, and priests, as well as the people of the land. To prepare the prophet for his difficult work, God transforms timid and reluctant Jeremiah into a "fortified city, an iron pillar, and a bronze wall." In lieu of one "fortified city" that would eventually go down in ruin (Jerusalem!), therefore, Jeremiah is presented by the text as a "surrogate" city.

These overtures toward Jeremiah in some respects correspond to the overtures extended to Judah. The lawsuit oracle in chap. 2 begins with a brief recital of God's gracious acts on behalf of Israel. Like Jeremiah, the community, when called by God at birth, is described as a "youth" who is "holy to the Lord," thus enjoying God's care and protection (2:2–3). During her time of betrothal, Israel wholeheartedly "followed" YHWH, her covenant partner, devoted only to his purposes. Even the hardships of the wilderness could not weaken this love relationship. YHWH, Israel's defender, protected the community from the onslaughts of dangerous enemies (both insider and outsider) by punishing all who would violate her.

Despite God's unwavering faithfulness, Judah's first love or youthful "devotion" quickly evaporated. In direct contrast to Jeremiah's reluctant obedience, Judah's flagrant rebellion and apostasy are portrayed unambiguously in the rest of the first scroll. The house of Israel and the house of Judah are bent on abandoning YHWH for other gods (see 2:4–37). The nation acts in character when it declines the many gracious invitations extended by God to "return." In fact, the community's recalcitrance and insubordination to YHWH are expressions of a history of obduracy.

The clearest and most poignant materials with which Jeremiah is cast as a foil character are without doubt the prophet's laments, especially when these prayers are read in conjunction with the prose sermons. It is precisely the juxtaposing of the two genres and their respective pieties that demonstrates the utter disparity between the righteous prophet, the surrogate nation and the idolatrous nation. In the coalescence of lament and sermon, Jeremiah's every move, his every word, his cries out of the depths—all bear witness both to the nation's arrant disobedience and his own "innocence" and alliance with YHWH. Each prose sermon sets forth various facets of the nation's wrongdoing while the adjoining lament clarifies the prophet's integrity and veracity. Accordingly, Jeremiah declares that he is unaware of the community's assault against him and that such aggression is entirely unjustified (11:18–23). The prophet complains that he is a "man of strife and contention to the whole land" (15:10). Even though he has "neither lent nor borrowed," all curse him (15:10). Jeremiah insists that he has been faithful to his prophetic vocation (15:16–17), yet he suffers excruciating pain (15:18). Moreover, he is recompensed evil for good (18:20) and encounters those who plot to kill him (18:22). The prophet faces scorn, abject humiliation, and reproach on account of his message of "violence and destruction" (20:7–12). The righteous prophet, especially in his role as a suffering servant of YHWH, unmasks the community's obduracy, thus justifying the ensuing desolation.

Finally, the nexus of prose sermon and complaint creates a milieu of death in which both the guilty community *and* the innocent prophet go down in apparent hopelessness. In doing so, the prose discourses and the Confessions in the first scroll descend into near oblivion as they depict God breaking down Judah's world. Whereas Jeremiah's suffering is cast in stark contrast to that of Judah's, both go down together. Like the prose sermons that broaden and intensify the scope of Judah's crumbling world, Jeremiah's laments, when read in succession, traverse "a road which leads step by step into ever greater despair" and "threaten[s] to end in some kind of metaphysical abyss" (G. von Rad, *Old Testament Theology*, 2.204). Together they testify to the descent of darkness upon the world. Indeed, now *the words and persona* of the prophet bear witness to the terrifying reality of cosmic crumbling. Any hope for the preservation of the old categories, any illusion of permanence, is totally dispelled by the confluence of the two.

In Jer 8:18–9:2, for instance, Jeremiah (and/or God) laments over Judah's pathetic and "fatuous complacency" (see especially 8:18–19b, 20–21). Although this passage is difficult to classify in terms of genre, it appears to be in part a personal lament, for it portrays Jeremiah's thoughts at the time the action takes place. As a parent who stands helplessly by the bed of a dying child, the poet (with God) can do nothing to head off imminent destruction. And so Jeremiah writhes in heartache and disappointment.

In contrast to Jeremiah's profound sadness in the face of desolation, Israel remains smug. As such, the nation maintains the same impudence and false security exemplified in the preceding Temple Sermon (which evidently serves as subtext for this lament). The community does not even perceive "that the temple claims are dead and have failed (cf. Jeremiah 7)" (Brueggemann, *A Commentary on Jeremiah*, 93). One can thus discern here clear echoes of the prose assertion that neither Jerusalem nor the temple will provide refuge from the soon-approaching destruction.

In Jer 15:10–21, Jeremiah rues his birth because he finds himself in conflict with "the whole land." The prophet, moreover, is tormented by the disparity between his conduct and his miserable condition. He testifies, as I noted earlier, that he has "not lent nor borrowed, yet all of them curse me" (15:10). He has embraced the vocation of prophet (15:16) and has accepted "the isolation and alienation from the community which have been imposed by the prophetic mission" (Diamond, *The Confessions of Jeremiah in Context*, 76). Nonetheless, he has yet to enjoy the anticipated protection and reparations from YHWH (Jer 15:18).

In context, the divine response to Jeremiah's complaint should not be limited to the poetic oracle in 15:19–21. The prose sermon that immediately follows (Jer 16:1–13) broadens the contextual base for understanding Jeremiah's Confession and YHWH's response. In addition to the brief poetic oracle in 15:19–21, which promises the prophet little respite from opposition, the prose sermon (in chap. 16) asserts that Jeremiah must relinquish all expectations for conventional structures, while the ordered universe unravels. The broader context appears to demand that the prophet abandon both the hope for normal social life

(16:2) and any prospect for an orderly symbol system (as the prophet longs for in 15:10–18). In spite of his obedience to God, Jeremiah is not exempt from the coming calamity. The prophet must participate fully in the demolition of Judah's world.

This participation is clearly illustrated in Jer 17:14–18, where the prophet once more cries out for divine aid and retribution against his enemies. Again we see that the suffering and turmoil of Jeremiah are not merely expressions of personal piety divorced from the prophetic office but are, rather, direct repercussions of the prophetic message.

> See how they say to me,
> "Where is the word of YHWH?
> Let it come!" (Jer 17:15)

K. M. O'Connor has argued that "this remark provides the key to the passage and reveals the nature of the prophet's predicament" (*Confessions of Jeremiah*, 49). Jeremiah's message of judgment has not yet come to pass, and so he is taunted by the community. In spite of the prophet's declaration of innocence (17:16) and his pleas for divine mercy (17:17) and vindication (17:18), he nonetheless is granted little reprieve. Instead, he is instructed by God (in the following prose sermon, Jer 17:19–27) to bring to the fore again (as he had in the bracketing section, Jer 11:1–13) the necessity of covenant observance and "hearing" Torah teachings. In the present literary setting, the alliance of Confession and prose sermon "emphasizes the failure of the people to heed YHWH's word" (ibid., 143), while entertaining some (faint) hope that the threatened disaster might yet be averted.

The penultimate Confession (18:18–23) is juxtaposed with yet another prose sermon (18:1–12). This prose discourse declares that Israel's election status can be reversed as a result of recalcitrance and disobedience. The potter allegory asserts that a once-rejected nation can change its ill-fated destiny if it "turns from its evil" (18:8). Conversely and more aptly, a nation that God "builds and plants" (18:9) can be rejected and destroyed if it "does not listen" (18:10). As potter and creator of Israel, God "shapes evil" against the community in order to bring "the people of Judah and the inhabitants of Jerusalem" to its senses (18:11). The text, however, contends forcefully that the people respond to the gracious invitation with an unequivocal "No" (18:12), thus sealing for itself, in the presence of the nations (18:13–17), its "horrifying" death.

The complaint of the people (18:18) and the subsequent prayer of the prophet (in 18:19–23) follow the prose indictment (18:1–12).

Although the prophet's persecutors are not explicitly identified, the obscure third-person-plural pronoun ("they" in 18:18) coincides with the ambiguous "they" in 18:12. In other words those who refuse to heed the prophet's assault on "insider privilege" now turn against him in a counteract of violence. This unnamed party within the community (a party apparently comprising of persons located at the upper tiers of the social hierarchy, because they perceive Jeremiah as posing a grave threat to "upper-tiered" structures [in 18:18]) attempt to bridle Jeremiah's (God's) "design for evil" (18:11) with their own evil "designs" (18:18). To thwart the threat of desolation and dismantling of the nation, this party engineers a plot that will "provide grounds for the slander, discrediting and ultimate destruction of the prophet before the nation." In response, Jeremiah prays to God for support (18:19), defends his innocence (18:20), and pleads for divine vengeance on his enemies (18:21–23). Notwithstanding such entreaties, Jeremiah's life remains in grave danger.

In the last Confession Jeremiah's despair and hopelessness reach a most critical level. Here we arrive at the final stage in the prophet's *via dolorosa*, the lowest point in his suffering:

> May the day of birth be cursed.
> The day when my mother brought me forth,
> may it not be blessed. (Jer 20:14)

"Night has now completely enveloped the prophet" (von Rad, "The Confessions of Jeremiah," 95). All hope for tomorrow has dissolved. The prophet is left alone to grieve the world that is gone. And yet he does not grieve in isolation. He stands alongside and inside a community that must face the loss of temple, covenant, election privileges, land, and king—that is to say, the deprivation of certitude and control.

So understood, the first scroll traverses a terrain that encompasses the prophet's call ("before I formed you in the womb," 1:5) and his longing for death (20:14–18). Intriguingly, both the call and death wish of Jeremiah are associated with the "womb" (cf. 1:5 and 20:17, 18). The womb—as a place of birth and as an abode of death—form the symbolic boundaries for the persona of Jeremiah as depicted in the first scroll. Paralleling the birth (2:1–3) and dissolution of Judah's social and symbolic universe, Jeremiah goes down to destruction in apparent hopelessness. Along with the people of Judah who must die in the presence of God, Jeremiah too stands under the severity of God's wrath. Jeremiah cannot escape the fate of the community. In fact he must embrace the dissolution and suffering of Judah as well as his suffering and disappointment with God. *By the conclusion of the first scroll, both the words and the persona of Jeremiah are eclipsed by darkness.* And together they testify that God's dangerous work of "plucking up and pulling down, destroying and overthrowing" is well underway.

The Persona of Jeremiah as Presented in Scroll Two

In the second scroll, the words and persona of Jeremiah still remain intractably knit together. While both are anchored firmly in the harsh realities of a crumbling world, the *messenger and the message* now testify to God's new work of "building and planting." Amid the desolation and unraveling of community life, the prophet heralds a *message* of restoration and promise for the future. Consequently, overtures of hope can be discerned throughout much of Jeremiah 26–52, but they are articulated most forcefully in the first macrostructural unit (chaps. 26–36), the oracles against the nations (chaps. 46–51), and in the "positive" prose endings of the book (chaps. 45, 51, 52). These blocks of material in particular assert the reestablishment of Israel as the very *telos* of history. The construction of the *literary persona of the prophet* in chaps. 26–52 echoes this message of hope and testifies that disaster and chaos are only penultimate realities. In other words, the literary persona of Jeremiah as configured in the second scroll corresponds to and buttresses the book's transition from what appears to be absolute hopelessness and judgment (in chaps. 1–25) to visions of transformation beyond exile. As such, Jeremiah *proclaims and embodies* the dual and paradoxical realization of death and resurrection, judgment and promise, threat and hope, exile and homecoming, endings and new beginnings. While the prophet can never elude the shadow of suffering and dislocation, he nonetheless comes forth in the second scroll as a "conflicted" messenger of YHWH whose persona pulsates with enormous possibilities for a yet-shapeless future.

This ambivalent characterization of Jeremiah—as one rooted in suffering and yet replete with potential for hope and promise—is evident in the introduction to the second scroll (chap. 26). Unlike the muted response to the Temple Sermon in the first scroll (in Jer 7:1–15), Jeremiah 26 describes an ambivalent reaction to the messenger of YHWH. Although many want to kill him for his assault on "the city" and its sacred shrine (26:7–11), others insist that Jeremiah is innocent of wrongdoing and is therefore undeserving of death (26:16–24). In doing so, they give him "mixed reviews," for the first time in this book, instead of flatly rejecting him. Like the people of Judah whom he represents, the prophet will survive and enjoy an opportunity to carve out a modest future. Moreover, his prophetic work will not come to a screeching halt, for the voice of God will not be silenced. Such modest allusions or "cracks" of hope contribute to the complex texture of the remainder of the book.

Without entering into an extensive discussion here, I will say that the subsequent chapters of the second scroll portray Jeremiah as a wounded survivor, who triumphs over adversity. So understood, the second scroll presents the persona of the prophet in an altogether distinct manner from that of the first scroll. In Jeremiah 26–36, the first macro-structural unit of the second scroll, the prophet is still battered and bruised by events and opponents over which he has little control. For instance, he faces stiff opposition from prophets and priests in Jerusalem and Babylon, whose configurations of the new world order are apparently still anchored in the old state religion's world view (chaps. 27–29). Nonetheless, he now emerges victorious over such hostilities. In a passionate confrontation between Jeremiah and the prophet Hananiah ben Azzur, Hananiah dies, thus revealing a "Deuteronomic vindication" of Jeremiah's message (chap. 28). The oracle against Shemaiah of Nehelam likewise corroborates the divine judgment on Jeremiah's enemies (29:24–32).

Moreover, while "landless" and "confined in the court of the guard" near the king's palace (chap. 32) and during the siege of Jerusalem by the Babylonian armies, Jeremiah is assured by God that "houses and fields and vineyards" will indeed come forth from the rubble and devastation. Despite present contingencies and the apparent cessation of history, Jeremiah, while still imprisoned, testifies in word and deed that God's salvific purposes on Judah's behalf have not ended.

In the pivotal chapter of the second scroll (36), Jeremiah finds himself under attack by the power brokers of the nation and in jeopardy of suffering a decisive defeat. The frenzied and dangerous scene is precipitated of course by a scroll read by Baruch to the assembly of royal officials and in the court scribe's office. While the royal officials are alarmed by the contents of the scroll (v. 16), King Jehoiakim and his hatchet men respond in a cold and calculated manner: they destroy the scroll and seek to arrest Baruch and Jeremiah in a cunning attempt to silence both message and messenger (v. 26). The text, however, asserts unequivocally that no exercise of control and domination can frustrate the sovereign purposes of God. And so YHWH hides Jeremiah and Baruch from their persecutors (v. 26), while the two collude to reproduce a scroll that is to include "many other (damning) words" (v. 32). Again, Jeremiah not only survives the conflict but he is triumphant.

In the Baruch narrative (chaps. [36] 37–45) Jeremiah suffers profoundly as Judah's world collapses under its own weight and under the heavy hand of the Babylonian armies. And yet even here, as the prophet suffers in solidarity with God and Judah, he nonetheless survives the offensive waged by dangerous insiders and encroaching outsiders. Like the community, Jeremiah would indeed go into exile but he, like Baruch, Ebed-melech, and the deportees in Babylon, would come through alive. The endangered prophet is rescued as a result of Ebed-melech's bold act of faith (38:7–13) and the ambivalent posturing of Zedekiah (e.g., Jeremiah 37), as well as by the kind overtures shown to him by Nebuzaradan (chap. 40). The latter liberates Jeremiah from "the fetters on his hands" and offers him asylum in Babylon, which he declines. In all this, the text heralds through the word and the literary persona of Jeremiah that new life and blessing would arise out of exile and death. Indeed, the present moment of social dislocation and symbolic anxiety, far from being the final act in the drama, provided enormous potential for new cosmic categories. Put more modestly, the community is assured of survival as a wounded yet reconfigured entity that would once again enjoy the blessings of God.

In the oracles against the nations [OAN], the final macrounit of the second scroll (in the MT), Jeremiah's appearance as a "prophet to the nations" balances and fulfills the call narrative in chap. 1. The OAN punctuate the second scroll and the book as a whole with hopeful oracles that "envisage(s) the destruction of the very power responsible for Judah's pathetic condition during the Babylonian hegemony" (Carroll, *Jeremiah* [OTG], 111). Interestingly the persona of the speaker is almost entirely absent in these texts because Jeremiah is eclipsed by the words he speaks. At the end of the OAN, however, he reappears as "writer" of "all the disasters that would come on Babylon, all these words that are written concerning Babylon" (51:60). And as such, the last words of the text depict Jeremiah as a strong opponent of the raw power responsible for Judah's wretched condition, thus heralding that the arrogant forces of oppression would be extinguished by the sovereign God. In the second half of the book, therefore, *the words and persona* of the prophet converge to declare that the dark valley of exile is not the final word of God but only a prelude and invitation to newness and hope.

The Scaffolding of the
Book of Jeremiah

MARTIN KESSLER
Danville, Pennsylvania

While the term *paradigm shift* has been overused at times, it seems to have some relevance to Jeremiah studies. Among widely used commentaries, some old standbys of the stripe of Rudolph and Bright are now being superseded by more recent studies, most notably the massive commentaries by Holladay, McKane, and Carroll. Brueggemann, commenting on these works, found them rather disappointing exegetically. His own, briefer, two-volume commentary on Jeremiah is, in significant ways, more helpful, particularly if read in conjunction with his magisterial work *Theology of the Old Testament: Testimony, Dispute, Advocacy* (1997). However, it seems as though the paradigm shift has not yet been completed, for there is no consensus on the interpretation of the book of Jeremiah. This is evident from the excellent work *Troubling Jeremiah* (ed. A. R. P. Diamond, K. M. O'Connor, and L. Stulman, 1999) which, while it offers much progress, also illustrates a continuing diffuseness in methodological focus.

The sheer size of the book of Jeremiah has not helped the situation. There is also the fact, not to be overlooked, that the book of Isaiah has always won the popularity contest with its neighbors Jeremiah and Ezekiel. Isaiah, for example, is one of the most heavily quoted books in the Greek New Testament, whereas Jeremiah is all too often (unfairly) associated with his lamentations (the so-called Confessions). Another important point worth noting is the progress that Isaiah scholarship has made in terms of cutting through the old shibboleths of multiple Isaiahs and Servant Songs. This does not mean returning to a single author but, rather, judging Isaiah to be a single book, even if it is appropriately characterized as "a complex unity." The work *New Visions of Isaiah*, edited by Melugin and Sweeney, is recommended reading for those who want to be up to date on the emerging consensus of Isaiah scholarship on the "unity" of this book, a unity not of authorship but of theme and coherence.

57

The present study pursues a synchronic path. It seems quite superfluous to offer a full-fledged defense for this procedure; this has been given
in countless ways by many writers. After over a century of genetic
criticism, it seems reasonable to attempt a different approach, though
it is quite understandable that there may still be a few who regard synchronic criticism as an enemy in the camp. The best result one might
hope for is that thorough and responsible literary analysis of the text will
not only reveal much about the surface structure of the book but even
provide us with some historical and sociological clues about the text.

Regarding Jeremiah, we are far from achieving a consensus or even
a majority view on the structure of the book except in very rough outlines. In the essays in this volume a number of attempts have been
made. Before offering some additional comments on structure, I wish
to make a few general points on the Jeremian material by way of literary and material distinctions, which may help us to gain an overview of
the book as a whole.

1. The most obvious distinction and also the most vulnerable is between *prose* and *poetry*. Newer biblical translations tend to print as poetry the parts of the text that are generally understood to be poetry.
One needs only to compare the King James Version's printing of the
text as if it all were prose with a more recent translation such as the
New Revised Standard Version, which presents much material as poetry. In an important sense, the prose-poetry dialogue has been carried
on by various modern Bible translations. Steven Weitzman, referring to
a number of studies on biblical poetry, writes: "These studies show that
there is no single trait that can be relied upon to distinguish biblical
prose from poetry—not meter, not rhyme, not even parallelism, since
the first two may not exist in biblical Hebrew and the latter also appears frequently in prose" (*Song and Story in Biblical Narrative* [1997],
143). Thus, the boundary between prose and poetry is nowhere near as
simple as often perceived, partly because every Hebrew biblical verse
(prose or poetry) is divided into parts. Moreover, unfortunately, prose
is generally judged to fall well below the literary quality of poetry; this
in turn adversely affects the judgment of the content.

Since this is a very basic topic in Jeremian scholarship, we may be
permitted to extend the discussion a bit by referring to the helpful discussion by F. Breukelman in *Bijbelse Theologie*, 1/1. concerning attempts
made in antiquity to facilitate the reading of the written text aloud.
Such reading was difficult because originally, words were not separated, and punctuation was lacking; the text was presented as *scriptio
continua*. This precluded rapid reading; for the text to be compre-

hended and remembered, a great deal of concentration on the part of the reader was required.

Two aids to reading were developed: *interpunction* and *colometry*. Interpunction refers to the placement of punctuation marks, the period (*punctum*) being the first one. As an aid to reading, a period was inserted between two words; hence the word *interpunctio*. Accordingly, reading aloud was called "oral interpunction." Clearly, this is about reading the text as given, regardless of whether it might be labeled prose or poetry.

Colometry refers to the segmenting of the text *on the basis of meaning without reference to length*. St. Jerome called it *per cola et commata*, the cola being the larger parts of a sentence and the comma the smaller parts. The great German theologians and translators Martin Buber and Franz Rosenzweig insisted that the German Bible must rid itself of punctuation systems, whether based on music or logic. For the sake of correct reading and hearing, we need to start all over again, they averred, which means that present punctuation systems need to be set aside at any cost, because the public has done a bad job of reading. Instead, these scholars felt, the segmenting of the text must depend on *breathing units*, which do not depend on logical or rhythmical considerations. Since breath is the stuff of speech, the drawing of breath should determine the natural segmenting of speech units.

Unfortunately, five centuries before printing was invented, colometry disappeared. Some attempts have been made to reinstitute this method of segmenting. The purpose of this excursus is to suggest that traditional distinctions of "poetry" and "prose," which have often been incorporated in print, and in turn have influenced reading and, for better or for worse, understanding—are due for revision. Colometry deserves to be resuscitated so that its services might contribute to reading and hearing with understanding. The model for this procedure is found in the concordant German translation of the Old Testament by Buber and Rosenzweig (*Die Schrift verdeutscht von Martin Buber gemeinsam mit Franz Rosenzweig*). An American attempt at a similar translation was made by Everett Fox: *The Five Books of Moses*.

2. Another clear distinction that we meet in the prophetic literature is between words that speak of "*good things*" coming ("salvation," "deliverance") and words that announce "*bad things*" ("judgment," "destruction"). Form critics have invented many labels, among them "oracles of salvation" or "promise oracles" versus "judgment oracles." The good things refer to blessings of all kinds grounded and reiterated in the patriarchal promises made to Abraham, Isaac, and Jacob. They pertain

fundamentally to land and offspring, blessed by fertility (in offspring, animals, and fields). The "bad things" (punishments, judgment) form a long list, such as the familiar trio of famine, war, and pestilence. The oracles against the nations (Jeremiah 46–51) dip very liberally into the massive inventory of items that describe the punishment meted out by YHWH, the God of Israel, on the foreign nations addressed. Additionally, the first half of the book of Jeremiah contains similar judgment oracles addressed to Judah, interspersed with other literary types and numerous calls to repentance. This literature (addressed to Judah) appears to be mostly in the "threat" mode; the indicated punishment is announced as a distinct possibility, or even a probability—but only to be executed if Judah does not mend its ways; in other words, this judgment speech is contingent by nature. It is quite clear that the implied hope, sometimes made explicit, is that Judah will avert the stated punishment by heeding the threat (cf. Jer 25:1–7).

3. Regarding the persons or nations addressed in Jeremiah, most of the material is intended for Judah and Jerusalem as a whole, but there are also judgment oracles addressed to specific classes, such as kings, prophets, and priests. On the other hand, there are also prophetic oracle collections clearly intended for foreign nations (chaps. 46–51).

4. The Jeremiah material gets quite complicated, if not confusing, when the two sets of oppositions (#2 and #3) cross over—that is, Judah versus the nations, and "good" versus "bad" (blessings versus punishments). Unless this dialectic of "promises" versus "punishments" and "Israel" versus "the nations" is grasped, the book will remain a hopeless confusion to the reader, and the expectation of any sort of coherence will remain an idle dream. It is best unraveled by sketching the scenario as it unfolds in the book on the surface level.

Judah and YHWH: Jeremiah 25

First, Judah had disobeyed YHWH and therefore was forced to hear the hard messages in which punishment was threatened unless moral improvement (repentance!) was forthcoming. This kind of speech virtually occupies the first half of the book.

In chap. 25, we encounter YHWH's overall program. This chapter, which I have described elsewhere as a "hinge" in the book of Jeremiah, is in effect the "key" to the book. Jer 25:1–7 contains a "motivation" (for the two-pronged judgment oracle that follows), which emphatically asserts that the Word of YHWH had come to Jeremiah for a period of 23 years (25:3). The prophet further reminds his hearers that he had faithfully communicated YHWH's word, that YHWH had sent him as he had other prophets (v. 4), and that he had reminded the people to follow the commandments (v. 7), but in each case there had been nothing but negative results: "You have not listened to [obeyed!] me, says YHWH" (vv. 3, 4, 7). It would be difficult to find a more apt and succinct characterization of the first half of the book.

The typical "therefore" (v. 8) prefaces the judgment oracle that follows the motivation (underscoring a necessary connection between the preceding [motivation] and the following [judgment oracle]), epitomizing as it were (in vv. 8–14) all of the punitive oracles in the preceding chapters. The oracle is introduced by the phrase carried over from the motivation: "because you have not obeyed [heard!] my words" (v. 8). Just as YHWH had previously "sent" prophets—though they went unheeded—so now he would "send" for the armies of the north, led by Nebuchadnezzar, king of Babylon, to punish the nation. This part of the oracle runs through 25:11, with the words: "This whole land shall become a ruin and a waste, and these nations [Judah and the surrounding nations] shall serve the king of Babylon seventy years." Indeed, this verse sums up and climaxes the first half of the book.

Judah and YHWH: Jeremiah 1

But the reader is also reminded powerfully of chap. 1, which contains the prophet's call narrative; it is another part of the book's scaffolding. Here the prophet is told in no uncertain terms that YHWH is commissioning him to execute his sovereignty *over the nations*: "See, I have set you this day over nations and over kingdoms, to pluck up and to break down, to destroy and to overthrow, to build and to plant" (1:10). Since this call, right up to 25:13, the story has been about YHWH's *threat* to "pluck up, break down, destroy, and overthrow," not only Judah, but (eventually) the surrounding nations as well. However, in chap. 25 the point is reached where threats (which functioned, as we have seen, as contingent oracles, the execution of which depended on the people's response) are replaced by genuine judgment oracles (bare predictions, though they too sometimes assume an air of contingency; cf. 38:17–18). In this chapter YHWH's plans, as they have been developing over many years, are specifically stated.

YHWH and Babylon

The agent whom YHWH expressly employed to execute his plans of destruction was the king of Babylon, who is therefore appropriately called YHWH's servant (25:9a), since he is, at this particular juncture of history, simply doing YHWH's bidding. All of this is predicated on the assumption that YHWH's sovereignty extends not only to Israel/Judah but to all nations (1:10). In effect, the text says that the king of Babylon has been appointed YHWH's (temporary) caretaker and that therefore all the nations (Judah included) are to serve King Nebuchadnezzar. What this mighty king did not seem to understand (judging from his subsequent behavior) was that YHWH retained ultimate sovereignty for himself, that he did not receive a blank check from YHWH, and that Babylon's sovereignty was strictly limited in time. He was only chosen *for his particular task, for a stated time period*; he was not chosen as a partner in covenant, as was Israel, the people of the covenant, who had been reminded again and again of their status as YHWH's "treasure people" (Exod 19:5). God's appointment of Nebuchadnezzar was not designated an election but an ad hoc appointment for a specific task: to mete out punishment to the people specified by YHWH. Again, YHWH was in no way obligated to "stay with" Babylon; in fact, quite the opposite was true. The "shocker" in this scenario is precisely this: after having used Babylon to demolish Jerusalem, YHWH assigned Babylon itself to irreversible destruction.

Accordingly, the judgment oracle in 25:8–14 is a curious one. Having accomplished its divinely-ordained task, Babylon, the punisher, is next in line for ordained judgment. As pointed out, the literary "hinge" is v. 12: "Then after seventy years are completed, I will punish the king of Babylon and that nation, the land of the Chaldeans, for their iniquity, says YHWH, making the land a perpetual waste."

This unexpected turn has puzzled many readers. Why should Babylon be punished for something that it was especially commissioned to do—by YHWH himself? This question needs to be borne in mind in the context of the book as a whole. More light is shed on it in the oracles against Babylon in Jeremiah 50 and 51, where this superpower is accused of pride, if not hubris (cf. 50:31). The reader is also referred to Brueggemann's article in this volume (pp. 117–134).

In the narratives describing the siege of Jerusalem, King Zedekiah asks the prophet for an oracle from YHWH, and the prophet tells him to submit to Babylon (38:14–18); in other words, to accept YHWH's plan for "the nations," including Judah. In fact, the prophet gave the king a choice: submit (to Babylon directly, but to YHWH indirectly) and all will be well; do not submit, and "this city shall be given into the hand of the Chaldeans, and they shall burn it with fire, and you shall not escape from their hand" (38:18). Not surprisingly, in view of the people's sustained opposition to Babylon's advances, Jeremiah was accused of treason (37:13). After Jerusalem was occupied by Nebuzaradan, the prophet was still regarded as being in league with the enemy. Jeremiah finally disappeared from sight when he was dragged along to Egypt to flee the Babylonian occupation (43:6). Once more, the motif "they did not obey the voice of YHWH" is sounded (43:7). Egypt was a paradigm for bondage and idolatry, and except for the sojourn by Joseph and his family to escape famine, it was not associated with YHWH's future blessings.

Oracles against the Nations: Babylon

The only way we can make sense out of the present text of the book of Jeremiah is to include—indeed, take seriously—the oracles against the nations collection (chaps. 46–51), in which the oracles against Babylon stand at the conclusion as a grand climax. It is crucial for our understanding of the book that we consider the judgment oracles against Babylon (chaps. 50–51) in the light of chap. 25. As we have seen, in chap. 25 also, Babylon receives much emphasis. In the cup of wrath pericope (25:15–29), the doom oracle is recast as a symbolic act. Again, the prophet is portrayed as being commissioned by YHWH, the sovereign of nations: "Take from my hand this cup of the wine of wrath, and make all the nations to whom I send you drink it. They shall drink and stagger and be crazed because of the sword that I am sending among them" (25:15–16).

The series corresponds superbly with the sequence of the book as a whole. The first one to drink the cup was "Jerusalem and the cities of Judah" (25:17). In the scenario described in the book of Jeremiah, the story of Judah, first threatened and then punished, stands first. In fact, it takes up most of the space in the book. Jeremiah 25 allows us a broader view of YHWH's plans for the nations, meaning all of Judah's 'neighbors, including Babylon. Chapter 25 is, moreover, in line with the prophetic commission in chap. 1, where the prophet is appointed "over nations and kingdoms" (Jer 1:10). Thus, after Judah has been punished for its sins, it is the other nations' turn. This is described by means of the metaphor of the cup of wrath. The prophet is told to let "the nations" drink, significantly, beginning with Egypt, the superpower to the west on whom many Judahites had pinned their hopes in vain. All known nations are included, with Babylon standing as the last one, for the climax (25:26).

The judgment is represented as inescapable. Now and again we hear tones of contingency, as though punishment could be avoided even at the very last moment. YHWH remained the God of the covenant, who had not abandoned his chosen people. But it was particularly for Babylon that the text says:

> And if they refuse to accept the cup from your hand to drink, then you shall say to them: "Thus says YHWH of hosts: You must drink! For behold, I begin to bring disaster on the city that is called by my name, and shall you go unpunished? (25:28–29)

Since Babylon is deliberately included twice in the punitive scenario (25:12, 26), first in the judgment oracle and then in the cup of wrath pericope, we should not be surprised to find it included, again with major emphasis, in the foreign oracle collection. The link-up has been admirably executed (between chap. 25 and chaps. 50 and 51). This, by far the longest oracle of the collection, is also the fiercest in tone and the most absolute in its destructive tendency. These oracles elaborate on the phrase epitomizing Babylon's announced destruction in 25:12: "perpetual *waste*" (compare "perpetual *reproach*" in 25:9, referring to Judah and its neighbor nations). In fact, the lengthy announcement and description of Babylon's doom is underscored by a symbolic act. The prophet orders Seraiah to sink a scroll in the Euphrates River in Babylon, after reading the oracle, with the ominous words: "Thus shall Babylon sink, to rise no more, because of the evil that I am bringing upon her" (51:64).

A Future for Judah

However, Babylon's punishment is only one aspect of this oracular material. The more important aspect is that, with the punishment of Babylon, the roles between it and Judah are reversed. First, it was Judah who was punished, namely, by Babylon; this time, since Babylon is being punished, Judah is encouraged to leave the city of captivity to return to Jerusalem: "Flee from the midst of Babylon, and go out of the land of the Chaldeans" (50:8; cf. 51:6, 45).

Just as YHWH had engaged Babylon against Judah, now he is stirring up "a company of great nations," later identified as the Medes, who will bring an end to Babylon. Clearly, the repeated "calls to flee" sounded in these oracles are the nexus between exile and return. These calls to return from exile in fact become one of the dominant notes in exilic and postexilic literature.

This scenario invites comparison with Isaiah 40ff. In Deutero-Isaiah the anti-Babylonian stance is considerably toned down, while the anti-idol polemics are heightened. However, the general exilic milieu of the two books is comparable. In fact, the Jeremian oracles contain such a plethora of motifs that it seems as if the writer has left no stone unturned, and every word or phrase expressing enmity toward Babylon should be included. However, Jeremiah 50–51 also includes a critique of idols, even if it is not as blatant as Isaiah 40. At the outset, the fate of Babylon's gods is announced as the introduction to the city's defeat. Babylon is defeated because its gods are finished; they cannot protect it because they are nothing:

> Babylon is taken,
> Bel is put to shame,
> Marduk is dismayed;
> her images are put to shame,
> her idols are dismayed. (50:2)

Just as Assyria was the international threat in Isaiah's time, Babylon is during the ministry of Jeremiah. When we consider the Old Testament as a whole, we have to conclude that the schematic role of Babylon is more crucial than that of Assyria. From the perspective of global politics, Israel/Judah was a small, insignificant people (cf. Deut 7:6ff.), wedged between the superpowers of the Nile Valley and Mesopotamia. The patriarchs had originated in Babylon (Abraham left Ur, Gen 11:31), traveled to Egypt temporarily, and had settled eventually in the land that YHWH had promised them. Both superpowers are represented as being addicted to idolatry and slavery. Though Abram had left as a free man, his descendants would be taken in exile to Mesopotamia against their wishes. The patriarchs had entered Egypt voluntarily, but they became enslaved because another pharaoh did not know Joseph, who had saved Egypt from famine. In both cases, YHWH acted the part of the liberator. After the forceful exodus out of Egypt, he led his people through a trackless wilderness to Mount Sinai, where he made a covenant with him. Similarly, out of Babylon he called them to return to Zion, to enter a covenant never to be forgotten. In both cases he set his imprisoned people free so that he might bind them to himself in freedom—a most amazing choice on YHWH's part. He chose not the great, leading, powerful nations of the world but Israel—not for its own sake or for the sake of its outstanding merit but because of his sovereign choice (Deut 7:6–11).

Conclusion

The book of Jeremiah, taken as a whole, is well structured, with a scaffolding composed of three "columns," on which the entire frame rests. Chapter 1 defines the nature of the prophetic office and the authority of the God of Israel as Lord not only of Judah but also of "the nations." Commissioned with the superhuman task of being YHWH's speaker and actor, Jeremiah is accordingly empowered with superhuman strength (Jer 1:6–10, 18–19), though even this seems insufficient at times. Chapter 25 stands in the middle, looking back as it summarizes the thrust of the prophetic message of the first twenty-four chapters, and summarizing what is ahead, at least for Babylon. The story is incomplete in chap. 25, for it only announces that Babylon will be punished as it has punished others. Nothing is yet said about what this will mean for Judah.

The massive punishment of Babylon to the point of extermination, is described "in living color" in chaps. 50 and 51, but the significant addition, not contained in the other oracles in the collection, are the promises of liberation extended to Judah. Accordingly, the repeated calls to flee become one of the most crucial elements of these oracles. The Babylon oracles not only list calls to flee, but they also add descriptions of groups of people actually exiting Babylon, en route to Zion:

> In those days and in that time, says YHWH, the people of Israel and the people of Judah shall come together, weeping as they come; and they shall seek YHWH their God. (50:4; cf. 50:28; 51:50)

With these three pieces of scaffolding, the book stands up well and illustrates coherence. Such a degree of coherence is not achievable, however, if chaps. 50 and 51 are not treated as part of the picture.

The Place of the Reader in Jeremiah

C. R. SEITZ

University of St. Andrews

The biblical prophetic books should first be read for their own sake—we might call this a per se reading—and then we should move forward to ask just how a book of Hebrew Scripture becomes Old Testament when interpreted in reciprocity with the New. The two tasks confronting Christian readers are: interpreting the Old Testament *per se* and the Old *in novo receptum*, as received in the New. My remarks in this essay deal with Jeremiah's own per se witness, without considering the relationship of this witness with the New Testament. We need to focus on the question: Does this book have a particular reader orientation that we are meant to identify and then orient ourselves around? Our goal shall be to determine *how consciously we as readers and hearers of this work of scriptural witness are actually anticipated by the literature itself* so that we might align ourselves with the natural expectations the literature has of us.

The issue may be illustrated in the following way. One of the domain assumptions of older critical approaches to reading the Bible was that we as readers of the finished products of biblical texts were only accidentally, or as latecomers or overhearers, anticipated by the literature itself. It is as though we had found ourselves "reading someone else's mail," as Paul van Buren[1] put it. The point of historical-critical labor was to recreate the situation in life in which the portion of the text under discussion was originally uttered and delivered. This task was not pursued for its own sake or because the task was challenging or because one could make a career doing it, but because it was never assumed that the material had been shaped to function as scripture for

---

Author's note: This essay is adapted from chap. 14, "Isaiah in Parish Bible Study: The Question of the Place of the Reader in Biblical Texts," in *Word without End: The Old Testament as Abiding Theological Witness* (Grand Rapids, Mich.: Eerdmans, 1998) 194–212.

1. Paul van Buren, "On Reading Someone Else's Mail: The Church and Israel's Scriptures," in *Die Hebräische Bibel und ihre zweifache Nachgeschichte* (Festschrift R. Rendtorff; Neukirchen-Vluyn: Neukirchener Verlag, 1990) 595–696.

just any audience who happened to show up and ask: What does this material have to say to me? Once the various situations-in-life that together constitute the book's complete history were imaginatively recreated, then the task would be to reapply the word once delivered to a changed but analogous modern context.

Now the strengths of such an approach are immediately apparent, especially in a book like Isaiah (but in Jeremiah as well), which Luther probably had in mind when he said, "[the prophets] have a queer way of talking, like people who, instead of proceeding in an orderly manner, ramble off from one thing to the next, so that you cannot make head or tail of them or see what they are getting at."[2] The notion that biblical books were not shaped in coherent ways so as to address later readers and hearers is not just a modern one; and the prophets are particularly challenging as Luther's statement implies. Critical method could make sense of a complex and confused text by assigning the material to its original setting and as an added bonus could show us our proper point of standing as readers and interpreters. Incidentally, this sort of approach, which might be called "subject oriented" (as against an approach focused on readers as objects of address), struggled to know if we were to relate to the prophet Jeremiah as prophetic subject or to the people Israel as subject, and at what particular point on the journey from sixth-century oral speech, to Nebuchadrezzar's capture of Jerusalem, to exile in Babylon, to the prospect of return to the land. To adapt this to a popular critical model, do we read with source A, B, or C? With exilic editors or with those who remained in Judah after 594 and 587?[3] But even this sort of concern was relatively minor measured against the strengths of an approach that could both make sense of an apparently randomly-organized text and also show us where to stand as readers and hearers of the word of God, spoken through a prophet and those who followed him.

Of course there was a practical question immediately felt in most Bible study. Just how did one go about assigning with confidence portions of text to original situations in life, granting even that such a goal was desirable? Would this not require very specialized skills and train-

---

2. Quoted in G. von Rad, *The Message of the Prophets* (New York: Harper and Row, 1967) 15.

3. See my *Theology in Conflict* (Berlin: de Gruyter, 1989). I regard the redactional-critical labor as properly preliminary in character and provisional. It helps us to gain a purchase on how the final canonical shaping took up the matter of previous audience—as a historical datum—and then recast it in the form of sacred literature. The process of textualization is at once a process of scripturalization, in the pregnant theological sense.

ing, of a sort either intimidating or overly academic for many readers, threatening to create a false dichotomy between "expert readings" (surely the Bible is not just for experts) and overly personalized or psychological ones? How was one to know for sure whether a text belonged to a specific period of history? In the case of the book of Jeremiah, to say that this book could be divided into a number of segments with perspicuous social-historical settings was grossly to oversimplify the problem of assigning texts, especially this book, to points in time. And of course it was also to insist that the key to proper interpretation had to be inferred through critical reconstruction and was not an obvious part of the book's own final literary presentation.

To say that such a task was difficult is not to say that the approach was wrongheaded from the start or that it had ignored quite obvious indices structured into the literature whose express purpose was to help us, here in the late twentieth century, know how to read and interpret a prophetic book like Jeremiah. The critical theory was itself an effort to respond to the very sorts of problems noted by Luther. But, in addition, the theory maximized the potential latent in a certain understanding of prophecy—namely, the prophets as individual, inspired speakers. Early historical-critical work operated under a distinctive set of theological and practical concerns, so that if such work is now to be set aside, new theological and practical parameters will have to be worked out. On the old model, traditional theories of inspiration that had insured a book's claim to faithfully report matters in time and space—even predicting the distant future—had been translated into a more diffuse understanding. But the same basic notion of inspiration applied: Word of God to inspired individuals, to receiving communities. On such a model, what was of utmost importance was not the actual book itself or its larger shape, since these could no longer with confidence be assigned to the traditional author, but rather a critical reconstruction of a variety of inspired individuals and the communities addressed by them. The focus had shifted from *inspired book* to *inspired individuals*.[4]

To shift the focus back to the book itself is not to ignore this significant, substituted theory of inspired individuals, but it is to shift attention to the possibility that the final shaping has itself crafted these various inspired voices into an organic whole, capable of speaking with one voice. But the chief point to be made here is that "capacity to speak with one voice" is not the same thing as either an obliteration of historical depth or the production of a static text with only one possible meaning.

---

4. See my remarks on Isaiah in *Word without End*, 113–29.

The process I am referring to, what Brevard Childs has called "canonical shaping," was not executed in the book of Jeremiah in this sort of manner. Efforts to anticipate and speak coherently to a readership explicitly outside the book's own historical frame of reference are not registered in such a way as to oppose participation in the book's coming-to-be. At the same time, however, it is Jeremiah's concrete, historical coming-to-be that also points in the direction of greater respect for the fact that the final organization and shaping—far from being random—has its own mysterious logic: a sum greater than the parts. That this logic is in Jeremiah neither chronological nor thematic should give one pause. In order to make sense of the book of Jeremiah's final form, we are inevitably drawn into a world of real historical reference, where distinctions between the Egyptians and the Babylonians, between Zedekiah and Nebuchadrezzar, between an intact temple and one destroyed are cleanly registered. But then the book does a surprising thing. Having made such distinctions, it begins to construct its own analogies and linkages, long before we get there as readers of this ancient witness, concerned with recasting the text chronologically, and then moving from ancient historical context to a modern, twentieth-century application. In Jeremiah's case, its logic is not chronological (anymore than in Isaiah), but we can come close to discerning a thematic logic.[5]

I have been speaking in theoretical terms up to this point. It is now time to read texts and illustrate exegetically what has been described hermeneutically. The concern is to comprehend the final shape of the book of Jeremiah without ignoring the fact of its complex prehistory, with the hope that by understanding this shaping, clues might be given about how readers might appropriate the message of the book. It is assumed here that the book was not just stumbled upon, like someone else's mail that must be decoded. Rather, a basic question is asked: How does the book function as a whole, directed toward potential readers? The answer that is given will involve regular, prayerful, chapter-by-chapter reading and reflection. I will make my own proposal here, and it is nothing more than the consequence of my own regular, prayerful, chapter-by-chapter reading. I am modeling my conclusions, but more important to me is the approach by which I reached them, which is what I wish to commend for parish Bible study.

I will be looking at Jeremiah to illustrate a perspective on reading the final form of a prophetic book. Moreover, Jeremiah's canonical

---

5. A number of essays in *Word without End* try to illustrate this point.

shape intrigues me, and I find it relatively easy to comprehend, easier for example than the more complex shape of Isaiah.[6]

The first six chapters of Jeremiah, in addition to speaking judgment on Northern and Southern Kingdoms, also hold out the possibility of repentance and a removal of the sentence of judgment.

> Return, faithless Israel, says the LORD.
> I will not look on you in anger, for I am merciful,
>   says the LORD;
> I will not be angry forever.
> Only acknowledge your guilt, that you have rebelled
>   against the LORD. . . .
> And I will take you, one from a city,
>   two from a family,
>   and I will bring you to Zion. (3:12–14)

Whether such calls for repentance were originally addressed only to Israel, the Northern Kingdom, is not so crucial as noting that such calls are in fact noticeably rare in the book. This is made clear as we leave the first six chapters and enter a new section in chap. 7, where the possibility of intercession on Jeremiah's part on behalf of Israel is withdrawn: "As for you, do not pray for this people . . . and do not intercede with me, for I will not hear you." This leads to awesome pictures of coming doom with no possibility of repentance and a Jeremiah wracked with anguish and dark foreboding. Now what could the reader discern here but sad testimony to the iniquity of prior generations, so vast as to demand a sentence of judgment virtually without rider. The lesson would be a chilling one, demanding repentance and a confession of guilt. And in fact, acknowledgments of just sentencing and personal confessions are woven into the text, both in this part of the book (9:12–16) and in the first section.

> Let us lie down in our shame, and let our dishonor cover us;
> for we have sinned against the LORD our God,
> we and our ancestors, from our youth even to this day;
> and we have not obeyed the voice of the LORD our God. (3:25)

The book has been shaped to allow the reader to participate in the refusal of an earlier generation to heed God's calls to repentance and to experience the judgment they eventually experienced, though now with a clear confession of wrongdoing and an acknowledgment that

---

6. See my "Prophet Moses and the Canonical Shape of the Book of Jeremiah," *Zeitschrift für die alttestamentliche Wissenschaft* 101 (1989) 1–15.

Jeremiah was a true prophet sent by God—something for which he was persecuted rather than honored and heeded.

To take another brief example from this section of the book, note how in chap. 16 eventual readers are addressed almost explicitly:

> And when you tell this people all these words, and they say to you,
> "Why has the LORD pronounced all this great evil against us?
> What is our iniquity?
> What is the sin that we have committed against the LORD our God?"
> then you shall say to them:
> "It is because your ancestors have forsaken me," says the LORD.
>   (16:10–11)

The indictment continues for another three verses. A response then appears in the form of a brief psalm toward the chapter's conclusion. The response is not Jeremiah's, but it is a model for the reader who confesses: "Our ancestors have inherited nothing but lies, worthless things in which there is no profit" (v. 19).

A very similar anticipation of readers who are recipients of the punishment of their ancestors can be seen in the closing chapters of Deuteronomy: "When all of these things have happened to you . . . and you call them to mind among all the nations where I have driven you, and you return and obey, then the LORD God will have compassion . . ." (30:1ff.). Not for nothing have scholars insisted on close links between Jeremiah's editing and the shaping of the Deuteronomic traditions. Both are concerned that lessons from the past continue to address future readers.

In chaps. 21–45, the next major section of Jeremiah, the situation of unmitigated judgment changes; at the same time a steady reader orientation is maintained. We still find clear sentences of judgment, though now with special emphasis on those exempted from the first exile of 597 who remained in the land with Jeremiah, in contrast to those already carried off to Babylon (especially 24:1–10). And now a timetable for judgment is also introduced: 70 years, after which time God will do a new thing with his people, all of them, whenever they were exiled from the land. But the reader will also note a change from chaps. 7–20. Where before we had clear sentences of judgment, now we find a subjunctive note: "*perhaps* the LORD will change his mind," we now hear. Two key chapters in this section (26 and 36) register this note up front. "It may be that they will turn and listen, all of them, and will turn from their evil way" (26:3); "It may be that when the house of Judah hears of all the disaster that I intend to do to them, all of them may turn from their evil ways, so that I may forgive their iniquity and their sin" (36:3).

That these are not just rhetorical flourishes meant to underscore the heinous nature of Israel's disobedience when that eventually occurs is made clear by the fact that specific individuals *do* heed God's word spoken through the prophet. Not all heed the word, as God has held out for, but instead only a few, whose names are obscure but whose actions clearly show forth exemplary behavior at a time of great hardship: the elders who stepped forth to defend Jeremiah when he was brought before the prophet-killer Jehoiakim; the lone Ahikam, son of Shaphan, who rescued Jeremiah from danger in that same trial scene; Jeremiah's loyal assistant, Baruch; and the obscure assembly of scribes and officials (Elishama, Delaiah ben Shemaiah, Elnathan ben Achbor, Gemariah ben Shaphan, Zedekiah ben Hananiah, Micaiah ben Gemariah) who in stark contrast to Jehoiakim and his servants shuddered when the king burned God's word in a brazier used to heat his winter house. Earlier, when they heard the scroll read, they knew that what they heard was the word of God, meant to bring about repentance and divine forgiveness.

Here in this section of Jeremiah, the reader sees the emergence of a small but courageous remnant, who in the midst of hardship and a sentence of divine judgment are still able to trust in God's infinite mercy at great risk to themselves but confident in exercising the choice that will give them the right to stand together with Jeremiah against those who refuse God's mercies as recipients of God's forgiveness. Their potential function as paradigms for a remnant in need of hope and forgiveness—a remnant confronted not by Jeremiah himself but by the book of Jeremiah as a word of scripture—seems clear. In the final section (chaps. 37–45) only two such figures stand out in the chiaroscuro of fear and equivocation on the eve of Judah's collapse. The foreigner Ebed-melech and the loyal Baruch were given their lives as a prize of war because of the trust they had shown in God.

Now the final shaping of Jeremiah has not forced all the material into a tidy scheme whose chief purpose is to confront readers approaching the material as a scriptural word of address. But it has made allowance for a word once addressed by the prophet to past generations to sound forth beyond its own temporal horizon, to address readers of Jeremiah as scripture in an intentional and not just a fortuitous manner. Moreover, the search for coherence in the final form, and even a direct reader orientation, has not just been artifically imposed, as though the choice were between the text as *Rorschach*, capable of an unlimited set of reader-imposed meanings, or a text with only one level of distinct intentionality. Rather, loose guidelines are set up to help the reader move through a very complex presentation, with a variety of past intentions whose force has not been obliterated in the final shaping process.

I have argued in another context for a similar sort of organizing lens, focused not so much on readers but on the figure of Jeremiah as a second Moses; an intercessor like Moses but forbidden to intercede; a prophet who like Moses shared in the judgment on a disobedient generation; the prophet who refashioned a burned scroll, as once-broken tablets were reconstituted at the foot of Sinai; one who singled out two special individuals exempt from the judgment on a generation, Ebedmelech and Baruch, just as once Joshua and Caleb were given their lives as a prize of war; and one who brought to a tragic conclusion a prophetic succession whose origins began with Moses in Egypt, now to be brought to conclusion there as well.[7]

Again, this larger organizing lens does not suppress the particularity of the individual chapters, nor is it the whim of readers looking for unity and larger shape that are not in fact intended. It is what it is: *a larger interpretive lens meant to provide loose organization and structure that will guide in interpreting the individual parts of the whole.*

It seems to me there are several clear implications for biblical study in this sort of approach. First, original authorial intention, difficult to reconstruct on an older, historical-critical model, is but one level of intentionality and it may well have been recast and reshaped in the final organization of a biblical book. Therefore, one needs to develop other sorts of instincts when reading biblical texts than instincts chiefly concerned with what was early or original. As you can see, in this reading of Jeremiah I have shifted the focus from author as subject to reader as intended object of address. I have not rejected intentionality but asked about it from the standpoint of the readers.

Second and related to this, it is important to try to find larger structure and coherence beyond the scope of an individual passage. This is especially difficult, since in the church's liturgical use of the Bible very rarely if ever do we read through a book chapter by chapter. But such a possibility is open to Bible study, even if it means paraphrasing and skipping over passages from time to time. Even then nothing prohibits one from at least raising the question of what the present organization of the material seems to be intending. And finally, it is always important to ask whether the material as it presently confronts us speaks a word to readers rather directly, and not just obliquely or through spe-

---

7. Ibid.

cial critical reconstruction. What I have in mind here is not lifting the plain sense of the text immediately into a higher spiritual or personal realm but, rather, asking how and why this text has, within the context of other texts, addressed previous generations of hearers, whose ranks have now swollen to include us, in the late twentieth century, in our particular corner of Christ's church.

The Polyphonic Jeremiah:
A Reading of the Book of Jeremiah

ROBERT P. CARROLL†
University of Glasgow

One of the most striking features of the book of Jeremiah is that it is a scroll full of many different and discrete voices. It is a book of voices held together by being attributed to the prophet Jeremiah, yet differentiated from the prophet's voice in many distinctive ways. Generally the books of the prophets in the Bible are collections of oracles, essentially anthologies of prophetic utterances, but the book of Jeremiah is different in that it contains stories and narratives in which other voices are represented as well as controlled accounts of the prophet's own voice (an anthology with commentary, as it were). Whatever these essential differences between the book of Jeremiah and other prophetic texts may represent, the polyphonic Jeremiah is an object of great interest in its own right.

Everything in the book of Jeremiah is held together by the opening lines, which insist on representing the book as "the words of Jeremiah . . . to whom the word of YHWH came in the days of Josiah . . . it came also in the days of Jehoiakim . . . until the deportation of Jerusalem . . ." (1:1–3), thus spanning the forty-year period when the Judahite kingdom came to an end. Words of Jeremiah as the word of YHWH? Word of YHWH as the words of Jeremiah? Words in a crisis, words for a crisis, words in crisis. As the kingdom collapsed under the weight of its own incompetence and in reaction to the onslaught of the Babylonian invading forces, the word of YHWH appeared in the form of the words of Jeremiah. Yet the book contains much more than the words of Jeremiah and therefore much more than the word of YHWH. It contains the words of others as well. The book also represents the polyphonic discourses of the warring factions that participated in Judah's downfall. The words of Jeremiah as the word of YHWH may dominate the book, but other voices may be heard throughout the book. As a polyphonic document it contributes strongly to deconstructing the notion of the word of YHWH tied to the words of a solitary controlling voice. From

1:4 to 51:64 the words of Jeremiah may represent the focus of the book, but there are words outside these words as well as other words inside the frame of Jeremiah's words. The words outside the words constitute the framework of the book; they undermine the sense of the book as being solely the words of Jeremiah. The dominant voice in the book of Jeremiah may be Jeremiah's (that is, YHWH's) but there are voices other than Jeremiah's and these contribute constructively to the making of Jeremiah's voice as well as making the book essentially and importantly polyphonic.

The different voices in the text reflect discrete interests and agencies in the book. These are mediated through various representations, oracular and narrative, and constitute a network of competing interests and conflicting voices that make Jeremiah one of the most interesting but difficult books to read in the prophetic collection of material in the Bible. I shall attempt to untangle the quilt, network, and web of voices by listing and discussing them briefly in what follows, before offering a few suggestions about how the polyphonic Jeremiah might be understood by modern readers. As a simplified but total reading of the book of Jeremiah, this attempt must be recognized as being an essay in reading beneath the surface of the text, with a concomitant high risk of misreading attached to it. It also represents an attempt to provide a "thick" description of the book of Jeremiah, being beyond the "thin" paraphrastic reproductions of the text that sometimes count as congenital readings of Jeremiah.

The Voices of YHWH and Jeremiah (1:4–19)

In the prologue to the book we are introduced to a dialogue between YHWH and Jeremiah as the means of settling the question of Jeremiah's legitimation. Once the problem of the legitimacy of his role as a prophet has been dealt with, we will be in a position to hear what that voice has to say. Already the tradition is being shaped by tension about his influences (Moses as model for Jeremiah's commissioning) and the problem of the legitimation of prophets (addressed more directly in 23:9–40 and chaps. 27–29). The context of Jeremiah's activity is set on the stage of international politics and the hegemony of the kingdoms of the north (1:15; 25:9; chaps. 50–51), but conflict between him and his own people is also singled out as a defining feature of the war between prophet and people (1:19; 15:10, 20; 43:1–7). Imbedded in the opening sections of the book are many of the themes that will constitute the heart of the scroll of Jeremiah.

A Voice Haranguing the Community (2:4–3:10)

The initial poetic sequences of Jeremiah's utterances represent a kvetching voice denigrating the community for its history of persistent rebellion against YHWH. The denunciatory tone of this voice appears to be designed to inculcate guilt about the past, while writing off the past and the bearers of that past, in order to prepare the ground for advocating radical change (3:12–4:4). The recital of the past as a history of idolatrous rebellion lays the foundation for the voice that will seek to justify the destruction of Jerusalem on the grounds of an idolatrous past (cf. 1:16; 19:1–13). Before voices can be heard speaking of the future, voices must condemn the past out of hand and eradicate its influence on present and future thinking. Many voices are heard within this section, though most of them may be the speaker's voice taking up different and competing positions: rhetorical questions are posed and answered, the people's voice is mimicked and words are put in the community's mouth (cf. 2:8, 20, 23, 25, 27, 29, 31, 35; 3:4–5). The internal dialogue seems to have one conversational partner, with the prophet's voice playing all the parts.

A Voice Calling for Repentance (3:12–4:4)

Given the representation of the nation's past in the poems leading up to 3:12, it is difficult for modern readers to grasp the logic of the voice commanding repentance. While the complex manipulation of words in 3:6–11 whereby "faithless Israel" has shown itself to be more righteous than "treacherous Judah" may be read as affording some grounds for the invitation to faithless Israel to return, it is a most curious discourse, and it sometimes backtracks on the overwhelming logic of the denunciations of Israel in 2:4–3:5. But the voice of return is one heard frequently in the book of Jeremiah (cf. 6:14–16; 23:7–8; chaps. 30–31) and must be judged to represent the voice of the diaspora, which belongs to the literature of the Second Temple Period (Persian–Hellenistic era). It also reflects the voice of the restoration-of-Jerusalem interests in the text (3:17; 31:38–40; 32:42–44). If YHWH's quarrel is with the succeeding generations of the community, from the past into the future ("I will contend with you . . . and with your children's children," 2:9), then the invitation to return to YHWH and to the homeland probably represents voices that were less persuaded that YHWH's quarrel would extend so far into the future.

Voices of Destruction (4:5–6:26)

Immediately following the voice calling for turning (repentance), the voice of destruction is heard. The transition from one voice to the other is managed by 4:3–4, where the ever-present threat of the fire of YHWH's anger is given as the motivation for circumcising the heart (the marriage figure of 2:2–3 is echoed in the figure of circumcision, with its echoes of the ritual preparation for marriage into the circumciser's family). Some of the poems in chaps. 4–6 reflect the theme of a powerful foreign nation advancing on the land and the city in order to besiege the city and to destroy the land. This is the "evil-out-of-the-north" theme prefigured in 1:13–14 and realized in these poems (4:6; 6:22). Other poems in the D cycle (according to Mowinckel, they are salvation oracles and oracles against foreign nations) represent the voices of the victims of the invasive forces and reflect horrified reactions to the suffering caused by the onslaught of such a powerful enemy. There are too many voices in this section to think of it as the simple production of one voice. Feminine voices are also heard in the section, as the land and the city (portrayed as women) cry out against the violation of invasion (4:19, 20, 31). These are the voices of "Daughter Zion" and will be heard elsewhere in the book (10:19, 20; 31:15). Whether they represent actual female voices or mimicked female voices is a matter for debate, but the social roles of women in such ancient cultures included the practice of professional mourning (cf. 9:17–19, 20–22), so it would be appropriate if we were able to detect the traces of "real" women's voices in the text here. While Jeremiah may represent the invading enemy's voice (reversed in chaps. 50–51), the city speaks with a female voice in protest against the outrageous violations of invasion (5:19–21, 31).

The Voice against the Cults (7:1–8:3)

Jeremiah is represented in a collection of prose pieces as speaking out against false notions of the temple and against various cults in and around Jerusalem. If these polemical diatribes against the practice of religion are taken in conjunction with the haranguing of the community in chaps. 2–3, then we may detect behind the text the voice of a kind of countercultic "orthodoxy" (Deuteronomistic or prophetic?) insisting on proper attitudes to the temple and correct cultic practices (one of the many subtexts of the book of Jeremiah?). It would go far beyond the available evidence to speculate on the identity of this voice, but it might not be very far removed from the Second Temple community's ideology of correct worship. The defamation of other and past cultic viewpoints would certainly serve such a purpose well. On the other hand, chap. 7 might serve a more radical purpose of criticizing the temple cult by means of challenging the voice that says, "the Temple of YHWH, the Temple of YHWH, the temple of YHWH are these" (7:4). Who can tell how these texts should be read? In the criticisms of the various cultic practices condemned in this section, different and discrete voices may be heard. The condemnation of the fire-cult of Topheth in the valley of ben Hinnom (7:30–32) could be taken to represent the voice of protest on behalf of the burning of the children there—a form of Rachel weeping for her children who are not (cf. 31:15). This reading of the text may take a conventional phrase in the wrong way, however, and assume that an "innocent ritual of dedication" was given a pejorative force by the writer of chap. 7 in order to present the past in the worst possible light. Yet the voice can also be heard as a very proper protest about cruel practices and the abuse of children—even polemical texts may include truthful accusations that cannot be dismissed as purely ideological statements. The voices in this chapter may be heard in very different ways, reminding modern readers that every hearing is also a contested hearing.

A Concatenation of Voices (8:4–10:25)

One way of grasping the essential point of this reading of the book of Jeremiah as a polyphonic production is to read chaps. 8–10 while paying attention to all the different voices represented in the text. A paradigm of this polyphonic feature of the text would be 8:4–7: "You shall say to them, Thus says YHWH . . . no man repents . . . saying . . . How can you say? . . ." (cf. 36:29). Here, imagined or invented conversations are represented as part of a polemic against competing claims of authority in society: the scroll of the wise versus the word of YHWH (pen versus word, 8:8–9). Different voices express different things in a context of dialogical deafness. In 8:19 Daughter Zion (Daughter [of] my People—the same thing, I think) speaks and in 9:3–6, 8 everybody in the community is represented as being a speaker of lies, deceit, and gossip. The concatenation of voices is a cacophony of voices in this over-voiced text.

Voices of Lamentation and Protest (chaps. 11–20)

Among the many different voices and topics running through chaps. 11–20 is a series of laments or complaints that has become known as the Prayers or Confessions of Jeremiah. Whatever category or description is given to these poems (11:18–20; 12:1–5; 15:15–18; 17:14–18; 18:19–23; 20:7–12, 14–18), the voice in them is certainly one much given to complaining and kvetching. The lament form is one of the major forms of expression in the book of Psalms and represents a fundamental voice of aggrieved piety in the Bible. It is also a form often associated with Jeremiah because of the traditional attribution of the book of Lamentations to him. The precise interpretation of the laments in the book of Jeremiah is a much-disputed matter in contemporary scholarship on Jeremiah, but my concern here is only with the topic of voices and not with either identifying the speaker of the laments or the minutiae of interpretation. The laments are about conflict and protest at the violation of the righteous. Echoes of the topic have already been heard in the texts representing the voice of Jerusalem protesting against violation. The feminine voice is invariably one of outraged protest at unconscionable violence (cf. 5:30–31; 13:20–27; 31:15), so it is a matter of poetic justice to hear the same cry from Jeremiah in these poems. The advocate of violence against the community (5:6; 6:11–12) is now himself the victim of violence and feels outraged by the experience (20:1–6). Some of the poems represent a cry against unjust oppression, and others appeal to YHWH for revenge. Narrative elements in the text relate some of the poems to aspects of Jeremiah's life, rather in the way that various psalms are associated with events in the life of King David. Other laments just appear in the middle of various poems and are not specifically related to the life of Jeremiah. Conflict with prophets (14:12–16) or prohibitions against prophesying (11:21; cf. 20:6) seem to have some bearing on the interpretation of these elements.

The protest against (unjust) suffering in the lament poems sits uneasily with the representation of Jeremiah in chaps. 2–10, where the prophet devotes much energy to condemning the community to justified suffering. Perhaps the tradition of laments incorporated at this point in the book represents a serious shift in reflective mood in the Jeremiah tradition, and the poems of lament should be read as second thoughts about the hasty judgment of chaps. 2–10. For if everybody is guilty of wrong—from the least to the greatest (5:1–6; 6:13; 8:10)—then how can there be any room for protest about the suffering of the just? I detect a very different voice in the laments from the dominant voice represented by the book of Jeremiah. The righteous are fighting back, and the blanket condemnation of a prophet such as Jeremiah just will not do. The Jeremiah tradition is deconstructing itself in the lament poems, as the community resists the rush-to-judgment factor expressed so explicitly in the first phase poems of the book (in chaps. 2–10).

Voices against the Prophets (23:9–40; chaps. 27–29)

A dominant voice throughout the book of Jeremiah is the one that speaks forthrightly against prophets. Few opportunities are lost in the book to attack prophets. In some cases the voice in the text appears to speak out against all the prophets; in other cases it is a matter of the prophet Jeremiah speaking against his competitor prophets. So there are at least two voices here: the voice against all prophets and the voice of Jeremiah against all the other prophets. In 27:9–18 the prophet Jeremiah is represented as saying "Do not listen to your prophets," where presumably he himself is exempted from the force of this warning. The tendency for the text to deconstruct itself at this point should be noted. The notion of *prophet* is a contested one in the book of Jeremiah and regularly poses problems and confusion for modern readers (cf. 23:22 with 25:1–7, where Jeremiah's criterion of 23:22 applied to himself would render him false!). At various points in the book the prophets are represented as being the voice of "peace" (*shalom*), 4:9–10; 5:12–13; 6:13–14; 14:13; 23:17; cf. 28:1–9, so Jeremiah as an opposing voice represents the voice of (divine) judgment. But in 29:11 Jeremiah is also represented as the voice of *shalom*, so not too much should be made of this contrast between judgment and *shalom*. What seems to emerge from a close reading of 23:9–32 is the voice against all prophets. Jeremiah as the bearer of the divine word may here be seen as the alternative to prophets.

Voices on Behalf of Babylon (25:8–14; chaps. 27–29)

Resistance to Babylon is represented in chaps. 27–29 as opposition to YHWH, so submission to the imperial power becomes obedience to the divine will. It goes further than that. The people deported to live in Babylonia are also commanded to seek the welfare of Babylon and to pray to YHWH for its *shalom* (29:7). While the Judahites may plot to overthrow Babylon, the deported people must learn to recognize that their own *shalom* depends on Babylon's *shalom*. This voice has a corollary voice in chaps. 24 and 29, where those who have been deported from Jerusalem to Babylon are represented as the hope of the future. They are, to use the metaphor of 24:1–3 that is used as a simile in 24:5, "good figs" compared with the "bad figs" of the Judahite community (24:8; 29:17).

The voice that speaks on behalf of the deportees in Babylonia parallels (if it is not the same voice) the voice that speaks against the people of Judah. One does not have to be a brilliant biblical scholar or even a skilled close reader to detect the contentious ideological claims lurking behind this set of voices.

The Voice against Babylon (chaps. 50–51)

If one voice in the book of Jeremiah represents the Babylonians as YHWH's instrument and the emperor Nebuchadrezzar as the servant of YHWH (25:9; 27:6), there is another voice in the book that speaks out against the emperor. For this voice, Nebuchadrezzar is not the servant of YHWH but is "like a dragon" or monster (51:34, Hebrew *tannin*; cf. Ps 74:13–14; Isa 27:1; 51:9; Ezek 29:3; 32:2). In the poems making up chaps. 50–51, Babylon is the voice of every nation and the destroyer of Israel, so the destruction of Babylon becomes "the vengeance of YHWH, the vengeance of his temple" (51:11). All the evil done in Zion by the Babylonians will be requited of them by YHWH (51:24). This voice of opposition to imperial oppression needs to be heard alongside the voice that adulates Babylon as YHWH's servant and vassal. While one voice may be thought to be the voice of the diaspora community in Babylon, where such *Realpolitik* attitudes were necessary for survival, the opposing voice is most likely to represent the Palestinian community, which had known the harshness of the imperial hegemony. Both voices are represented in the text as belonging to the prophet Jeremiah: that prophet, *he speaks with a forked tongue!*

Voices of the Future (chaps. 30–31, with 32–33)

In spite of the preponderance of oracles of woe and judgment and the poems of lament in the book of Jeremiah, there are happier voices to be heard throughout the book. Songs of redemption are to be heard throughout the text (3:15–18; 12:14–17; 16:14–15; 23:1–8; 30:18–22; 31:1–6, 7–9, 10–14). Hope has not entirely died out in ancient Judah or Jerusalem, nor are grounds for hope completely banished from the tradition. Life in the community could not be lived without hope and, for all its negativity and focus on destruction, the book of Jeremiah reaffirms hope. This aspect of the book may be summed up in the words of 31:17: "There is hope for your future, says YHWH, and your children shall come back to their own country." There is hope for the repopulation of the land, for the rebuilding of the community and the city of

Jerusalem, for the celebration of the vintage when young and old will dance and make merry together, for the return of the children, and for the making of a new covenant between YHWH and the houses of Israel and Judah. But it is attenuated hope. It is focused in the diaspora. Hope for the future seems mainly to reside in hope for the reversal of the deportations, which have devastated land and cities. In the future, land deals and transactions will take place again (32:6–15). Yet mostly the vision of hope seems to relate to the descendants of those who were deported by the Babylonians (24:4–7; 29:10–14). For those who survived the invasions, onslaughts, and deportations of the Babylonian armies, little hope is held out (24:8–10). Even the possibility of hope, briefly raised for the Palestinian communities (42:1–12), is dashed by any plan to flee to Egypt (42:13–22), and the communities that flee to Egypt become the target for extremely virulent hostility (44:26–30). Only forcible deportation to Babylonia seems to be valued in the book, and any form of voluntary emigration elsewhere is condemned outright.

The Function of Jeremiah 50 and 51 in the Book of Jeremiah

KLAAS A. D. SMELIK

Protestant Theological Faculty, Brussels

Doubt arose in the nineteenth century about whether the prophetic books of the Old Testament contained only the *ipsissima verba* of the prophet named in the book. Are there passages that definitely did not originate with the prophet in question? In the book of Jeremiah, chaps. 50 and 51 are a clear example of a part of which the authenticity was doubted. C. Budde, who wrote a very detailed article on the subject in 1878, concluded that these two chapters were written by a postexilic author. This unknown writer—inspired by Isaiah 13 and other texts— attempted to compose a prophecy in the style of Jeremiah. Budde claimed that these two chapters were therefore irrelevant in our investigation concerning the "authentic" Jeremiah.

Budde's detailed study has not discouraged later scholars in the search for an "authentic Jeremian" kernel in chaps. 50 and 51. More recent examples may be found in the dissertations by D. L. Christensen (1971) and C. de Jong (1978). Both believe that they can identify passages in Jeremiah 50 and 51 that go back to the prophet himself.

We might question, however, whether such research for the *ipsissima verba* leads to convincing results. The problem remains that outside of the book of Jeremiah we have no data concerning the prophet by this name. He is not named in the books of Kings. The references to him in Daniel, Ezra, and Chronicles are dependent on the book of Jeremiah. The possibility that he is exclusively a literary figure may not be ruled out. Each ascription of passages to the historical Jeremiah rests on a circular argument: first, a certain type of texts is characterized as "Jeremian"; next, other passages are investigated to determine whether they demonstrate sufficient similarity to the parts already ascribed to Jeremiah. If they do, they are then considered to be Jeremian, too. Clearly, different starting points may produce different results.

Author's note: This essay was first published in *Nederlands Theologisch Tijdschrift* 41 (1987) 265–78, and is used with permission. Translation by Martin Kessler.

It is presently assumed that the poetic parts of Jeremiah 1–25 are more likely to have originated with Jeremiah. However, based on the fact that date and context is often indicated in prose narratives (while such information is often lacking in a poetic fragment), it might also be argued that it is precisely the prose passages that originated with Jeremiah, while the poetic sections are by unknown authors. If we start, however, with Jer 1:5, where Jeremiah was appointed a prophet to the nations, one might be tempted to ascribe the oracles against the nations to Jeremiah. There are even more possibilities. In each of such cases, the chosen point of departure largely determines the ultimate result of the investigation.

To move beyond this impasse, it might be more sensible to cease the search for the *ipsissima verba* of the historical Jeremiah and to concentrate on the question of the composition of the book of Jeremiah and on the literary persona of "Jeremiah." We do not need any external data to gain answers to such questions; neither has the search for answers reached a saturation point.

Point of Departure

Instead of searching for possible "Jeremian" passages in chaps. 50–51, I prefer to question why the editors of the book of Jeremiah have included the prophecy against Babylon in their work. Though scholars often designate the composers by the term "redactors," I prefer to call them "authors" because I have a higher view of their literary activity than most exegetes do. Moreover, I presuppose that this prophecy is not a later addition to the book of Jeremiah but that the authors produced it themselves in one or other phase of their writing, with the aid of existing material. Moreover, I work with the MT and not the LXX, because we are not dealing here with a reconstruction of the manner in which the text might have originated but with the function of these chapters in the book as a whole. When necessary, differences with the LXX will be discussed. There is a possibility of later interpolations in the text, but I prefer to be quite reticent on this point.

Attitude toward Babylon

Jeremiah's attitude toward Babylon is illustrated throughout the book. First, we turn to chaps. 27, 28, and 29. These chapters clearly illustrate a mutual relationship and originally were dated the same year. In chap. 27 "Jeremiah" turns against a plot to cast off the yoke of Babylon, by means of a threefold prophecy. According to "Jeremiah," a revolt against Nebuchadnezzar would be a revolt against YHWH under the circumstances, since YHWH had granted world dominion to the Babylonian king as his servant, thereby guaranteeing his power. This lordship is temporary, however, and limited to three generations. Then Babylon will in turn be subjected to another kingdom. In chap. 28 Jeremiah is confronted by a fellow-prophet, who claims that YHWH has already broken the yoke of the king of Babylon. At the end of the chapter YHWH settles the conflict in Jeremiah's favor. Chapter 29 introduces a letter by "Jeremiah" to the exiles in Babylon, who are summoned to settle in Babylon and pray for the welfare of the city. After 70 years, the exiles will be allowed to return. A violent end awaits prophets who proclaim another message.

In spite of a difference in the time span allotted for the Babylonian dominion, these chapters are clearly in agreement regarding their judgment of Babylon. The close of the prophecy against Babylon in chaps. 50 and 51 (51:59–64) is dated in the same (fourth) regnal year of King Zedekiah as the events narrated in chaps. 27–29. This correspondence may be explained by assuming that these events actually took place in the same year (594 B.C.E.), but this does not seem likely, as we will see. If on the other hand we assume that these dates are consciously chosen by the authors, such agreement in dating must have a literary purpose—for example, as an indication to the reader that the prophecy of chaps. 50–51 must be related to chaps. 27–29 (the reverse possibility—that the authors of chaps. 27–29 wish to refer to the prophecy against Babylon—seems less likely).

Reading the well-constructed chaps. 27–29 first and then turning to the "hurricane" of chaps. 50 and 51 leaves one amazed. Instead of a call to subjection to King Nebuchadnezzar and a prayer for the welfare of Babylon, "Jeremiah" proclaims in 50–51 that Babylon is about to be destroyed and warns the exiles to leave the city as quickly as possible. Carroll writes: "If such a poem were to be attributed to the 'historical Jeremiah' it would raise the insuperable problem of reconciling the speaker of this anti-Babylonian outburst with the image of Jeremiah as the friend of Babylon portrayed in 27–29, 39–40. Babylon would not have trusted a man who could utter such things *against* Babylon" (Carroll, *Jeremiah*, 816). On a historical level one might question, moreover, whether Baruch's brother Seraiah, who as quartermaster was to organize King Zedekiah's journey to Babylon in 594 B.C.E., would have been ready to carry out such a dangerous order. The public reading of a text such as Jeremiah 50 and 51 on the banks of the Euphrates only appears to make sense as an attempt at suicide.

What may be historically excluded does not need to be so on a literary level. After all, an author is not bound to what is historically possible. One might question what purpose the author had in doing violence to history.

General Tendenz *of the Prophecy*

At first sight, the prophecy against Babylon in Jeremiah 50 and 51 makes a minimally accessible impression. Rudolph writes in his commentary: "This is not a piece of closed structure but falls in a series of individual passages" (Rudolph, *Jeremia*, 3.297). This comment does inadequate justice to the authors, however. No matter how poorly organized their approach may appear, these chapters were intended to carry a specific message in a manner that they expected to be successful.

It is important to grasp the particular manner in which the authors develop their argument. Clearly, they do not develop a continuous, systematically ordered narrative. The text consists of brief episodes around central themes that keep returning in the text. The authors do not finish one theme in order to continue with another one, but they do move from one theme to another. With each treatment, other aspects of the text come to the fore, so that the repetitions indeed make sense. As such, Jeremiah 50 and 51 structurally looks more like a musical composition than a political manifesto.

First off, the prophecy appears to contain the following five basic elements:

1. description of the beginning of enemy action against Babylon
2. call to war against Babylon
3. description of the destruction of Babylon in all its aspects
4. call to destroy Babylon
5. call to flee Babylon.

It is clear from this overview that the prophecy keeps shifting its temporal perspective: in the one case, Babylon's enemies still need to mobilize, in an other verse there is heavy fighting, and in a third Babylon has become an uninhabitable pile of rubble. These temporal changes may impress the reader rather chaotically; they surely contribute to the liveliness of the text. The same may be said concerning the change between descriptive parts and passages directly targeted to different groups, such as the nations, the exiles, Judah/Israel, and Babylon itself. A form-critical analysis demonstrates that the authors have richly developed the many possibilities offered by the prophetic genre. Clearly, they wished to make this text the zenith of Jeremiah's prophecies against the nations. The reason is clear: since 586 B.C.E., Babylon had become Judah's enemy par excellence.

The five basic elements named above are military-political in nature. We are dealing with poetic descriptions of the type of warfare that was common at that time. One may suppose that if the position of the last Babylonian king, Nabonidus, had been stronger, the city would indeed have been besieged, taken, and destroyed in such a manner. However, because Nabonidus has become radically estranged from the priests and the population of Babylon, the city was not militarily defended, enabling Cyrus the Persian king to take it in 539 B.C.E. without lifting a finger.

Ideological Level

In addition to this military-political level, the text also knows an ideological aspect. Central is the question why the God of Israel allows such events to happen. On this level we are not concerned with the attacking power of the peoples from the north or the defeatism of the Babylonians, but with YHWH, who actively invades history. We need to remind ourselves that the authors wrote all of this at a time in which YHWH was still seen as the national God of Judah/Israel, a nation that had lost its independence a short time ago and was partly dispersed in an area considered large at that time. This God of a group of losers in the historical powerplay is now represented as the One determining history. It seems amazing that these writers, in their difficult circumstances, were able to make such a bold mental leap and, even more, that their vision eventually found worldwide resonance.

On an ideological level one notes different poles in the text, with YHWH in the center. Judah/Israel, Babylon (and its gods) and the peoples from the north stand in mutual contrast and at the same time in a relationship with YHWH. Past, present, and future are all dominated by him. No sharp division is made between present and future, but there is a division between past and present.

In regard to Judah/Israel, we see the following contrast between past and present/future: in the *past* Israel was a flock of lost sheep. Misled by their leaders, they took wrong paths (idolatry is probably meant) so that they easily fell prey to their enemies, who devoured them (50:6–7). The image of a chased sheep that is devoured returns in 50:17, where the Assyrian king and Nebuchadnezzar are named as Israel's enemies. The motif "devour" returns in 51:34, where it is developed in a description of how Nebuchadnezzar treated Judah/Israel.

Opposed to this somber image of the past is the joyous *present*, in
which YHWH brings Israel back to its pasture (50:19, again the metaphor
of "small cattle"—sheep and goats). The description of Israel's future ter-
ritory demonstrates that the authors assumed a "Great Israel," including
Transjordan. The reason that YHWH shows mercy toward his people lies
in the forgiveness he grants, so that they will be without sin anymore. In
50:33–34, the emphasis lies still more on YHWH's faithfulness toward his
people: he is their strong redeemer, who liberates Israel and Judah from
the power of their enemies, who hold them captive. Here we also meet
the motif of the lawsuit that YHWH executes in favor of Judah/Israel,
while we read in 51:10 that he demonstrates Judah's righteousness. As
indicated above, when a theme is repeated, additional aspects come to
the fore. While 50:19–20 deals with God forgiving Israel's guilt, in
50:33–34 the image of YHWH as redeemer is central. In 51:5, both aspects are joined: even if Israel and Judah were full of guilt, YHWH would
not leave them alone.

The changed relationship between YHWH and his people is described quite briefly in this prophecy. More attention is directed to the
relationship between YHWH and Babylon. In the *past* Babylon has
sinned against YHWH (50:14), has fought with YHWH (50:24), and has
been arrogant toward YHWH (50:29). However, in addition to emphasizing the guilt of the Babylonians, Babylon's function in God's plan is
mentioned. In 51:7 Babylon is described as a gold cup in YHWH's hand,
whereby the nations are made drunk and foolish. We find a variation of
the cup motif in the fragment in which Babylon is praised as a war club
in God's hand (51:20–23). Babylon is here seen as an instrument of God
to act in world history. However, without taking into consideration the
rest of the book of Jeremiah, this image would remain quite unclear.

As opposed to the might and pride of Babylon in the past is its complete ruin in the *present*. The Babylonian gods are ashamed (50:2). After all, the destruction is the work of Israel's God (50:45), who puts the
idols (50:38) to shame (51:17–19, 47, 52). The comment that YHWH is
visiting Babylon or taking vengeance on Babylon, requiting Babylon
for what it did to others (50:15, 29) recurs as a refrain.

Why this requital? The text points out several violent acts that are
now avenged: the destruction of the temple (50:28; 51:11) and of Zion/
Jerusalem (51:24, 35), the plunder and destruction of the whole earth
(51:25, 44, 49) and idolatry (51:47, 52).

This approach attracts attention to the paradox between the images
of Babylon as a cup/hammer of God on the one hand, and the overcon-
fident destroyer of the whole world, fighting against God, on the other

hand. Are these images consistent? Their juxtaposition is an example of the authors' method. They juxtapose images and leave it to the reader to make the mutual connection. In this, the approach of Isa 10:5–19 differs. It attempts to work out the same paradox within a single text: Assyria is the rod of God's anger without realizing it. Therefore, Assyria acts pridefully and rapaciously. For this it will be punished by God, though he has used Assyria to punish the people of Israel. But even in the structure of this Isaian passage (particularly the end), one notes that the author has difficulty maintaining both aspects of the matter in a single image.

The Image of the Cup

As we have seen, the image of Babylon as a cup in God's hand is hardly developed in 51:7. It seems therefore that this passage intends to refer to an already familiar metaphor. This metaphor is found in a series of Old Testament texts, of which Jer 25:15–29 is the most interesting for our investigation. Could the metaphor in 51:7 be intended as a pointer to the reader to relate Jeremiah 50 and 51, not only to chaps. 27–29, but also to chap. 25? Indeed, when we relate Jeremiah 25 to this investigation, the connection between the prophecy against Babylon and the rest of the book of Jeremiah becomes remarkably clearer.

Jeremiah 25 may be divided into five parts. The first part (25:1–7) provides a brief summary of Jeremiah's prophetic career. Because Judah did not want to listen, an announcement of judgment follows (25:8–11a). YHWH will summon Nebuchadnezzar to execute his justice. Thereafter follows a passage on Babylon's future (25:11b–14) and a prophecy concerning the cup of judgment (25:15–29). The chapter closes by a quite general prophecy of judgment against the nations (25:30–38).

When we compare the passage about the cup of judgment here with 51:7, we note that in chap. 51 Babylon itself is the cup whereby YHWH makes the nations drunk, while in chap. 25 God hands the cup to the prophet to let the nations drink of it. In other words, the cup is not further identified in chap. 25.

A large part of the prophecy concerning the cup is filled by a lengthy list of nations who must drink from it. Babylon does not appear in this list. At the end of v. 26 it is said that the king of Sheshak (= Babylon) must drink after the nations. This notable placement of Babylon after the list of the nations may point to a later interpolation. This suggests that Babylon was not originally mentioned in the text, from which

inference one might deduce that there is an implicit connection between the cup of wrath and Babylon, in the sense that the cup is a symbol for Babylon. If this supposition is true, 25:15–29 corresponds
perfectly with both 25:8–11a and 51:7.

The remark in 25:29 that the nations do not go free when Yнwн
brings disaster on Jerusalem is interesting. When God's own city of Jerusalem is punished, the nations will be punished all the more. We find
this emphasis on Israel's election in chaps. 50 and 51 as well (50:11, 28,
34; 51:10, 19, 24, 36, 49). Moreover, we find a clear parallel to this
verse in the prophecy against Edom (Jer 49:12).

The Intention of Jeremiah 25

Scholars tend to regard Jer 25:8–14 MT as secondary. A primary reason is the LXX, which deviates significantly from the MT, in that references to Babylon and Nebuchadnezzar are lacking in vv. 9, 11, and 12
of the LXX. There is only a reference to the "generation from the
north." Moreover, v. 14 is completely lacking. The LXX of v. 13 deals
with the prophecies against the nations, which the MT places at the end
of the book of Jeremiah. In itself, the placement in the LXX gives more
relief to v. 13, which speaks of "this book," which contains all the words
that Jeremiah spoke against "that land." In view of the context of the
LXX, the subject must be a prophecy against "the generation from the
north," one of the foreign nations; and one may assume that by "this
book" is meant a grouping of prophecies against the nations. Thus,
v. 13 in the LXX forms a fitting introduction to the part of Jeremiah in
which these prophecies have been collected.

However, the difference between the LXX and the MT is not as great
as it appears. One may assume that it was clear to the reader of the
LXX which nation was meant by "the generation from the north," certainly if we take v. 11 in view, which indicates the same number of years
as 36:10 (MT: 29:10), where Babylon is named. The notion that this nation would be punished by Yнwн is present in the LXX of chap. 25,
though on a more limited scale than in the MT.

Things change drastically if one suspects that there was a more original text behind the LXX: "The original address was presumably much
briefer, and concerned exclusively with warning Judah of the ruin and
exile shortly to overtake her. . . . Thus the nation threatened in v. 13
was originally Judah, while 'this book' was the scroll of Jeremiah's
prophecies . . . now underlying chapters i–xxv" (Bright, *Jeremiah*, 163).

The chief objection to these attempts to reconstruct a (supposed) original version of 25:1–14 is that one not only abandons the *Tendenz* of the MT but also of the LXX. If we delete all references to "the generations from the north," that is, Babylon, from 25:1–14, a judgment prophecy against Judah remains that has so little character of its own that it could never have fulfilled a function within the total composition, since it had nothing new to offer. There appears therefore little reason for assuming the existence of such an original version. The imperfections of this passage are not caused by a later editing of the text but by the authors of chap. 25 wishing to connect a variety of separate themes in the book of Jeremiah. The function of this chapter is chiefly redactional. As a connecting part roughly in the middle of the book, it points both backward (particularly to chaps. 1 and 4–6) and forward (particularly chaps. 36 and 46–51 MT). It appears likely that the MT offers an editing of the *Vorlage* of the LXX that nevertheless represents the *Tendenz* of the earlier version in a correct way.

Jer 25:11b–14 offers the prospect that servitude to Babylon will last 70 years, as is also mentioned in 29:10. The difference, however, is that chap. 25 (MT) speaks explicitly about Babylon's guilt. Moreover, the expectation that Babylon will experience servitude is combined with the prophecy of judgment that Babylon will be totally destroyed. Logically, the one more or less excludes the other, but the author wishes to combine two separate themes. The idea of the termination of Babylon's dominion is typical of chaps. 27 and 28; the doom prophecy concerning Babylon's destruction is typical of chaps. 50 and 51, where the theme of Babylon's servitude to other nations does not occur. The correspondence between chaps. 25 and 50/51 becomes still clearer if "this book" in 25:13 indeed refers to Jeremiah's prophecies against the nations, particularly Babylon, for the expression "this book" returns in 51:63, while the preceding verses (both 25:12 and 51:62) mention that Babylon will become a "perpetual desolation." This is obviously an explicit reference within the book of Jeremiah.

Lacking in chap. 25 is the notion that YHWH will have mercy on his people in spite of the sins that they have committed. But this idea is found in chap. 29 (in addition to other chapters in Jeremiah). Thus, if we combine chaps. 25 and 29, we encounter several elements of the ideology of chaps. 50/51. There is clearly not as great a contradiction between the prophecy against Babylon and the rest of the book of Jeremiah as is sometimes claimed. To the contrary, the prophecy agrees reasonably well with the chapters to which the authors themselves have drawn connecting lines.

The Function of Jeremiah 50 and 51

Typically, scholars have paid very little attention to the function of Jeremiah 50–51. Instead, they have concentrated on the question of whether Jeremiah 50/51 might or might not go back to the historical Jeremiah. We have pointed out that 51:59–64 does not make a convincing historical impression. It is also difficult to imagine that—given that the historical Jeremiah tried hard to oppose the opinions of Hananiah—he at the same time might have written a prophecy in which the fall of Babylon was said to be imminent. Moreover, this prophecy contains a number of citations not only from the book of Jeremiah but also from Isaiah 13 and Hab 2:13.

However, this argument does not exclude the possibility that the prophecy against Babylon was the work of authors who composed the book of Jeremiah as a whole. These authors wrote in a situation in which a rebellion against Babylon was out of the question, and they could freely quote from the sources and traditions at their disposal.

We may quite confidently date the prophecy against Babylon between 560 and 555 B.C.E.[1] This also appears to be the probable dating of the book of Jeremiah as a whole (disregarding a few later interpolations). Thus, also in respect to date, there is no objection to ascribing the prophecy to the authors of the book.

However, if this part originated with the authors of the book, why did they produce this long prophecy and include it in their work? In the first place, a prophecy against Babylon could hardly be left out of a series of prophecies against foreign nations, particularly since the events of 586 B.C.E. had made Babylon into Judah's greatest enemy.

There was more, however. I now venture to take a leap from the literary to the historical plain. If the description of Jeremiah's experiences during the reign of Zedekiah that we find in the book of Jeremiah and that is often ascribed to Baruch goes back to historical events to a certain extent, one has to conclude that Jeremiah, at least in the eyes of a number of contemporaries, was a traitor. We are told in 37:11–16 that Jeremiah made an attempt to leave the city during a break in the siege of Jerusalem but was apprehended and accused of wanting to defect to the Babylonians. In spite of his protests, he was then imprisoned.

---

1. From 51:46, we gather that the struggle for power after Nebuchadnezzar's death (562 B.C.E.) was still going on. This struggle ended with Nabonidus's ascension to the throne in 555 B.C.E.

The suspicion against Jeremiah does not appear to be groundless when one reads Jer 39:11–14 concerning the preferential treatment that Jeremiah received from the Babylonians after they had taken Jerusalem. According to 40:1, Jeremiah appears to have landed after a few weeks among the captive exiles, but then he also received special treatment by order of the high Babylonian officer, Nebuzaradan. To be sure, 40:1–6 presents a clear fictional element: in view of the words that are put in his mouth, the author wants to persuade us that Nebuzaradan was a pupil of Jeremiah (40:2–3). On the other hand, it is difficult to think of a reason why the authors would have fully imagined such events, which put their hero in a rather unfavorable light.

Whoever the authors of the book of Jeremiah may have been, they obviously had a particular veneration for this prophet. They therefore had a problem with the traditions and (possible) written sources about Jeremiah at their disposal, since the prophet's pro-Babylonian attitude was undeniable. This attitude indeed turned out to be good insight into the international politics of his time, but would have been considered quite dubious after 586 B.C.E. If the authors wished to be successful with their representation of Jeremiah as the ideal prophet, they could not just let him remain a partisan of Babylon. Thus we see that the authors let Jeremiah sigh in 28:6, wishing that YHWH would make Hananiah's words of salvation true. The reader should not doubt Jeremiah's patriotic attitude. The prophet longed as much for the fall of Babylon as the reader, but patience was needed. The 70-year period was not yet past. The remarks in chap. 25—that Babylon was indeed sent by God to bring devastation but will be punished for what it did—are on the same level. What the authors wish subtly to make clear to the reader is that Jeremiah did indeed plead for subjection to Babylon but that this did not mean that he was also an accomplice of the Babylonian king.

To exclude misunderstanding, the authors moreover composed an extensive prophecy against Babylon in which they introduced no new thoughts but in which they could broadly showcase Jeremiah's repugnance toward Babylon. They therefore dated this prophecy to the same year as Jeremiah's apparent pro-Babylonian activity described in chaps. 27–29, and in 50–51 they also placed accents clearly different from the rest of the book: the guilt of Judah/Israel is mentioned in a few places, as well as the concept that Babylon was an instrument in God's hand, but the emphasis lies on the punishment of Babylon's pride and on revenge for the Babylonians' destruction of enemy territories. Their actions will be avenged: a new enemy is coming from the north, this time not to bring disaster on Judah but on Babylon.

For this reason the authors could not omit this prophecy in their painting of the (literary) figure of Jeremiah. Whether the historical Jeremiah would have been happy with this reinterpretation of his career will always remain a puzzle. When his admirers wrote this prophecy against Babylon in his name, the prophet had probably been dead for some 20 years.

A God of Vengeance?
Comparing YHWH's Dealings with Judah and Babylon in the Book of Jeremiah

J. G. AMESZ

Rotterdam, The Netherlands

Introduction

In their search for an "authentic Jeremiah" kernel in the Oracles against the Nations (Jeremiah 46–51), nineteenth-century scholars were keenly concerned with the *ipsissima verba* of the prophet. Another one of their vital concerns was the representation of God, since it was thought to have occupied a crucial place in the prophets' thought world. The question was asked whether the representation of YHWH in the Oracles against the Nations agreed with the representation in texts that were considered to have been written by the "historical" Jeremiah.

As is amply evident from research, Jeremiah viewed YHWH as the God of Israel. He is highly exalted above the heathen gods and merciful and gracious toward his people. Because of the proud and ungrateful attitude of the people, YHWH threatened them through his prophet with destruction of the land and deportation of the inhabitants if they persisted in their refusal to listen to the prophetic proclamation and did not repent. If they, on the other hand, would listen to YHWH's voice, he would permit them to continue to live in the land. In the prophetic oracles addressed to Israel and Judah, YHWH is represented as a God who is willing to forgive and who is inclined to revoke his former threats. In the oracles addressed to the nations, however, YHWH appears as an irreconcilable God of vengeance who announces ruin to the nations. These oracles contain threats of destruction exclusively, while the preaching of repentance is completely lacking. Since these representations of YHWH were found to diverge so radically, scholars concluded that the Oracles against the Nations cannot be ascribed to Jeremiah.

Author's note: The text was translated by the editor. The author thanks Prof. Dr. K. A. D. Smelik for his comments on this essay.

It might be questioned, however, whether preaching of repentance is a fixed component of Jeremiah's oracles. The problem is that the book of Jeremiah contains no information about the provenance of "Jeremian" prophecy. The comparison of other oracles with texts containing supposedly "genuine" words of the "historical" Jeremiah always rests on circular reasoning because we have no firm, undisputed knowledge about a historical Jeremiah. The result of the comparison is always dependent on which texts we ascribe to the historical Jeremiah. The fact remains, however, that for historical data we depend virtually completely on the book that bears his name.

To break through this circular reasoning, the starting point of our investigation of the composition of the book of Jeremiah should not be the words ascribed to a putative historical Jeremiah but the words of the "literary" figure after whom the book of Jeremiah is named. As the figure of a Harry "Rabbit" Anstrom is a literary creation of a writer named John Updike in his Rabbit tetralogy, Jeremiah is a literary creation of the authors of the book bearing his name. When comparing representations of God in texts that are addressed to different nations, it is important to note the consistency of such representations by the literary figure of a "Jeremiah." How is YHWH represented within the different texts in the book of Jeremiah? How does YHWH act toward Judah and toward the peoples outside of Judah? To what extent do the images of God or representations of God in the oracles mutually agree and where do they differ? Can the differences between the investigated oracles be explained? In this essay I plan to answer these questions, based on two comparable judgment oracles.

The first oracle material is addressed to the inhabitants of Judah and Jerusalem (4:3–6:30); the second is an oracle directed to the superpower Babylon (chaps. 50–51). Both oracles contain monologues of YHWH concerning the destruction of the addressed people by him or by an enemy that he would call for that purpose. Characteristic for these (war) texts are the calls containing imperatives, such as the call to battle against a nation, the call to flee, and the call to lament by the threatened people. Another characteristic of both texts is that the structure does not form a running, systematically ordered whole. To communicate a message, the authors have structured the texts from brief episodes based on a number of themes that keep recurring with regularity. Such themes tend to be only partly developed when the author proceeds to another episode containing a different theme.

Repetitions in both oracles are usually related to the desire for emphasis. This essay begins with a description of both oracles, with the aid of segments (such as acting figures, the announcement and the result of destruction, anxiety, and imagery) that appear in both oracles. Subsequently, we examine the way that YHWH deals with both nations. Coupled with this is the question of why YHWH intervenes against Judah and Babylon. The conclusions will center on the agreement of the representations of YHWH in the two oracles discussed.

A Prophecy in Jerusalem

The prophecy addressed to Judah and Jerusalem (4:3–6:30) is part of a long speech (chaps. 2–6) that the man of Anathoth gave to an audience in Jerusalem (2:1–2). In the superscription YHWH addresses himself to the I-figure (the prophet) with the commission to go to Jerusalem to speak his words there in the hearing of the city. In the first part (2:2–4:2) YHWH speaks to "the house of Jacob and all generations of the house of Israel" (2:4). He formulates a complaint against Israel that they have forsaken their God (2:13). The prophet points to different moments from Israel's history (2:5–8). For their behavior he had punished Israel with exile (3:8), but the possibility of return to him is mentioned (3:10). With his call to return he gives the assurance that he will no longer be angry because he is just (3:12). Israel is called upon to acknowledge their guilt: they have broken fellowship with YHWH, their own God, and given their favors to foreign gods and nations (3:13).

Though this speech is addressed to a Judahite audience, the name of Israel recurs with regularity. The reader's question is: Which Israel does YHWH mean?

1. Is he speaking to fugitives from the Northern Kingdom of Israel who had taken refuge in the city of Jerusalem?
2. Does he mean the "Confessional" name that Judah took over from the North?
3. Or did YHWH want to warn his Judahite audience about their future fate by comparing their present behavior toward him with Israel's behavior in the past?

A number of times Israel is named in combination with Judah. The first time is when Israel had turned from YHWH and made other gods of wood and stone to serve them. Israel was disappointed in their expectations, however, since not every appeal to YHWH in time of disaster was answered. Judah would also appeal to their gods in vain; YHWH remarked ironically that these gods were as numerous as Judah's cities (2:28).

The second time YHWH referred to both the former Northern Kingdom of Israel and Judah is when he portrayed them as two unfaithful
women: Israel whom YHWH named "Faithless One" led in prostitution,
and Judah, whom YHWH called her "False Sister," followed her example
(3:6ff.). In both admonitions YHWH offered a possibility of repentance.
In the one case the "Confessional" community of Israel refused to accept the message of YHWH. YHWH therefore complained that Israel had
forsaken him (2:19). Moreover, he showed them the results of their rejection in societal and political life (2:34–37). In the other case YHWH
refused to accept the fact that Israel had broken fellowship with him.
With his call: "Go, and call these words to the North. . . . Return, faithless Israel" (3:12), he wished to restore this fellowship. In the first instance this call appeared destined for the exiles from the Northern
Kingdom. However, the entire speech was directed to Judahite ears.
Before this call to return, YHWH judged Judah negatively, compared
with Israel (3:11). By YHWH's judgment against Israel, an urgent call
was directed to Judah. Because Israel did not return, YHWH afflicted
them with exile, though they were judged less guilty than Judah (3:10);
how much the more Judah would be punished if they would not return
to YHWH!

When Israel and Judah were named together for the third time,
there was a new situation to consider (3:18). Both were promised a future return, they would unite as brothers, they would return from exile
and take possession of the land that was given to their fathers. This
promise presupposed, however, that Judah would go into exile as Israel
had. Though Israel was mentioned frequently in the first part of
YHWH's speech, its subject was really Judah and particularly their relationship to YHWH. Israel's history was actualized for Judahite ears as a
warning against the consequences of their behavior. If they persisted in
forsaking YHWH, Judah would also be taken into exile. In the sequel,
which aimed entirely at Jerusalem and Judah, their future fate, threatening disaster from the north, was reported.

Disaster from the North

After a sustained portrayal of Israel's history as a mirror for Judah's
behavior, in the second part of his speech YHWH turned directly to his
hearers in Jerusalem with a threatening report of the coming of an enemy to Judah: "I bring evil from the north, great destruction" (4:6b).
This message of disaster, "the threat from the north" recurs repeatedly

in the text in different words. The coming of an ancient people (5:15), speaking an unknown language was part of the execution of an irrevocable judgment (4:12, 28) that YHWH had spoken concerning Judah. The land would be destroyed; every city would be deserted (4:27–28). That the enemy is not named in this prophecy may be significant, underscoring that it is really YHWH who acts. In addition to summoning help from the north to destroy his people (6:1, 22–23), he made an afflictive visitation of his own (5:9) to the inhabitants of the land, avenging himself (5:29). He stretched out his hand and caused his people to stumble (6:15, 21).

An obvious way of describing the ruin of a people is to sketch the destruction of their habitat. It begins with the threat of the cities and their inhabitants (4:16) along with their fields and meadows, by the enemy from the north (5:17). After the war activities, the fortified cities were destroyed (5:17), their inhabitants either were killed or fled (4:25), and the arable land was destroyed (4:26). Total destruction made Jerusalem and Judah uninhabitable: "Every city is forsaken; it has no more inhabitants" (4:29).

The ruin of Judah and its cities is presented by varied *imagery*. The inhabitants had fallen prey to aggressive predators. They were threatened by their enemy as if by a lion, a wolf, or a panther. The common image of a lion is often used: he rises in the bushes to fall on his prey, destroying the cities, which lose all their inhabitants (4:7). Another image spelling disaster is the natural phenomenon of the "desert wind," which leaves a trail of destruction behind (4:11).

The prophet also employs *metaphors* for the besieged in their threatening situation. These express the powerlessness and the total destruction of Judah; with the hearing of the rumor that the enemy was moving in, anxiety seized her: anguish "as of a woman in labor" (6:24). At the beginning of the battle Judah was likened to a vineyard given up to plundering (5:10); elsewhere the destruction of the "rest of Israel" was like a vineyard whose tendrils needed to be examined before the harvest (6:9), and the "daughter of Zion" is portrayed as a field that the shepherds let their cattle graze bare (6:3).

The different images for attacker and attacked, of the cause and of the victim of disaster, intensify the description of the hopelessness of Judah's situation. It appears as though Judah cannot expect help from anywhere. How did Judah land in such a distressing position? To answer this question we need to analyze the relationship between the one calling for and the one affected by disaster.

Accusations against Jerusalem and Judah

In addition to this military-political aspect, the prophet's speech also touches an ideological level. The central question is why YHWH allowed these events against Jerusalem and Judah to occur. How are YHWH's motives in his international intervention in Judah's national history legitimized? YHWH, as the national deity of Judah, participates in the historical powerplay in which his people lose their independence. Surprisingly, YHWH, the God of the losers, is also the one who determines the course of history.

Thus, YHWH appears to assume an opposing posture in relationship to the inhabitants of Judah. On the one hand he accuses them of straining their relationship with him, for which they are threatened with punishment by an enemy from the north. On the other hand he calls on them to restore their relationship to their God (to be demonstrated in their behavior) by turning to him. Both the complaints and the appeals are expressed by YHWH at different times in the text.

Generally speaking, three types of complaints may be distinguished.

1. In the first group of complaints, YHWH calls attention to the *external behavior* of Judah's inhabitants in the past. In his complaint he describes their "walk (literally, way) and acts" toward him (4:18) as rebellious (4:17), utterly faithless (5:11), and stubborn (5:23). They have wandered away from YHWH by turning their backs on him (5:23). From young to old, all were greedy, seeking their own gain (6:13). They only thought of their own advantage, without any concern for the well-being of others. On the contrary, they did not hesitate to exploit and extort others. Injustice and the misuse of power, particularly by the rich, are exposed with a few concrete examples. Instead of putting their power and prosperity at the service of orphans and the poor (according to the divine commandment) they used their influence to enrich themselves. They failed to acknowledge the rights of the poor and socially disadvantaged in society (5:28). They were as hard as metal (6:28). All of this prompted YHWH to ask, "Would I not punish them for these things, or avenge myself on such a people?" (5:29).

2. The second group contains complaints relating to *how the people have forsaken him*. Forsaking God implies a turning to other gods:

> Your children have forsaken me
> and swear by those who are not gods. (5:7)

Using imagery pertaining to adultery, YHWH accused the inhabitants of Jerusalem of prostituting themselves with other gods. In spite of the fact that he provided them with everything good, they committed adultery. Like "stallions in heat" they took their refuge in brothels, the temples of other gods. The serving of other gods in their own land, is referred to once more. This time YHWH attached a judgment to the complaint by announcing their future fate:

> As you have forsaken me
> and served foreign gods in your land,
> so you shall serve strangers in a land
> that is not yours. (5:19)

In his judgment YHWH turned the situation for the inhabitants upside down: serving other gods in the land resulted in subservience to foreign rulers with other gods.

3. The final group of complaints refers to *estrangement* between YHWH and the people. The inhabitants of Judah no longer knew YHWH. This was not intellectual knowledge (4:22) but rather the failure to acknowledge him and to act according to his "way" (that is, his commandments), by which YHWH bound his people to himself. However, the people no longer listened to the word of YHWH. They did not take it seriously (6:10, 19).

> My people are foolish,
> they do not know me.
> They are stupid children,
> they have no understanding.
> They are skilled in doing evil,
> but how to do good they do not know. (4:22)

Roaming through the streets of Jerusalem (5:1), the prophet thought that he would only find this attitude among the socially weak, since their life is occupied by the care of daily existence (5:4); however, the affluent were worse than the poor. YHWH himself described the behavior of priests and prophets, the spiritual leaders of the people, as "appalling and horrible" (5:30). Though they had been appointed as watchmen (6:17) of the people, prophets aided by priests spoke falsely (5:31). Like Jeremiah, they claimed to prophesy in the name of YHWH, but their message was false:

> No evil will come upon us;
> we shall see neither sword nor famine. (5:12)

Instead of showing the people the cause of social abuses and warning them, they claimed that all was well (6:14). When the enemy would come whom YHWH called from the north, their message would prove to be a delusion (5:13) and they would be ashamed before their hearers (6:15).

The Search for a Righteous One

Besides admonishing them several times, YHWH called the Judahites three times to return and to show remorse for their "walk and actions" so that they might forestall the threatening calamity. By this appeal he wished to remind the people of the agreement existing between them and God.

1. At the beginning of the prophecy, a call to return is sounded:

> Circumcise yourselves to YHWH,
> and remove the foreskin of your hearts. (4:4a)

A reference to the circumcision ritual points to the sign of YHWH's relationship to his people. YHWH called the inhabitants to cut away the "foreskin" of their hearts, just as a farmer plows fallow land and removes thorn bushes (4:3) because young plants cannot grow between thorns. Thus, the heart of the inhabitants needed to be cultivated to make room for new fruit.

2. In his second call to return, YHWH again addressed the hearts of the Jerusalem inhabitants:

> Wash your heart of wickedness,
> Jerusalem, that you may be saved. (4:14a)

Jerusalem, addressed as a woman, must wash her heart (as one washes clothes) since sinful thoughts and considerations are lodged in her heart (4:14b). In Hebrew linguistic usage, the heart is above all the place of general sentiment and understanding, the will, and the making of decisions—functions that Western culture associates with the head. When YHWH called for circumcision and washing of the heart, he desired that the Judahites again direct their efforts to keeping his commandments. The calls refer to a renewed dedication to YHWH's ordinances so that they might be his people again. The conversion of their hearts signifies the restoration of his relationship with them.

3. In the final call, in which he addressed the city as a woman again, YHWH gave Jerusalem room for conversion in spite of fact that the threat from the north was inevitable:

> Take warning, O Jerusalem,
> so that I will not be alienated from you
> and make you a desolation,
> a land without inhabitants. (6:8)

YHWH's warning to the Jerusalem community implied his wish to withdraw his threat. If they would accept reproof, the enemy might be stopped. It was "not yet" too late for the inhabitants to change their ways. Even when YHWH announced the destruction of the land, there was likewise the implication of a "not yet," when the threat of destruction would "not yet" be realized in its totality (4:27; 5:10, 18b). Apparently, YHWH reserved the right to change his mind—specifically, his earlier announcement of doom. He hoped that his speeches would bring about a change of attitude so that he did not need to execute his plan; however, if they would not change their ways and show remorse, he still would not totally destroy the land.

In any event, YHWH might change his mind and reconsider his judgment of the people. The possibility that YHWH might change his attitude was based on his relationship with them. In his final appeal YHWH reminded the Judahites of this relationship, which he now wished to break. He threatened to turn away from the city. It is perhaps ironic that the break of this relationship is expressed in the language of love. As a husband leaves his wife after making love, so YHWH would leave Jerusalem (6:8). However, his bond with Jerusalem and Judah was so important to him that he, in faithfulness to their relationship, kept inviting them to return.

That YHWH wished to maintain the covenant relationship in spite of the fact that he condemned the life and works of the people of Jerusalem also appears from his commission to the prophet:

> Roam through the streets of Jerusalem,
> look and take note.
> Search its squares to see
> if you can find a man,
> whether there is one person who does justice
> and seeks honesty,
> so that I may pardon Jerusalem. (5:1)

In a dialogue YHWH commanded Jeremiah to look for a man, just as Abraham asked (Gen 18:22–33), who kept his commandments and observed righteousness. The purpose of this search was so that not only the entire city might thus be saved but also the relationship between the city-dwellers and YHWH. However, Jeremiah's search for righteousness was in vain (5:3).

The Oracles against the Nations

The oracle collection directed against Babylon is found in Jeremiah 50 and 51; it closes a collection of ten oracles directed to the nations that comprises six chapters (chaps. 46–51). This complex of oracles has its own superscription: "The word of YHWH that came to Jeremiah the prophet concerning the nations" (46:1), and its own closure: "Thus far are the words of Jeremiah" (51:64). The collection opens with an oracle against Egypt and closes with one against Babylon. Between the oracles against Egypt (chap. 46) and Babylon (chaps. 50–51), the following peoples are addressed: the Philistines (chap. 47), Moab (chap. 48), Ammon (49:1–6), Edom (49:7–22), Damascus (49:23–27), Hazor (49:28–33), and Elam (49:34–39). Egypt and Babylon, as the two most important nations in the book of Jeremiah, frame the oracle collection.

In his proclamation, the prophet had declared to his hearers in Jerusalem that an enemy from the north had been sent by YHWH to punish Judah for its failures. Later he named the enemy: Nebuchadnezzar (chap. 21). Rebellion against Nebuchadnezzar to remove the Babylonian yoke and to choose another major power (Egypt at that time) would be rebellion against YHWH, according to Jeremiah (chap. 27). After all, YHWH had granted the Babylonian king world hegemony and guaranteed his power. However, the judgment oracles against Babylon and Egypt suggest that the prophet did not make a choice for one or against another. Egypt suffered defeat by YHWH and the army of Nebuchadnezzar, but after that the land would be inhabitable again (46:26). Nebuchadnezzar and his land were also threatened with ruin by YHWH and by an unknown enemy from the north.

A Letter at the Euphrates

The oracle collection closes with a letter for the exiles in Babylon (51:59–64). The prophet gave this letter to Seraiah, a brother of Baruch (Jeremiah's scribe), to take along when he [Seraiah] accompanied King Zedekiah, serving as quartermaster on a journey to Babylon (51:59). Having arrived in Babylon, Seraiah, as he had been told by the prophet, read aloud the document (51:61) and then, weighting it down with a stone, threw it into the Euphrates—symbolizing the ruin of Babylon (51:63). In the letter, written by Jeremiah, YHWH announced his plan to destroy Babylon and the land of the Chaldeans totally and permanently (51:60). The summary statement regarding the letter (51:60) refers back to the long oracle against Babylon. In the oracle the prophet announced the disaster called for by YHWH against Babylon and the land of the Chaldeans (50:1). He did not offer a chronological timetable for the execution of his message of doom. He changed theme and time even more than in his speech against Jerusalem. The prophecy frequently cites parts of the battle for the city of Babylon, but no attention is paid to events preceding the course of the battle. If there is heavy fighting at a given moment, at the next moment the enemy still has to besiege the city, and at another moment the city has already become a ruin. Such changes contribute to the liveliness of the text.

In the prophecy Jeremiah announced that YHWH was bringing a multitude of people against Babylon (50:9), as he had done against Jerusalem and Judah. They were arrayed against the city to raze it from all sides. The enemy was armed with bow and arrow (50:14), sword (50:35), spear (50:42), and shield (51:11) and was equipped with horses (50:42). Twice Jeremiah named Media as the enemy (51:11, 28). In the battle the enemy laid bare the broad fortress walls of Babylon and set its high gates on fire (51:58). The towers of the city had fallen down (50:15). The enemy pursued its defenders in the city streets and cut them down (50:30; 51:4). Its heroes were taken prisoner (51:56). Subsequently, the enemy plundered all of the city and the entire country (50:10). Meanwhile, the foreigners in Babylon, among whom were the Judahite exiles, were summoned by YHWH to leave (50:8). Babylon was no longer the place toward which people were streaming (51:44). No one came to aid the city in the enormous violence of the war (50:32), for "the patient was incurable" (51:9).

The command to the enemy of the north to mobilize (50:21) was part of the decision that YHWH made to wreak vengeance on Babylon (50:45). The city would be made a desolation (51:29). YHWH was himself actively involved in executing the plan: he opened his armory and took out the tools of his anger (50:25). In this case the storage chamber of arms was in the north, in the hands of the people who were coming down. The prophet viewed Babylon's ruin as the result of YHWH's "visitation" of the city (50:18). The day of Babylon's downfall had come (50:31).

YHWH's destructive acts against the city were drawn in different images. He would ignite a fire around the city that would destroy it (50:32). He would catch it in a snare and seize it (50:24). He would stretch out his hand to it and roll it off a crag (51:25). He would make it drunk so that it would sleep forever (51:39). In his revenge he would overpower it as a tyrant so that its mighty voice would be silenced (51:55). The area had become like a desert without habitation (50:12). The destructiveness of YHWH's intervention against the city appears from the way the inhabitants lived after the destruction. Before the coming of the armies from the north, Babylon was a mighty city, favorably located on a river (51:13), protected by a broad fortress wall with high gates (51:58) and towers (50:15). Strongholds for defense surrounded the city (51:30).

During the zenith of its power, population groups from nations, including Jerusalem, had been taken in exile to Babylon (51:44). After the war of destruction, the once mighty realm would become a ruin among the nations (50:23). In his judgment YHWH compared the ruin of the city with the fate of Sodom and Gomorrah (50:40a):

> Therefore wild beasts shall dwell with hyenas,
> and ostriches shall dwell in her;
> she shall be peopled no more forever,
> nor be inhabited for all generations. (50:39)

Babylon would become a heap of ruins and a haunt for jackals (51:37). The land would be uninhabited (51:43). The future appearance of the city would be like a desert, a barren and arid land (50:12). Anyone passing the destroyed city would be amazed and whistle at its blows (50:13). Its destruction was so total that whatever was left of the city could not be used for any purpose (51:26). To Jeremiah, the point of the prophecy was that the city would be made forever uninhabitable, for he commissioned Seraiah to announce the ruin of Babylon with the words:

> YHWH, you have threatened this place to cut it off,
> so that nothing shall dwell in it,
> neither human nor beast,
> and it shall be desolate forever. (51:62)

Human beings and animals would disappear from Babylon, even if it meant filling it with troops like locusts (51:14). To flee the threatening danger, the exiles were called to leave the city (50:8). Local citizens reacted, for the rumor was spreading that Babylon had been taken, as a woman in labor (50:43). Panic had broken out in the city. The king had lost his courage and his soldiers were alarmed (51:32); their heroism had shriveled up and they had become as "women" (51:30). Since the Babylonian god Marduk had also been defeated, the inhabitants' trust in their god was shamed (50:2). A universal cry for help arose from the destroyed city (50:46).

To clarify his words of doom to the reader, the authors used imagery like the imagery in chaps. 4–6. Like a lion, the multitude of enemies was approaching (50:44). Their arrows (aimed at the city's defenders) were like those of a skilled hero (50:9). Another image of the coming of the enemy was the preparation of the threshing floor when harvesttime arrived (51:33).

Various images are used for the battle. The hammer—which Babylon once was in YHWH's hands (51:20–23)—had been destroyed (50:23). The golden cup that Babylon used to be and by which YHWH made the nations drunk (25:15–29), Babylon herself now needed to drink to the dregs (51:7). She was made drunk (51:39) and would sleep a perpetual sleep (51:57). In the final phase of the battle, Babylon was like a woman who had broken her leg through a fall. No balm would heal her; her ruin was unavoidable (51:8–9).

An ideological question suggests itself: why this practice of vengeance? To answer this question, the relationship between Babylon and YHWH, *past* and *present*, will be examined.

YHWH's Inheritance in Babylon

Although Babylon is described in the oracle as the instrument to execute YHWH's will in world history, it appears from the flashbacks to the literature of Israel and Judah (50:6–7, 17, 33) that YHWH held Babylon solely responsible for the robbing and looting (50:11). As far as YHWH was concerned, Babylon remained responsible for its misdeeds even if it was at one time the hammer or the golden cup in his hand. However, Babylon defended itself against this accusation by pointing out to YHWH the attitude of his people toward him:

> We are not guilty,
> for they have sinned against YHWH. (50:7)

Babylon did not fear revenge by a god whose property rights had been violated, since there was no longer any bond between the people and their god. After all, a people does not forsake its god; foreign nations know this as well (2:10–11). In the *past* Israel/Judah were:

> . . . lost sheep;
> their shepherds led them astray,
> turning them away on the mountains;
> from mountain to hill they went,
> they forgot their fold.
> All who found them ate them. (50:6–7)

Misled by their leaders, the people of Judah took wrong roads, wandering from the fields of righteousness to the heights of idolatry. They forgot YHWH their God. No longer protected by their God, they were delivered defenselessly to their enemies. Assyrian and Babylonian kings are mentioned explicitly as Israel's enemies (50:17). The latter particularly had done Judah enormous harm:

> Nebuchadnezzar, the king of Babylon,
> has devoured me;
> he has crushed me . . .
> he has swallowed me like a dragon;
> he has filled his belly with my delicacies. (51:34)

Nebuchadnezzar took everything of any worth to his city of Babylon.

The Descendants of Israel and Judah Seek YHWH

Contrary to the pathetic image of the past is the joyful *present* in which YHWH brings his people back to their pasture (50:19). He calls on them to flee Babylon before the enemy from the north arrives. In the descriptions of the flight and the return to Zion, the sheep metaphor recurs:

> Flee from the midst of Babylon . . .
> and be as male goats leading the flock. (50:8)

YHWH has had mercy on his people. The reason for his changed attitude toward his people is that he has granted them forgiveness so that they will be without sin (50:20). As the oracle continues, Jeremiah emphasizes another aspect of the relationship between YHWH and Israel/Judah—YHWH's faithfulness toward his people:

> Oppressed are the sons of Israel
> and the sons of Judah together;
> all who took them captive, held them fast;
> they refused to let them go.
> Their redeemer is strong,
> YHWH of hosts is his name.
> He will plead, yes, plead their cause. (50:33–34)

As in a judicial proceeding, YHWH leads a trial for his heritage. The trial will make it clear that he is the only redeemer of his people, who liberated them from the power of enemies that held them captive. Even though Israel and Judah were full of guilt by leaving their God, YHWH did not leave them (51:5). In this verse, YHWH moves the guilt question from Israel/Judah to Babylon. The enemies violated what was holy to YHWH,

> for [Babylon] proudly defied YHWH,
> the Holy One of Israel. (50:29)
> For the land of the Chaldeans is full of guilt
> against the Holy One of Israel. (51:5)

Though Israel and Judah were humbled and oppressed, they were not left to their fate. After all, YHWH was and will remain their spouse. To express YHWH's faithfulness to his people, the writer uses the metaphor of marriage:

> For Israel and Judah have not been forsaken
> by their God. (51:5)

The idea of a trial is referred to once more when YHWH speaks of Judah's righteousness (51:10). By his liberating act of justice his people are able to return to Jerusalem. The children of Israel and Judah will go together, weeping, to Zion to seek their God YHWH and to tell of his works (50:4–5). After a temporary stay in Babylon, Israel/Judah will return to Zion to bind themselves again to YHWH. The approaching disaster in Babylon by the coming of the enemy from the north reminds the exiles that their God YHWH has not forgotten his eternal covenant with them (50:5). When in the past the people, through the influence of their leaders, became unfaithful to him, he punished them by disaster from the north; but in taking his requital, he never forsook his faithfulness to them.

Jerusalem and Babylon: An Answer

These two texts, Jeremiah 4–6 and 50–51, appear to describe a similar event and even appear to link up in various details. In the same manner as Judah, Babylon would become a victim of the enemy from the north, summoned by YHWH, precisely because Judah had also become a victim.

The fate of Babylon, the same as that of other nations in the Oracle against the Nations, is the same as the fate of Judah. The prophecy of the Cup of Wrath (25:15–29), which contains a long list of nations who must drink from it (to be led away drunk), closes with an interesting comment that the nations would not go free if YHWH had not spared Jerusalem. However, the name of Babylon is lacking in the list, though it does say that the king of Sheshach (a code name for Babylon) will be the last one to drink the cup. Thus, Babylon is assigned a unique place in the decision that YHWH makes in regard to his people as well as other nations. Certainly, it could not be that only Judah would be destroyed by YHWH and that other nations would remain unpunished. After all, for YHWH, Jerusalem and Judah remain his eternal heritage.

The oracles against Jerusalem and Babylon share an identical detail that assumes an important place, namely, the *vengeance of YHWH*. The meaning of this expression differs in these texts. For Jerusalem/Judah, vengeance refers to YHWH's requital for their sins: the forsaking of their God in exchange for idolatry, and the practice of social injustice. In the beginning, his attitude toward judging his people was not resolute. Before punishment was executed, he commissioned the prophet to seek a righteous man. Furthermore, the destructive judgment to come will not be the end for Judah. The prophet's preaching of imminent judgment was aimed at Judah's return to YHWH, for he has not forgotten his covenant with them.

Against Babylon also, YHWH expressed a number of complaints on which his vengeance on that kingdom was based. His vengeance was requital for their insolent attitude toward YHWH, the violent deeds against Israel and Judah, and the oppression of the nations. The latter motif, combined with the vengeance of YHWH, appears in another oracle in the collection, the oracle against Egypt (46:2–12). In both cases the aim of YHWH's punitive intervention was to keep world hegemony in his own hands (46:9–10; 51:25). While the people of Judah were carried off to Babylon, the writers wished to proclaim that their God, YHWH, was Creator of heaven and earth (51:15) and also remained world sovereign after the fall of Jerusalem. The king of Babylon did not owe his throne to his god Marduk but to the national god of one of the nations he thought he had destroyed. Babylon's hegemony would last as long as YHWH thought he needed it as an instrument (cup/hammer) for the execution of his plan. After that, his kingdom would be totally destroyed and his god Marduk would be put to shame (50:2), as opposed to the Creator of all things, the God of Israel and Judah (51:19). For both Jerusalem and Babylon, the punishment for their attitude toward YHWH would be essentially identical: the coming of an enemy from the north, summoned by YHWH.

Moreover, both oracles contain an identical passage describing the coming of the enemy (6:22ff. = 50:41ff.). The prophetic oracles, originally directed against Jerusalem, are now directed against Babylon. This reapplication of the words of the prophet provides a (literary) hint about some kind of connection between the oracles against Judah and Babylon. The flashbacks in the oracles against Babylon suggest that Jeremiah viewed Babylon as an instrument (servant!) of YHWH. However, in a confrontation with his opponents the prophet was accused of a pro-Babylonian stance in his preaching (chaps. 27–29). After the fall of Jerusalem he even received preferential treatment from the Babylonian occupation (39:11–14). In spite of these events, the reader must not doubt Jeremiah's "nationalist" (pro-Judahite) attitude. Indeed, Jeremiah pleaded for subjection to Babylon, but this does not mean that he was an accomplice of the Babylonian king. The prophet longed just as much as his fellow-Judahites for the fall of Babylon, but he also realized that patience was needed (25:11). The writers of the book, by their re-application of the words of the prophet, wished to counteract a misunderstanding about Jeremiah's attitude. No new thoughts appear in the oracles against Babylon, but instead Jeremiah's aversion of Babylon is strongly emphasized. In the lengthy oracle against Babylon filled with hostile speech, unlike the oracles against Jerusalem (and the rest of the book), little attention is paid to the guilt of Israel/Judah or to the concept of Babylon as an instrument in YHWH's hands. Attention is paid instead to the punishment of Babylon's pride and insolence and its large-scale destruction on earth. Its actions would be avenged: a new enemy from the north was coming, this time not to bring disaster on Jerusalem but on Babylon.

A remarkable point of difference between the oracles against Jerusalem and Babylon is the *possibility of restoration*. Opposed to the power of Babylon in the past stands the total ruin of the present. After YHWH's visitation on Babylon, it had become an eternal ruin, in which no one could live any longer (51:26). Restoration was impossible for Babylon after all its misdeeds. The same lot was assigned to Edom (49:13) and Hazor (49:33). No reason was given for their permanent destruction, however. Neither was a reason for restoration given for the nations to whom it was promised: Egypt (46:26), Moab (48:47), Ammon (49:6), and Elam (49:39).

The oracle directed to Babylon announces the change of YHWH's plan for Jerusalem: *from judgment to deliverance*. Interspersed among YHWH's doom oracles against Babylon are *oracles of promise* to the Jerusalem exiles who live in Babylon:

> [Israel and Judah] shall come together, weeping.
> They shall seek YHWH their God. (50:4)

In the oracles against Jerusalem in which YHWH calls his people to return, the phrase "not yet" appears a number of times, suggesting that the judgment of the city and the land is temporary. The starting point of YHWH's words is the possible return of his people. As he once spoke to Abraham, so he now called on Jeremiah to look for a righteous man. Even after the execution of judgment, YHWH's faithfulness to his people remained, for an eternal covenant cannot be forgotten (50:5). In the oracle against Babylon, YHWH received a response to his commission. A return was taking place. After the fall of their enemy, the people of Israel and Judah together looked for righteousness: their God Yʜᴡʜ on Mount Zion.

At the Mercy of Babylon:
A Subversive Rereading of the Empire

WALTER BRUEGGEMANN
Columbia Theological Seminary

Biblical theology as a study of Israel's faithful speech may be said to revolve around two organizing questions. The first question of biblical theology is, "How does Israel speak about God?" Israel characteristically does not speak about God unless it speaks at the same time about the world in which God is present and over which God governs. For that reason, the second question of biblical theology is, "What else must Israel talk about when it talks about God?" It belongs decisively to the character of this God, as artistically rendered in Israel's text, always to be engaged in ways that impinge both upon God and upon God's "other." One aspect of that God-other engagement that is typical of Israel's theological speech is God in relation to the nations. The God of Israel is a God who deals with the nations, and the nations inescapably deal with the God of Israel. Together they form a common subject in Israel's theological speech.

Israel's Theological Imagination

The great powers, north and south, dominate Israel's public life and policy. In this chapter, I will pay attention to one of the great northern powers, Babylon, and the way in which Babylon enters into Israel's speech about God. While Babylon may be regarded as simply one among several great powers that concern Israel, it is also clear that Babylon peculiarly occupies the imagination of Israel.

Babylon goads and challenges Israel's theological imagination in remarkably varied ways. As a theological metaphor, Babylon is not readily dismissed or easily categorized. Indeed, in the postexilic period, it is Babylon and not Persia that continues to function as a powerful

---

Author's note: This essay was first published in *Journal of Biblical Literature* 110 (1991) 3–22, and is used by permission.

117

theological metaphor for Israel. Babylon operates in a supple way in Israel's theological speech because Babylon is a partner and antagonist in Israel's political life and is perceived as a partner and antagonist worthy of YHWH. As YHWH cannot be settled or reduced in Israel's discernment, so Babylon cannot be settled or reduced, but remains a tensive, energizing force in Israel's faith and imagination. Moreover, if the experience of exile was decisive for the canonizing process, as seems most probable, then it is equally probable that Babylon takes on imaginative power that is not simply historical and political but canonical in force, significance, and density.

By considering the theological function of Babylon, we are concerned with the question, What happens to *speech about Babylon* when it is drawn into the sphere of speech about God? In a lesser fashion, we will also ask, What happens to *speech about God* when God is drawn into the sphere of speech about the empire? In posing these questions, it is clear that we are taking up issues of artistic construal that are not fully contained in historical and political categories. As George Steiner has said of great art in general, we are dealing in the Bible not simply with a formulation but with a reformulation and a rethinking. We are concerned with a canonizing process whereby Israel voices its normative, paradigmatic construal of imperial power. Israel's rhetoric at the interface of God and empire is a concrete attempt to hold together the inscrutable reality of God (which is at the center of its rethought world) and the raw power of the empire (which is the daily reality of its life). Israel's self-identity, presence in the world, and chance for free action depend upon how these two are held together.

By joining speech about God to speech about Babylon, Israel's faith radically rereads the character of the empire, consistently subverting every conventional reading of the empire in which complacent Babylon and intimidated Israel must have colluded. That is, Babylon presented itself as autonomous, invincible, and permanent. When Israel entered fully into the ideology of Babylon (and abandoned its own covenantal definitions of reality), it accepted this characterization of Babylon and, derivatively, its own fate as completely defined by Babylonian reality. This is a classic example of the phenomenon, noted by Marx, of the victim willingly participating in the ideology of the perpetrator. This conventional collusion about power practiced by perpetrators and victims is controverted, however, in Israel's alternative reading, which is deeply and inherently subversive. When Israel, in a Yahwistic context, could discern that Babylon was not as it presented itself, then Israel did not need to define its own situation so hopelessly. Thus

Yahwistic faith makes an alternative to imperial ideology available to those who live from this counterrhetoric.

Select Rhetoric about Babylon

I have selected six texts concerning Babylon on which to focus. These texts are: Jer 42:9–17; 50:41–43; Isa 47:5–7; 1 Kgs 8:46–53; 2 Chr 36:15–21; and Dan 4:19–27. My thesis, which I will explicate in relation to these texts, is that when Israel's speech about Babylon is drawn into Israel's speech about God, the power of the empire is envisioned and reconstructed around the issue of mercy (*rḥm*). The intrusion of the rhetoric of mercy into the *Realpolitik* of Babylon derives from the uncompromising character of God. It also arises from the deepest yearning of the exilic community, which must have mercy to live, which expects mercy from God, and which by venturesome rhetoric dares to insist that the promised, yearned-for mercy cannot be ignored by the empire.

1. *Jeremiah 42:9–17*.   In its final form the book of Jeremiah has a decidedly pro-Babylonian slant, mediated through the Baruch document and perhaps powered by the authority and influence of the family of Shaphan. The sustained urging of the text is that the people of Jerusalem must stay in the jeopardized city and submit to the occupying presence of Babylon and not flee to Egypt. This announcement reflects a political judgment and a political interest that cooperation with Babylon is a safer way to survival. This voice of advocacy also concluded that cooperation with Egypt would only cause heavier, more destructive Babylonian pressure. That political judgment, however, is given as an oracle of God. The urging, therefore, is not simply political strategy but is offered as the intent of God for God's people. Thus the oracle is not simply speech concerning the empire but also speech about God.

The oracle of Jeremiah 42 is cast in two conditional clauses: one positive, "if" you remain in the city (vv. 10–12); the other negative, "if" you flee to Egypt (vv. 13–17). The positive conditional clause is cast as a promise that God will repent of evil and issues in a salvation oracle:

> Do not fear the king of Babylon
> of whom you are afraid.
> Do not fear him, says the Lord, for I am with you
> to deliver you from his hand. (v. 11)

The Jeremiah tradition takes a conventional speech form, the salvation oracle, and presses it into new use. The conventional form is "do not fear," followed by an assurance. Here, however, the form is daringly extended to identify the one not to be feared, the king of Babylon. Moreover, the speech form is utilized exactly to juxtapose the fearsome power of Nebuchadnezzar and the resolve of the Lord, "Do not fear him . . . I will deliver." The oracle counters the empire with God's good resolve. The assurance of God continues:

> I will grant you mercy [*raḥămîm*]
> that [*wĕ*] he will have mercy on you,
> and let you remain in the land. (v. 12)

The connection between "I" and "he" (the king of Babylon) is elusive, bridged only by a waw consecutive. The oracle does, however, insist upon this decisive, albeit elusive, link between Yhwh's resolve and anticipated imperial policy. The oracle asserts that Babylon can indeed be a source of mercy to Jerusalem when the empire subscribes to God's own intention. The negative counterpart of vv. 13–17 indicates that if there is flight to Egypt and away from Babylon, the same Babylonian king who is capable of mercy will indeed be "the sword which you fear" (v. 16).

Our historical-critical propensity is to say that the oracle of Jer 42:9–17 simply reflects a wise, pragmatic political decision. Such reading, however, ignores the casting of the speech in which the "I" of God's mercy directly shapes the "he" of Nebuchadnezzar's policy. That rhetorical linkage is crucial for the argument of the whole of the tradition. This rhetorical maneuver recasts the empire as an agent who is compelled, under the right circumstance, to show mercy. The speech practice of the Jeremiah-Baruch-Shaphan tradition includes Babylon in the sphere where mercy will be practiced as a public reality.

2. *Jeremiah 50:41–43.*   Scholars tend to read these "Oracles against the Nations" as a separate literary unit and in terms of historical, political developments. In distinction from the Greek, the Hebrew text places the Oracles against the Nations, and especially chaps. 50–51 against Babylon, at the end of the book; this arrangement invites us to pay attention to their canonical intention, that is, to move beyond historical, political concerns to notice the connection between these oracles and other parts of the Jeremiah tradition.

In this ordering of materials, the midterm verdict of the book of Jeremiah is that Nebuchadnezzar will triumph and rule, even in Jerusalem (25:8–11; 27:5–7b). That midterm verdict, however, is overcome by the final verdict of the Hebrew book of Jeremiah (see also 25:12–14; 27:7b). In the end, it will be God and not Nebuchadnezzar who prevails in the historical process. Again, we can read this assertion simply in relation to the politics of the nations, so that we anticipate (in retrospect) that the Persians will have defeated and succeeded the Babylonians.

Israel's way of speaking, however, is not rooted simply in historical analysis. The ominous verdict against Babylon in Jer 50:41–43 is rather an intentional rhetorical effort that intends to answer and resolve the so-called Scythian Song of 6:22–24. This is not simply a conventional recycling of poetic images, but this reuse of poetic material intends to counter and refute the first use. The purpose of the Scythian Song (6:22–24) is to invoke in the most threatening fashion the coming of the intruder from the north. The coming threat is portrayed in this way:

> They lay hold on bow and spear;
> they are cruel and have no mercy [*rḥm*]. (6:23)

In contrast to the anticipated Babylonian accommodation of chap. 42, the poetry of 6:23 knows there will be "no mercy" from the invading army. The coming of the invader with "no mercy" in chap. 6 is God's resolve to punish recalcitrant Jerusalem.

Chapter 50 uses the same rhetoric to reverse the earlier verdict of 6:23. Now the threatening intruder from the north is not Babylon, but one who comes against Babylon. This coming people, like Babylon, is savage in its invasion:

> They lay hold on bow and spear;
> they are cruel and have no mercy [*rḥm*]. (50:42)

The ones who come against Babylon have "no mercy." Thus the poem threatens and destabilizes Babylon with the same phrasing that authorized Babylon in 6:22–23.

The use of the same phrasing in 6:22–23 and 50:41–43 greatly illuminates the way in which Yhwh relates to the nations. On the one hand, Yhwh is in both situations the one who takes initiative, the one with authority. On the other hand, Yhwh's purpose is multidimensional, so that in different times and circumstances, the rule of God may be evidenced both for Babylon and against Babylon. In both postures, the way of Yhwh is the implementation of a policy of "no mercy."

The prose commentary that follows this oracle in 50:44–46 interprets the poetry. It makes a sweeping theological claim: God has a plan (*ʿṣh*) and a purpose (*mḥšb*) and can appoint and summon "whomever I choose" (v. 44). The retention and exercise of imperial power are tentative and provisional. Even the great Nebuchadnezzar, the rhetoric asserts, is subject to the rule of Yhwh, which concerns the practice of "mercy" and "no mercy." Thus the oracle of Jeremiah 50–51 at the end of the canonical book asserts the rule of God over international affairs. The reuse of 6:22–23 is, for our purposes, particularly important. The double use connects the dispatch of Babylon by God with "no mercy," and then the destruction of Babylon with "no mercy."

Two things strike us in this construal of Babylon's destiny. First, God deals directly with Babylon and Persia, without any reference to Judah or Jerusalem. God is indeed the God of the nations. Second, the exercise of God's sovereignty concerns matters of mercy and no mercy. The destiny of Babylon turns on YHWH's various initiatives with mercy. Thus the rhetoric of Israel reconstitutes the geopolitics of the Fertile Crescent with reference to mercy.

The sequence of 6:22–24 (which anticipates Babylon) and 50:41–43 (which dismisses Babylon) stands in an odd relation to the salvation oracle of chap. 42. The editing of the book of Jeremiah is complex, so that we may indeed have different editorial hands. In the text as we have it, the Baruch document promises mercy from Babylon, though that mercy is conditional (42:9–17). The poetic units, both the "early" poem (6:22–23) and the oracle against the Babylonians (50:41–43), refute the option of mercy. Yet in all of the texts, whatever their origin, the rise and fall of empires has been drawn into the language of mercy. The tradition insists—as regards Babylon, Persia, Jerusalem, and God's assurance—that the play of power around the city of Jerusalem raises the question and the possibility of mercy.

3. *Isaiah 47:5–7.* Because we do not know when to date the Jeremiah materials, we do not know about the relative dating of Jeremiah 50 and Isaiah 47. I take up Isaiah 47 after the Jeremiah text because conventionally, Second Isaiah is placed after Jeremiah, though Jeremiah 50 may indeed be later. In any case, Isaiah 47 permits a more comprehensive and reflective commentary on the mercy questions posed in the Jeremiah tradition. In brief form, Isaiah 47 permits a more comprehensive and reflective commentary on the mercy questions posed in the Jeremiah tradition. In brief form, Isaiah 47 offers one of the most comprehensive statements of Israel's theology of the nations. God's dealing with the empire is elaborated in four stages:

a. The first element is:

> I was angry with my people. (v. 6a)

The tradition insists that the destruction of Jerusalem was not an accomplishment of Babylonian policy but happened at the behest of God (cf. Jer 25:8–11; 27:5–6; Isa 40:1–2). The destruction is a sovereign act of God, only implemented by Nebuchadnezzar.

b. The second element is:

> I profaned my heritage;
> I gave them into your hand. (v. 6b, c)

It is God who submits Jerusalem to the invasion of Babylon. These first two elements of the speech of God constitute a conventional prophetic lawsuit. Israel is indicted for its failure to obey God. Israel is placed under the judgment of foreign invasion. The coming of the invader is God's stance of "no mercy" toward Jerusalem.

c. The third element of this oracle is unexpected and moves well beyond the conventional lawsuit speech:

> You [Babylon] showed no mercy [*rḥm*]. (v. 6d)

The text offers no grammatical connection between this statement and what has just preceded. We expect "but" or "nevertheless," but we get nothing.

d. This parataxis then leads to a rebuke of the empire:

> You said, "I will be mistress forever,"
> so that you did not lay these things to heart
> or remember their end. (v. 7)

The first two elements in Isa 47:5–7, then, are conventional: God is angry with Israel. God punishes Israel by summoning a punishing nations, in this case Babylon. We are not prepared fror the third and fourth elements, however. The speech is constructed as though Nebuchadnezzar (and Babylonian policy) was all along supposed to have known that mercy toward Jerusalem was in order and expected, appropriate even in light of God's anger. I imagine that inside the drama of the text, Nebuchadnezzar could react to these third and fourth elements in God's speech in indignation, "Mercy? You never mentioned mercy!" Of course, Nebuchadnezzar is not permitted to speak at all, except in the poetic self-indictment of v. 7a.

The turn in the third element of Isa 47:5–7 is precisely pertinent to our thesis. "Mercy" readily intrudes into political talk where it is not expected. Mercy impinges upon the policies and destiny even of the empire. In conversation about God and empire, mercy operates as a nonnegotiable factor. Nebuchadnezzar should have known that YHWH is that kind of God. From the beginning, YHWH has been a God of mercy, and mercy is characteristically present where YHWH is present. In the end, even the empire stands or fails in terms of God's resilient commitment to mercy. Ruthless power cannot circumvent that resolve of God.

It is clear that rhetorically, something decisive has happened between the second and third elements of this oracle. The first two phrases look back to 587 and echo the predictable claims of lawsuit, long anticipated by the prophets. In the third and fourth phrases, however, the poet has turned away from conventional lawsuit claims, away from 587, away from destruction and judgment. Now the poet looks forward, out beyond the exile. Now God's very tool of exile has become the object of God's indignation. In this moment, God's old, old agenda of mercy reemerges (cf. Exod 34:6–7). The practice of this rhetoric, on the horizon of the poet, destabilizes the empire. Israel's speech knows that empires, in their imagined autonomy, will always have to come to terms with God's alternative governance. The empire is never even close to being ultimate but always lives under the threat of this rhetoric that rejects every imperial complacency, every act of autonomy, every gesture of self-sufficiency. The poem of Isaiah 47 ends with an awesome verdict emerging from this exchange about arrogant autonomy and mercy: "There is no one to save you!" (v. 15).

4. *1 Kings 8:46–53.* This text is commonly taken to belong to the latest layer of Deuteronomistic interpretation. It is cast as part of the prayer of Solomon. It is structured as an "if-then" formulation, echoed in 2 Chr 30:9. The petition anticipates a conditional exile. It contains an "if" of repentance in exile (v. 48) and a "then" followed by four imperatives addressed to God on the basis of repentance:

> [H]ear thou in heaven . . . ,
> maintain their cause,
> and forgive thy people; . . .
> grant them mercy [*rḥm*]. (vv. 49–50)

A motivation is offered to God in v. 51; an additional petition is voiced in v. 52; and a final motivational clause is given in v. 53. What interests us is the fourth imperative of the petition in vv. 49–50:

> grant them compassion [*rḥm*] in the sight of those who carried them away captive, that they may have compassion [*rḥm*] on them.

It is clear in the prayer that it is God and only God who gives mercy. God is the only subject of the verb, *ntn*. God must grant [*ntn*] mercy if any is to be given. The last word of the petition adds, however, "that they [the captors] may have compassion [or mercy]." Again the inclination of God and the disposition of Babylon are intimately related to each other. It is not doubted that the Babylonian Empire could be a place of mercy. The exile can be a place of compassion, but that can only be because God hears prayers and attends to the needs of the exiles. The empire is a place where God's inclination for mercy can indeed be effected in a concrete, public way. Babylon can enact what God grants. The claim of this text is close to the affirmation of Jer 42:12.

5. *2 Chronicles 36:15–21.* This text is the penultimate paragraph of 2 Chronicles. In these verses, the Chronicler gives closure to the narrative and engages in a sweeping retrospective. The term "mercy" [*ḥml*] occurs twice in this concluding and ominous statement. First, the God of Israel is a God of mercy who has practiced long-term, persistent mercy toward Israel:

> The Lord, the God of their fathers, sent persistently to them by his messengers, because he had mercy [*ḥml*] on his people and on his dwelling place. (v. 15)

The whole history of prophecy is an act of mercy. In this usage, however, mercy is not rescue but warning, to deter Jerusalem from its self-destructive action. Israel, however, refused and resisted, until God's wrath arose and there was "no remedy" [*ʾên marpēʾ*], v. 16.

This passage is constructed so that Babylon does not appear in the text until God's mercy is spent. Only then does the empire enter the scene:

> Therefore, he [God] brought up against them the king of the Chaldeans, who slew their young men with the sword in the house of their sanctuary, and had no mercy [*ḥml*] on young man or virgin, old man or aged; he gave them all into his hand. (v. 17)

It was the designated work of Babylon to destroy, reflective of God's exhausted mercy. The statement is framed so that the active subject at the beginning and end is God; only in between these statements is the king of Babylon permitted as an active agent. Thus far the argument with the double use of "mercy" closely parallels the first two elements of the argument in Isaiah 47.

It is to be recognized that the key term in this text is *ḥml* and not *rḥm*, as elsewhere in our analysis. However, the explicit reference to Jeremiah in 36:21 suggests that this text in the Chronicler is an intentional development of the Jeremiah tradition. The Chronicler reiterates the assertions of the Jeremiah tradition that justify the catastrophe of 587. Yet the Chronicler also moves beyond the reflections of the Jeremiah tradition. Thus, the text of Jeremiah is cited as an anticipation that now comes to fresh fulfillment. This penultimate paragraph with the double, albeit negative, reference to "mercy" prepares the way for the final paragraph of vv. 22–23, which moves dramatically beyond judgment to God's new act of mercy among the nations:

> Now in the first year of Cyrus, king of Persia, that the word of the Lord
> in the mouth of Jeremiah might be accomplished, the Lord stirred up the
> spirit of Cyrus the Persian so that he made a proclamation throughout all
> his kingdom and also put it in writing. (v. 22)

Even this new world power is to fulfill the word of Jeremiah. Now begins the new phase of Jewish history with Cyrus. It is a new beginning
to which Jeremiah 50 has made negative reference and to which Isaiah
44–47 makes positive reference. Our pivotal point of interpretation
juxtaposes *the exhaustive mercy of YHWH* and *the lacking mercy of Babylon*.

These texts from Jeremiah, Isaiah, 1 Kings, and the Chronicler seem
to be intimately connected to one another in a sustained reflection on
the destiny of Israel vis-à-vis Babylon and the working of God. The sa-
lient point is that mercy from God and mercy from Babylon live in an
odd and tense relation; neither will work effectively without the other.
That is, when Babylon has mercy, it is derivative from the mercy of
God. Conversely, when God has no mercy left, there will be none from
Babylon. This straightforward connection, however, is disrupted by the
discernment of Isa 47:6. It is this text that creates tension between the
mercy of heaven and the mercy of earth. The tension occurs because
the empire can indeed exercise autonomy. That autonomy characteristically is self-serving, against mercy, and sure to bring self-destruction,
even upon the empire.

In all these texts, Israel is now prepared to move toward the newness
embodied in Cyrus the Persian. Thanks to Second Isaiah, the Persian period, contrasted to that of the Babylonians, is perceived as a new saving
action of God that permits the survival and modest prosperity of Jerusalem. Yet Persia never takes on the imaginative power or metaphorical
force of Babylon. In the Old Testament, the theological struggle concerning public power and divine purpose remains focused on the reality, memory, experience, and symbolization of Babylon.

6. *Daniel 4:19–27.*   When we come to the book of Daniel, we see
that Israel's theological reflection cannot finally finish with Babylon. It
is clear that by the time of the Daniel texts, we have broken free of historical reference; Nebuchadnezzar now looms on the horizon of Israel
as a cipher for a power counter to the Lord. It is evident, moreover, that
Babylon is not a reduced or flattened metaphor, for then Nebuchadnezzar could be defeated and dismissed in the literature. Nebuchadnezzar,
however, is kept very much alive and present by the rhetoric of Israel.

The narrative of Daniel 4 concerns the dream of Nebuchadnezzar
that the "great tree" will be cut down. As Daniel interprets this dream,
it anticipates Nebuchadnezzar's loss of power. Two assumptions oper-

ate for the narrator that make the story possible. First, it is proper, legitimate, and acceptable for Jewish lore to entertain a story about
Nebuchadnezzar. As we might expect, such a story is told in order to
mock and deride the great king. As we shall see, the narrative is not finally a mocking or dismissal of Nebuchadnezzar but in fact portrays his
remarkable rehabilitation. Thus, the horizon of the Bible does not
flatly dismiss the empire but entertains its possible transformation to
agent of obedience.

Second, the narrative assumes that the great king and his govern-
mental apparatus are dysfunctional. In the end, the great king must
step outside his own official circles of power and influence for the guidance he needs. On one level the narrative is a rather conventional contrast between the stupid wielder of power and the shrewd outsider who
is able to turn the tables. As we shall see, however, the narrator moves
in a different, somewhat unexpected, direction. This story is not primarily about how a Jew prevails over Babylon. It is a story, in the end,
about the well-being of Babylon and its power.

Daniel's interpretation of the dream of the king turns on three crucial affirmations. First, "It is you, O king" (v. 22). The interpretation by
Daniel brings the dream into immediate political risk, with rhetoric
that recalls Nathan's indictment of David (2 Sam 12:7). Second, the
purpose of the dream is that the king will "know that the Most High has
sovereignty over the kingdom of mortals, and gives it to whom he will"
(v. 25). This formula dominates the narrative occurring in vv. 14, 22, 29,
and, with greater variation, 34. Moreover, the formulation contains an
echo of Jer 50:44, to which we have already made reference (cf. 49:19):

> I will appoint over him whomever I choose. For who is like me? Who will
> summon me? What shepherd can stand before me? Therefore, hear the
> plan which the Lord has made against Babylon.

In the Jeremiah usage, the transfer of power away from Babylon to "a
people from the north" is sure and settled. In the Daniel narrative,
however, there is a third point that leads the narrative in a surprising
direction. At the end of this interpretative account, Daniel says:

> Therefore, O king, let my counsel be acceptable to you; break off your
> sins by practicing righteousness and your iniquities by showing mercy
> [*hn*] to the oppressed. (v. 24)

Daniel's counsel to the king is unexpected in this context. We have been
given no reason to anticipate this narrative development. Daniel ceases

here to be an interpreter and becomes a moral instructor of and witness to the great king. For our purposes, it is important to recognize that the empire is understood by the narrative as a potential place of mercy; Nebuchadnezzar is presented as a ruler who is capable of mercy to the oppressed and would be wise to practice such mercy and righteousness.

In the unfolding of the narrative, we are never told that Nebuchadnezzar heeded Daniel and practiced righteousness and mercy. We are told, however, that his "reason" [*mandĕʿî*] returned" (v. 34). He submitted in praise to the Most High (vv. 34–35). Thus, it is legitimate to imagine that the narrative understands the "return of reason," the capacity to praise, and the restoration of majesty and splendor to Nebuchadnezzar (v. 36) as evidence of the practice of mercy as urged by Daniel.

We may now consider the sequence of texts we have discussed concerning the recurring interplay of God, mercy, and the destiny of the empire:

a. In Jer 6:23 and 2 Chr 36:15, there is no mercy because God intended that there should be no mercy.
b. In Isa 47:6, there is no mercy, and Nebuchadnezzar is sharply admonished for this lack that violates God's intention.
c. In Jer 42:12 and 1 Kgs 8:50, Babylon is judged to be capable of mercy, and Jews legitimately expect mercy.
d. In Dan 4:27, which is a late, perhaps climactic word on Babylon in the Old Testament, the hope of Daniel again counts on the mercy of the empire, as that mercy is anticipated in Jer 42:12 and 1 Kgs 8:50.

To be sure, this good word about Nebuchadnezzar and Babylon may be simply part of a Jewish strategy of political quietism and cooperation. We should not, however, neglect the theological force of Dan 4:22 and its fruition in vv. 34–37. The theological claim of the narrative, regardless of what it may mean for Jewish conduct and hope, is that the empire is transformable and can become a place of mercy and righteousness. This transformation happens when the God of Israel is accepted as the Most High, that is, when the empire is brought under the rule of the Lord. Thus, the nations, given this example of Babylon, are redeemable, transformable, and capable of salvage for the human purposes of God. Moreover, the narrative of Daniel 4 is a warning to all would-be Nebuchadnezzars that the exercise of power uninformed by righteousness and mercy will lead to insanity and loss of authority. The empire is a place that may host mercy. It is a place that, in its self-interest, must host mercy. There is no alternative strategy for royal power that can possibly succeed.

Babylon's Role in Israel's Theological Rhetoric

At the outset, I offered two questions that may focus the task of theological interpretation: (1) How does Israel speak about God? and (2) What else must Israel talk about when it talks about God? The answer to the first question, given our topic, is that Israel talks about God in terms of the reality of mercy. The answer to the second question, I have suggested, is that when Israel speaks of the mercy of God, it first speaks of the nations, specifically *Babylon*, more specifically, *the mercy of Babylon*. To say that Israel's speech about God entails speech about the mercy of the Babylonian Empire evidences the delicate, daring enterprise that Israel's theological speech inescapably is. In its theological speech, Israel recharacterizes God. At the same time, it recharacterizes the empire and the meaning of worldly power.

Israel's speech about God requires and permits Israel to say that the empire is not what it is usually thought to be. It is not what it is thought to be by Israelites who fear and are intimidated by the empire. Conversely, it is not what it is thought to be by the wielders of power themselves, in their presumed self-sufficiency. Negatively, this claim of mercy asserts that imperial rule is not rooted simply in raw power. Israel, when it is theologically intentional, will not entertain the notion that "might makes right." Positively, this claim asserts that political power inherently and intrinsically has in its very fabric the reality of mercy, the practice of humanness, or as Daniel dares to say to Nebuchadnezzar, the care of the oppressed (Dan 4:27). This daring rhetoric, which follows from Israel's speech about God, does not mean that the holder of power will always accept this characterization of power. Israel, nonetheless, refuses to allow any enterprise of power to exist and function outside the zone of its theological rhetoric.

This claim about imperial power is even more stunning when the subject of such speech is characteristically Babylon. The same playful, ambiguous, venturesome rhetoric of Israel is also employed concerning Egypt and Assyria, but perhaps not as extensively. While Babylon functions in this regards as a metaphor for all such power, no doubt Babylon, in and of itself, occupies a peculiar and distinctive role in Israel's theological horizon. In the Bible, Israel would never finish with Babylon, and therefore its speech about Babylon is of peculiar importance.

We may suggest two reasons for this odd focus. First, there is good historical reason for such an insistence concerning Babylon. The deportation of the Jerusalem elite required honest and alarming theological reflection by the makers of Judaism. It was Babylon that had the capacity to create a situation in which God's mercy was experienced as null and void; Israel was left to wonder what that nullification signified (cf. Lam 5:20–22). Second, there is surely canonical reason for such a focus on Babylon. It is most plausible that the process of displacement in the sixth century not only was decisive for the community that experienced it but also became, through the process of canonization, a decisive and paradigmatic reality for continuing regeneration of Jews.

Thus the exile became paradigmatic for all Jews, including the God of the Jews. Jews and the God of the Jews must come to terms with the definitional role of Babylon. It was exactly the experience and metaphor of *Babylonian exile* that made the question of *mercy* so acute. It was exactly the mercy of God, remembered, experienced, and anticipated, that made a redefinition of Babylon so urgent and so problematic.

Israel's rhetoric accomplished a stunning claim. It asserted that no savage power in the world could separate Israel from God's mercy. It did more than that, however; it also asserted that no savage power, no matter its own self-discernment, can ever be cut off from the reality of God's mercy. It is for that reason that the burden of mercy is repeatedly thrust upon Nebuchadnezzar; and for that reason, Daniel finally, at the end of this literature, has Nebuchadnezzar's "reason return" (Dan 4:31). Now Nebuchadnezzar "knows." What he knows is that power is held by the God who gives it as God wills. Moreover, "God wills" always toward mercy. No amount of cunning or force can escape this intentionality of God. The rhetoric of Israel about the nations is rooted in the very character of Israel's God. The very character of God, however, lives in this rhetoric that is not negotiable. The rhetoric assures that God is bound to Babylon even in the work of mercy. The rhetoric assures as well that Babylon is bound to mercy because it is the purpose of this God who gives power to whom God wills. Nebuchadnezzar persistently has refused this reality of Gods powerful resolve for mercy. His rule culminates in sanity, praise, majesty, splendor, and more greatness, however, only when he accepts God's rule of justice and abandons the option of autonomous pride. Nebuchadnezzar's reason is his "knowing," knowing the truth of Israel's rhetoric and knowing the one who is the primal subject of that rhetoric.

The Politics of Theological Rhetoric

I want now to situate my comments in relation to two addresses given by past presidents of the Society of Biblical Literature. I suggest that a contrast between the presidential addresses of James Muilenburg and Elisabeth Schüssler Fiorenza will illuminate the claim I am making for the theological intentionality of Israel's rhetoric.

On the one hand, James Muilenburg delivered his remarkable and extremely influential address on rhetorical criticism in 1968. It was Muilenburg who both noted and, in my view, enacted the decisive methodological turn in the guild toward literary analysis. One can hardly overstate the cruciality of what Muilenburg accomplished in his address and more generally in his work.

Nonetheless, it is fair to say that Muilenburg's presentation of the importance of speech and of rhetoric was quite restricted. There is no hint in his presidential address of an awareness that speech is characteristically and inevitably a political act, an assertion of power that seeks to override some other rhetorical proposal of reality. One can rightly say of Muilenburg's horizon either that he was not interested in such issues or that the whole critical awareness of the political dimension of speech came much later to the discipline of biblical interpretation. In any case, it is time to move beyond such innocence in rhetorical criticism, as many in the field have done, to an awareness that the text entrusted to us is a major act of power. Our own interpretation is derivatively an act of power even as we pose, or perhaps especially as we pose, as objective in our interpretation. One can detect Muilenburg's lack of interest or attention to this issue at the end of his address, when, in juxtaposition to T. S. Eliot's phrase "raid on the inarticulate," he speaks of a "raid on the ultimate." I suggest that such a formulation bespeaks a kind of untroubled transcendentalism. Of course, Muilenburg was not untroubled, and he knew the text was not untroubled. Nonetheless, he moves directly from the text to "the ultimate." Given what we know of the political power of rhetoric, we dare not speak of a "raid on the ultimate" unless we first speak of a "raid on the proximate."

There is available to us a variety of theories of speech and rhetoric. The move beyond Muilenburg's innocent analysis of rhetoric can benefit from Jean-François Lyotard's presence in the conversation. Lyotard suggests that speech is fundamentally agonistic, that it intends to enter into conflict with other speech-claims. One figure he uses for this agonistic understanding is that speech is like the taking of tricks,

the trumping of a communicational adversary, an assertively conflict-
ual relation between tricksters.

Without following Lyotard's complete postmodern program, I suggest that in the guild of scholars, we shall more fully face the danger
and significance of the texts entrusted to us if we notice how these texts
enter into conflict with other rhetorical options. Concerning my theme
of *mercy and empire*, the several texts I have cited and their shared rhetorical claim do not constitute an innocent, neutral, or casual act. In
each case the text is a deliberate act of combat against other views of
public reality that live through other forms of rhetoric. Thus, the
"trump" of this rhetoric seeks to override the assured autonomy of
Babylon that dares to say, "I am and there is no other" (Isa 47:10). Conversely, this rhetoric enters into combat with Israel's rhetoric of complaint, which asserts that "there is none to comfort" (Lam 1:2, 17, 21),
that "the hand of the Lord is shortened" (Isa 50:2; 59:1), and that "my
way is hid from the Lord, and my right is disregarded by my God" (Isa
40:27). Both the arrogance of autonomous Babylon and the despair of
doubting Israel generate, authorize, and commend a politics of brutal-
ity and intimidation.

The rhetorical trajectory I have traced refuses to leave either Israel
or the empire at peace in its mistaken rhetoric. This counter-rhetoric,
this "strong poetry," that seeks to reread the empire and the faith community is a radically subversive urging. Aside from the specific argument I have made about empire and mercy, I suggest that our scholarly
work requires a theory of rhetoric that is more in keeping with the re-
lentlessly critical, subversive, and ironic voice of the text, which sets itself endlessly against more conventional and consensual speech. Thus,
we are at a moment not only "beyond form criticism," which Muilenburg had judged to be flat and mostly sterile, but also beyond rhetorical analysts that are too enamored of style to notice speech as a means
and source of power.

On the other hand, in 1987, nineteen years after Muilenburg, Elisabeth Schüssler Fiorenza delivered a major challenge to the Society of
Biblical Literature. Alluding to the presidential addresses of James
Montgomery in 1919, Henry Cadbury in 1937, and Leroy Waterman
in 1947 as the only exceptions in presidential addresses, Schüssler
Fiorenza protested against scholarly detachment and urged that members of the society have public responsibility in the midst of their scholarship. She proposed that attention to rhetorical rather than scientific
categories of scholarship would raise ethical-political issues as constitu-
tive of the interpretative process. Moreover, she observed that no pres-

idential address since 1947 had made any gesture in the direction of public responsibility.

It is not my purpose to enter directly into an assessment of previous presidential addresses. It is, however, my purpose to reflect on the task and possibility of biblical theology. The dominant line of scholarly argument has insisted that biblical theology must be a descriptive and not normative enterprise. Or to put it with Krister Stendahl, it must be concerned with what the text "meant" and not what the text "means." In my judgment, that urging contains within it not only a considerable fear of authoritarianism but also a decision about "strict constructionism" concerning the text, a preoccupation with "authorial intent," and a positive notion of rhetoric, of image, of metaphor, and, finally, of text.

If we move in Muilenburg's direction of rhetoric and in Schüssler Fiorenza's direction of public rhetoric, and if we understand that the rhetoric of a classic text is always and again a political act, then it is, in my judgment, impossible to confine interpretation to a descriptive activity. The text, when we attend to it as a serious act of rhetoric, is inherently agonistic and makes its advocacy in the face of other advocacies.

The trajectory of texts I have cited may be taken as a case in point. There is no doubt that the primary references in these texts are the God of Israel and the Babylonian Empire, a datable, locatable, identifiable historical entity. There is also no doubt, however, that the term "Babylon" has become a metaphor for great public power and that the term spills over endlessly into new contexts. A primary example of such spilling over is the power of the metaphor "Babylon" in the book of Revelation. The Babylon metaphor has exercised enormous influence in the church's thinking about "church and state." There is no doubt that that spilling over happens in the text itself and, as W. Sibley Towner has shown, that spillover has continued in any but the most flattened historical interpretation. Thus we never have in the text the concrete historical reference to Babylon without at the same time the potential for spillover into other contexts. That spillover, I suggest, is not evoked simply by willful, imaginative interpreters but is also rooted in the metaphors and images themselves, which reach out in relentless sense making.

Thus, we have before us in these six texts concern for the God of Israel, who is the God of mercy, and the empire, which must be endlessly concerned with mercy. In attending to these texts, we seek to enter Israel's rhetoric and to notice Israel's agonistic intent in this set of metaphors. We read the text where we are. We read the text, as we are bound to read it, on the horizon of China's Tienamen Square and Berlin's wall, of Panama's canal and South Africa's changing situation, of Kuwait's lure of oil. Or among us, when we are daring, we may read the text in relation to the politics of publication, the play of power in promotion and tenure, the ambiguities of acquiring grants, and the seductions of institutional funding. We inevitably read the text where we sit. What happens in the act of theological interpretation is not an "application" of the text, nor an argument about contemporary policy, but an opening of a rhetorical field in which an urgent voice other than our own is set in the midst of imperial self-sufficiency and "colonial" despair. We continue to listen while the voice of this text has its say against other voices that claim counterauthority.

Thus, the agenda that Schüssler Fiorenza proposes is not extrinsic to the work of the Society of Biblical Literature. The spillover of the text into present social reality is not an "add-on" for relevance; rather, it is a scholarly responsibility that the text should have a hearing as a serious voice on its own terms. One need subscribe to no particular ideology to conclude that our public condition is one of deep crisis. And since we as biblical scholars have invested our lives in these texts, one may ask directly how or in what way this text is an important voice in the contemporary array of competing rhetorics. Or less directly, one may ask if we want to be the generation that withholds the text from its contemporary context, the generation that blocks the spillover that belongs intrinsically and inherently to the text. It is possible that we would be the generation that withholds the text from our contemporary world in the interest of objectivity and in the name of our privileged neutrality. Such an act, I should imagine, is a disservice not only to our time and place but also to our text. Such "objective" and "neutral" readings are themselves political acts in the service of entrenched and "safe" interpretation.

It can, however, be otherwise. Without diminishing the importance of our critical work, it is possible that the text will be permitted freedom for its own fresh say. That, it seems to me, is a major interpretative issue among biblical scholars. The possibility of a fresh reading requires attentiveness to the politics of rhetoric, to the strange, relentless power of these words to subvert and astonish. When our criticism allows the rhetoric of the text to be voiced, the way mercy crowds Babylon continues to be a crucial oddity, even in our own reading. Those of us who care most about criticism may attend with greater grace to readings of the text that move even beyond our criticism.

Jeremiah's Message of Hope:
Public Faith and Private Anguish

RONALD CLEMENTS

Emeritus Professor of Old Testament, King's College, University of London

From the point of view of a modern reader of the book of Jeremiah, its preserved structure and arrangement poses some alluring possibilities as well as some significant problems. Chapters 1–25 form a quite plausible book all by themselves, in which Jeremiah presents a series of severe warnings and threats against religious complacency, especially idolatry. Even the great temple of Jerusalem may be destroyed if those who worship there put their trust in it in the manner of a superstitious fetish (Jer 7:1–15)! Interspersed with these warnings, we encounter a series of complaints and inner reflections that end in chap. 20, when the prophet utters an almost suicidal curse upon himself and his very existence. Denouncing the folly of others was clearly no easy path to high self-esteem! There was a price that had to be paid.

Following these chapters, which really come to an end in chap. 24, where Jeremiah looks away from his fellow-citizens in Judah to contemplate the future role of those who had been deported to Babylon (chap. 25 is an important transition piece), are a series of narratives in chaps. 26–45. These at first glance appear readily accessible to a preacher's interpretation because they report a series of events in which Jeremiah was deeply involved as a courageous and even heroic figure who spoke out against a group of complacent and faint-hearted political leaders. They openly opposed him by confining him to cruel imprisonment but secretly appear to have believed that he was probably right in his diagnoses of Judah's problems. Even more useful for the preacher is the fact that Jeremiah is soon proved to have been wholly correct in his fearful forebodings concerning Judah's fate. At the vital moment when everybody else was about to abandon all hope for Judah's future after the cataclysm, this lonely prophet made a significant gesture by purchasing a plot of land in his hometown of Anathoth, at a time when its value appears to have fallen to near worthlessness. So there is hope

135

after all, but it is not a traditional, this-wordly, kind of hope—it is hope that rests wholly on God and on a deep and far-seeing faith in the divine purpose for the people of God.

The Prophet behind the Book

Putting the two presentations of Jeremiah's inner self side by side—the private feelings of torment and despair and the public message of hope—gives us a powerful paradox, but not one that is unresolvable. Quite the contrary! It is the kind of paradox with which we are all too familiar and which drives home some vital truths. On one side we learn of the prophet's deep inner turmoil and anguish, plunging him into a maelstrom of confusion and self-doubt; on the other side we discover that there came a moment of breakthrough when the very pain of a prolonged period of uncertainty and questioning was set at rest. This occurred through an event that conveyed meaning far beyond its own domestic simplicity—it was a revelation from God, arriving in almost unexpected fashion. It is not surprising therefore that the primary goal of the earliest period of critical interpretation of the book of Jeremiah should have strived to present this in the form of a biography. Moreover, such a biography was not simply a chronicle of outward events but the kind of inward-looking, soul-searching biography of a personal spiritual pilgrimage that retains contemporary appeal. It bears all the hallmarks of the kind of story that still makes for some of the very best nonfiction reading. The passage from a faith shaped by received conventional dogmas, stripped bare by the experience of pain and disillusionment, and then ultimately refashioned to recover hope at a much deeper level appears as a private pilgrimage that gives to religion realism and integrity. Without these it cannot survive and we feel that, even in a very minor fashion, we have had similar experiences.

Not surprisingly we can trace a long period (almost a century in fact) during which this biographical approach to the book of Jeremiah held sway and which enabled serious biblical scholarship to fulfill a useful servant-role in sorting and reassembling the various materials in the book to create a credible and attractive biographical portrait of a courageous man of God. Yet all has never been well with such a criticial reconstruction, and the questions and uncertainties that really began in earnest with B. Duhm's commentary of 1902 have become louder and more insistent in their challenge. Certainly the initial assumption that all that was needed was for scholars to identify and match up the prophecies of chaps. 1–24 with the narratives of 26–45 has proved to be mistaken and oversimplistic. Similarly the assumption that a prophetic "biography" could be written, illustrating the struggles of the prophet's life against the background of the tragedies of his times, has proved to be a dangerous model for the interpreter to adopt. The contents of the literature have almost invariably been squeezed into a most unsuitable container.

Yet the model of a biography is not a wholly mistaken or unsuitable genre of writing to pursue in an effort to understand the nature of prophecy. In some measure an individual "life," with all its attendant experiences, must underlie so influential a book as that of Jeremiah. Committees do not write this kind of work, nor even assemble such from snippets and cuttings! Nor is the tension between the public face of a messenger of hope and the private anguish of a tormented soul, striving to keep his head above the waters of chaos, an implausible reality to examine. The human condition is repeatedly a condition of pain and renewing of hope so that the expectation that the pursuit of virtue and truth will necessarily be rewarded with applause and happiness appears largely to be vain. In no small measure it has been the broad universal appeal of the assumed Jeremiah-like experience that has made this book such an attractive one within the biblical literature. So the effort to reconstruct the events that shaped the course of Jeremiah's life and that brought together the somber and disturbing sounds of his cries of lamentation with the trumpet chords of hope and assurance about the future is a worthwhile undertaking.

In no small degree the idea of a prophetic biography is too grand an illusion to pursue for it to be readily accessible to us. The wealth of material that would be necessary for such an undertaking is simply no longer there. There is no preserved diary, and even letters are recalled only in brief extracts. What is preserved for the modern reader has been carefully edited and selected to focus the issues that appeared to matter most. In part the reader is easily misled by the wealth of detail and background color that is woven into several of the scenes of Jeremiah's experience to suppose that a similar fullness of information must be applicable to all. That these revealing scenes were culled from reminiscences of a confidant or close observer (usually identified with the figure of the scribe Baruch) is wholly plausible. Unfortunately such reminiscenses cover only a very short period of the prophet's career. The very span of years that the biblical text ascribes to the period of Jeremiah's prophesying—approximately forty years beginning in the thirteenth year of King Josiah (639–609 B.C.E.) and extending to sometime after the disaster of 587 B.C.E.—has led a surprisingly large number of scholars to believe that a mistake exists about the date of the prophet's sense of call. The fact that nothing very much at all can be gleaned about what he was saying and doing in the first twenty years has created the belief that the date must have been mis-recorded. Yet there is no firm reason for supposing this to have happened. It is simply that we have no record from that early period of Jeremiah's work.

Clearly the notion of a biography in the modern sense is impossible. Yet the material that has been preserved reveals outlines of a shape and structure that make it more than a jumbled anthology. There appears to be good reason why the brief records of what Jeremiah said and reflected upon, couched in the first-person "I" form, have been combined with reports recorded in the third person. The terrible onrush of only dimly premeditated events brought new trials and difficulties. Even when they brought some sort of vindication for the ignominy and hostility that had been heaped upon the prophet, they led to no ultimate popular accolades. His only memorial is his book, though it can never have been designed by the prophet himself for that purpose. It is rather a memorial that devoted admirers pieced together concerning his work from whatever materials had been preserved about him after he had departed this life.

If then we have to bid farewell to the hope of constructing a biography of this great prophet, we should not let go of the expectation of recovering a knowledge of the prophetic bios, the life behind the images and feeling that the book discloses. Clearly in prime place in this, as in all the prophetic literature, the major concern has been to indicate and preserve the word that God had given regarding Israel and its future. The message was paramount, and the messenger was only incidental to this. Yet this is not an absolute categorization, and with Jeremiah in particular it clearly became evident that the trials and sufferings of the messenger were intimately bound up with the nature and truth of the message. Fresh impulses that have made biography such an important genre of historical literature were being powerfully felt. No other explanation is convincing for preservation of the wealth of circumstantial details uncovering the strange and often unexpected scenes of Jeremiah's words and actions during Jerusalem's twilight days. The prophet's misfortunes mirror those of the general populace when starvation, hopelessness, and fear racked the city.

Similarly no better explanation has been put forward to explain the retention of the reports of the private struggles and inner conflicts that Jeremiah experienced before the final catastrophe overtook his people with a growing inevitability. It is true that these reports represent cries of angry resistance and anguish with which the reader can sympathize, but they are not simply part of a dramatic dialogue that enables the reader to give vent to pent up anger. They indicate far more than this since they make explicit the inner tension of faith that belongs to the painful realism of spiritual commitment. They represent a genuine foreshadowing of the cross of Jesus Christ because they reflect the pain at the heart of the complex reality of sin in human decision-making and its consequences.

If we are, in deference to the sheer lack of suitable resources, compelled to abandon the idea of any biography of Jeremiah, save an imaginative reconstruction, then we should nonetheless refuse to abandon with it the hope of understanding the real life experiences that have led to the extant shaping of this remarkable book. Perhaps the most suitable classification is the one suggested by P. R. Ackroyd in relationship to the prophet Isaiah: what we are offered here constitutes a "presentation" of Jeremiah.

It is a reflection of the life of the prophet himself that comes to us through his book, which is neither a shapeless anthology nor yet a biography. Nor is it simply a collection of important addresses given on prominent public occasions. At times the feelings of author and reader coalesce so that we cannot tell whether the words are a laying bare of the prophet's inner thoughts or whether they represent a kind of liturgical response, offering the reader a moment for reflection and empathy with the fearful import of the subject matter. A real life figure of flesh and blood stands behind these words, whose reality holds our attention because he felt in full measure what the reader feels in part.

The reader is asked to accept that fears had engulfed Jeremiah and doubts had torn away the received assurances that had supported him since his youth. When he felt he deserved applause and recognition, he had instead received shame and degradation. All the things that brought reassurance and hope to others appeared to be denied to him. He justifiably complained repeatedly and bitterly about such a fate! Yet, in the moment of supreme crisis, when these conventional resources failed to sustain the remnants of his nation, he had found a renewal of hope in the fact of God's reality. This hope was given expression through some of the most universal and unspectacular features of human existence. Since Jeremiah had followed such a path to spiritual renewal, so the reader too is bidden to follow in his steps.

To lose sight of the real human being behind the book in the face of the undoubted awkwardnessses and intricacies that have arisen with the recording of these experiences in words, and the fashioning of these words into text, would be to lose a vital perspective concerning the nature of the book itself. The reader is invited to penetrate behind the prophetic text to uncover its struggle to articulate the human need for faith. Prophecy becomes more than knowing what will happen next and takes on the task of bringing insight into the human condition that the outward history of events cannot uncover.

The Private Anguish

The first half of the book of Jeremiah contains a significant number of passages in which cries of anguish and lamentation burst through the more conventional forms of the delivery of prophetic invective and message. Exactly how many passages are properly to be reckoned as belonging to this category of the so-called "Confessions" has been variously reckoned. That they follow closely the established lament form of psalmody was ably demonstrated by Walther Baumgartner in a classic study. To suppose that they once formed a separate collection, a kind of private diary of spiritual struggle, is wholly unlikely and there seems no reason for relocating them to anywhere other than their present positions in their relationship to other prophecies. Where many scholars have classified them as intensely autobiographical, others have recognized that they serve a more editorial and literary purpose in providing a response to the stark nature of the doom-laden pronouncements made by the prophet.

The first of these passages is found in 8:18–9:1 [8:23 in the Hebrew], and the concluding example appears in 20:14–18. In between these two framing instances we should note 12:1–5; 15:16–21; and 20:7–9. We may note the suddenness with which the first such cry of anguish bursts forth in the wake of the sharp threats that have preceded it in 8:4–17:

> My joy is gone, grief is upon me,
>   my heart is sick.
> Hark, the cry of my poor people
>   from far and wide in the land:
> "Is the LORD not in Zion?
>   Is her King not in her?"
> ("Why have they provoked me
>   to anger with their images,
> with their foreign idols?")
> "The harvest is past, the summer is ended,
>   and we are not saved."
> For the hurt of my poor people I am hurt,
>   I mourn, and dismay has taken hold of me.

Is there no balm in Gilead?
  Is there no physician there?
Why then has the health of my poor people
  not been restored?
O that my head were a spring of water,
  and my eyes a fountain of tears,
so that I might weep day and night
  for the slain of my poor people!
                    (Jer 8:18–9:1[Hebrew 8:18–23])

The hurt that the message of judgment inflicts upon both the prophet himself and the reader of the book cannot be mistaken. Heard as the prophet's anguished reflection, the sense that judgment and doom had now become inevitable hangs heavily over the words. For the reader the pain is no less, since the very heart of the book echoes with warnings and forebodings that went unheeded and that bore no obvious fruit. Judgment had become an accomplished fact even though the very essence of prophecy was to provide an avenue of divine foreknowledge that could turn an errant nation back from its headlong dash to destruction.

Careful examination of the dialogic form of the passages in 12:1–5; 15:10–12; and 15:21 reveals a prophet wrestling with an inner struggle, born out of self-doubt and striving, to find some way of escape from the consequences of his warnings. Yet no relief is made evident. Instead, when we move ahead to the complaints and warnings of 20:7–12, these threats are followed by an outburst of prophetic anger at the isolation and humiliation that his message-bearing has occasioned. There is no way out! Doom must come, and the messenger will be inescapably embroiled in it.

Jeremiah's curse upon the day of his birth in 20:14–18 brings to a conclusion the series of reflections and complaints, highlighting the awfulness of the threat that hangs over Jerusalem, the inner shrinking of the prophet from proclaiming its inevitability, and the pain it has brought to him. At one stroke the reader is made aware that this is no triumphant vindication of one who could declare "I told you so!" when disaster struck. It is instead the record of a soul who suffered in trying to spare others the misery of that suffering. Though the prophet could not take away the suffering of others, he could nonetheless share it with them.

Much scholarly effort has been expended in the concern to find some reasoned meaning and purpose behind the retention of these unique prophetic lamentations. Do they provide some deepening grasp of the intensity of the divine grief over Jerusalem's sin and its consequences? In some measure they seem to show a figure who still hoped in the face of all past experience that his warnings would be heeded and that Judah would turn from its path of folly. It is as though some scarcely perceptible chink of light still encouraged the prophet to believe that his threats would bring about a change of attitude and a wholesale movement for reform. Hope was dying, but it was not yet dead.

At the point when hope finally fades for Judah's deliverance, the prophet too despairs of all hope for himself and curses the day of his birth and the very parents who had given him life. One source of light is gradually extinguished for him.

Certainly the deepening tones of these laments mark a growing sense of loss and the closing of a door that could not thereafter be reopened. The pain intensifies and does not become easier to bear. Whether this was precisely how the prophet himself had felt during these drama-filled days, or whether it is simply how the final editors of his prophecies have strived to present him, it is undoubtedly the picture that is given. The darkness deepened, and there is no compensating relief in the knowledge of God's presence supporting him in any way.

So we are not entitled from the text of these Confessions to draw the conclusion that Jeremiah had found some comfort and consolation in the belief that, painful as the experience had been, his isolation and humiliation had intensifed his awareness that God was close at hand. Quite the contrary, when the sequence of the material is carefully traced, the last and starkest of the Confessions shows the prophet confronted with an impenetrable wall of despondency and doubt.

Jeremiah was not a fatalist, and all his artistry and skill must have been employed in the service of the hope that his people would, even in some imperfect way, find a path to penitence and renewal. The verdict for him appears, at least for a period, to have been one in which he stared blankly and hopelessly at the barriers of rejection and hostility that the future presented. The last rays of light had flickered and gone out. He was alone in spiritual darkness. Whether or not we are entitled to speak of some form of inner spiritual crisis, akin to the mystic's "dark night of the soul," has to be set aside as a question that cannot be answered.

Since we cannot prove that we are faced here with a genuine record of Jeremiah's feelings, it is pointless to pursue the biographical quest. Nevertheless we are, on even the most cautious reckoning, given a presentation of a personal inward response to the message of divine judgment. It is one that the editors of this prophetic scroll clearly saw as a wholly appropriate and credible reaction to its import. The text itself becomes a liturgy in which God and the prophetic messenger engage in a heart-searching dialogue. So the prophet and the reader similarly share a dialogue of admonition and response. God speaks, and the words are too painful for the reader to bear. Yet they must be listened to, for they declare a truth that cannot be contradicted or denied. However, in place of a dumb and awestruck resentment at the harshness of God, the laments take in the fact of Jerusalem's judgment and teach the reader to see its pain-filled necessity. Since such judgment cannot be denied, it must be accommodated into the factual reality of human existence.

The Message of Hope

Is it against such a background of anguish that the breaking through of the message of hope for the prophet can best be understood? As the book is now constructed, there has evidently been an editorial intent of gathering together a major collection of reassuring prophecies of hope for the future in chaps. 30–33. They then constitute an independent unit that has acquired the title "The Little Book of Consolation." Its location is not inappropriate since, as now preserved, the "Letter to the Exiles" of 29:4–28 offers a guarded word of hope for the citizens deported to Babylon in 598 B.C.E. (especially 29:10–14). That there was such a letter to the exiles seems highly probable, although its core content concerning the lifetime of exile to be spent in Babylon must have been, when it was first delivered, more in the nature of a warning than a word of reassurance (the "seventy years" of v. 10 [cf. further Jer 25:12] can only have been construed as a warning to abandon any immediate hope of return such as the prophets mentioned in Jer 29:15–23 had declared). It is the passage of many years that has softened the harshness of the original judgment by establishing a temporal limit to its harsh terms.

Much of the force of the extended sequence of prophecies set out in Jeremiah 30–31 lies in the breadth and general character of their assurance rather than in the detail or precision of what they promise. They draw their assurance from the nature of God and from the record of his dealings with Israel from the beginning. That they owe much to a broad editorial desire to spell out with the utmost conviction the confidence that Israel can be reborn and can again find grace in the present wilderness years seems certain. Similarly the broad nature of the promises concerning the eventual restoration of the Davidic monarchy in

33:14–26 gives no hint regarding the manner or circumstances in which such a restoration could be accomplished. This is particularly noteworthy when set against the background of Jeremiah's earlier fore-closing on the contemporary expressions of such hope, which had arisen and been swept aside during the final period of Judah's collapse.

Overall the message of hope is both a central feature of the final shape of the book of Jeremiah as well as one of the most enigmatic keys to the complex nature of the book's construction. The events of 32:1–15 are central to the concern to locate and define the circumstances of the hope that came with such electrifying effect as a divine revelation to Jeremiah. During the terrible months when Jerusalem was under siege for the second time by the Babylonian armies in the years 588–587 B.C.E., Jeremiah's cousin Hanamel came to him in Jerusalem with the request that he honor the code of family loyalty by buying a field in Anathoth, belonging to his cousin, that was up for sale. The fact of pur-chasing the deeds of the field then became for him a sacrament of hope, giving assurance as the very word of God to him:

> For thus says the LORD of hosts, the God of Israel:
> Houses and vineyards shall again be bought in this land.
> (Jer 32:15)

The simple assurance that this brought personally to Jeremiah could then be enlarged, as it has been at the hands of the prophet's editors, into a larger expression of hope for the future of Israel:

> For thus says the LORD: Just as I have brought all this great disaster upon this people, so I will bring upon them all the good fortune that I now promise them. Fields shall be bought in this land of which you are saying, It is a desolation, without human beings or animals; it has been given into the hands of the Chaldeans. Fields shall be bought for money, and deeds shall be signed and sealed and witnessed, in the land of Benjamin, in the places around Jerusalem, and in the cities of Judah, of the hill country, of the Shephelah, and of the Negeb; for I will restore their fortunes, says the LORD. (Jer 32:42–44)

The arrival of his cousin Hanamel and the significance attached to his purchase of the plot of ancestral land in Anathoth mark the moment of greatest breakthrough for Jeremiah. For the first time, even while Jeru-salem was under siege by the Babylonian forces, some ray of light had begun to penetrate through the gloom of despair and hopelessness to which the Confessions testify. This brief but informative narrative pro-vides the core text around which all other prophecies of hope in the book have now been grouped. The evidence points us to recognize that any earlier hopes Jeremiah had nursed had taken the form that somehow the disaster threatening Judah and Jerusalem might be averted. Only when that hope had finally been eliminated, as they so clearly had by the time of the anguish expressed in 8:20, could the ground be prepared for a new and deeper basis of hope to appear. The particular forms of hope had to be swept aside in order to expose the fundamental basis of all hope as a principle that resides only in God and in awareness of a divine purpose for humanity. The private anguish that Jeremiah had suffered was the only path that could lay bare the more fundamental truth that lies with the knowledge that human existence itself demands faith.

Even so, the complexity of the book of Jeremiah makes plain that this new hope itself needed to be tempered with fresh challenges and with an ever-widening horizon. This comes to the fore in chap. 25, which marks a further shifting of perspective that has given to the book its major hinge-point. The import of this shifting of viewpoint lies in the fact that, after the catastrophe had fallen upon Jerusalem and the city lay in ruins, Jeremiah chose to stay amid these ruins to savor the reality of a new beginning. The details of this are recorded in 40:1–6, which makes explicit that, given the choice of either staying in the devastated land of Judah or going with the exiles to Babylon, Jeremiah chose to stay.

The brief interlude of respite for the miseries of Judah under the governorship of Gedaliah and its new administrative center at Mizpah appears to have held sufficient promise to provide a basis for the hope Jeremiah had voiced when he purchased the plot of ancestral land in Anathoth. Yet such a brief interlude of hope was short-lived and, after Gedaliah's untimely murder recorded in 41:1–18, a major reorientation was needed. After this further national tragedy, the remnant in Judah fled to Egypt, compelling the unwilling Jeremiah to accompany them (42:1–22). The last prophecies we hear from him constituted a warning concerning the idolatry and spiritual death that would inevitably ensue for those who had fled there (43:8–13; 44:1–30). Far from Egypt's providing a new birthplace of hope, it would provide a graveyard for Judah's aspirations.

This unexpected series of events in which the narrator shows clearly Jeremiah's choice to stay in Judah and the unwillingness with which his ultimate removal to Egypt took place, has an important bearing on understanding the circumstances of Jeremiah's hope for Israel's renewal and also of the complex literary structure of the book. Already we have noted that chap. 25 marks an important transition—undoubtedly the most instructive of all such units that are found in the entire book. It takes the form of an editorial review of the substance of Jeremiah's prophesying from his earliest years with its sharp admonitions and summons to national repentance (25:3–7). It records that such warnings had gone unheeded and that the consequence was the Babylonian destruction of Judah and Jerusalem at the hands of King Nebuchadrezzar of Babylon. All this is spelled out firmly in summary form in 25:8–11—as a record of events that had already taken place by the time this report came to be written.

What is significantly new in this review of the import of Jeremiah's message of hope concerning the future is the insistence that a period of 70 years must elapse during which Nebuchadrezzar, and the Babylonian Empire he represents, will rule for 70 years over the nations, until eventually the time of judgment upon Babylon itself arrives. Then it too will fall and its land suffer devastation (25:12). The same message is spelled out with even more detail as a summary of a divine "plan" for punishment upon the nations in 27:1–22. In this, the changed perspective of hope points directly to those who had been deported to Babylon as the remnant of hope (27:22), whose return would be consequent upon Babylon's downfall and through whom the restoration of Israel could be accomplished.

It is this making concrete of the manner and circumstances in which hope for Israel's restoration would occur that has led to the detailed elaboration of the parable of the good and bad figs in 24:1–10 and the letter to the exiles in 29:1–28. The most significant expression of this new perspective of hope is found in 29:10–14.

Conclusion

If this attempt to reconstruct the path of Jeremiah's pilgrimage of hope is valid, then we can see that it possesses a measure of coherence and transparency. It also provides some of the most illuminating insights into the grounds of hope as the antidote to human despair that are to be found anywhere in the Bible.

That its origins lie in the spiritual pilgrimage of the prophet's own experience is a contention that appears adequately justified. What makes it remarkable is that it arose from an inward experience of illumination that made it a revelation from God. It took as its key convictions not a catalogue of traditions concerning covenants, dynastic promises, and all the familiar focal points of a great nation and tradition, even though it recognizes their existence. Rather, it found hope to lie in the very ordinariness and seeming unpretentiousness of human activities. Just as the misery of human suffering and hopelessness could be described in terms of the suppression of all normal signs of day-to-day activities,

> I will banish from them the sound of mirth and the sound of gladness,
> the voice of the bridegroom and the voice of the bride,
> the sound of millstones and the light of the lamp (25:10),

so the breakthrough of hope took on tangible form in the signing of a simple deed of purchase of a plot of land—itself very plausibly of no great size (32:14–15). The foundations of hope were to be seen in the divine meaning and dignity of the naturalness of life and its opportunities. In creating human beings God had planted the seeds of hope in their very humanness! In no small measure it is this simplicity and poetic sensitivity that has made the book of Jeremiah one of the great biblical expressions of hope. That this hope suffered setbacks and found fulfillment in very different ways from the ways that the prophet's original expectations had envisaged highlights all the more its deep significance. It drew its meaning and inspiration from God—a faith that had to come out into the open because of the trials of anguish imposed upon Jeremiah. Hope built on less than this can only remain a fragile and weak echo of its proper theological foundation.

"Your Exile Will Be Long":
The Book of Jeremiah and the Unended Exile

JOHN HILL
Yarra Theological Union
Box Hill, Victoria, Australia

A fundamental belief in Second Temple Judaism was that the community, although living in the land of Judah, was still in exile. The historical experience of a sixth-century exile in Babylon had been transformed into a paradigmatic event that the postexilic community used to interpret the events of their own times. The aim of this essay is to explain how the seeds of a belief in an unended exile are found in the book of Jeremiah.

The first part of the essay is an analysis of Jeremiah's letter to the exiles in Babylon (Jeremiah 29). What is important here is the prophet's directives to the exiles: they are to regard life in Babylon as being on a par with life in the promised land. The second part of the essay is about the book's portrayal of Babylon. The figure of Babylon is presented in a much more positive light than in other places in the Old Testament. Although the Babylonian Empire had disappeared by the time the book of Jeremiah reached its final form, it is presented in the book as a here-and-now reality. The third section analyzes the final form of the Masoretic Text of Jeremiah (MT) and shows that the idea of an unended exile is embedded in the very structure of the book. The fourth section takes up the familiar Jeremian prediction that Babylon will be dominant for 70 years and shows how the 70-year theme contributes to the postexilic understanding of the unended exile. These four strands of thought in the book contribute to the belief in an unended exile.

1. Jeremiah's Letter to the Exiles (Jeremiah 29)

Set in the years after the first deportation to Babylon in 597 B.C.E. (v. 1), the letter is a response to unrest in the exilic community. Jeremiah's prophetic opponents believed that the exile would be short.

Opposing this view, Jeremiah gives the exiles directions about their life in Babylon:

> Build houses and live in them;
> plant gardens and eat what they produce.
> Take wives and have sons and daughters;
> take wives for your sons,
> and give your daughters in marriage,
> that they may bear sons and daughters;
> multiply there, and do not decrease.
> But seek the welfare of the city
> where I have sent you into exile,
> and pray to the LORD on its behalf,
> for in its welfare you will find your welfare. (29:5–7)

An initial reading reveals a positive view of Babylon. A closer reading of the text makes us realize how startling and radical such a view is. The prophet's directives about life in exile contain direct references or allusions to texts in the Old Testament that speak about life in the promised land.

The letter first alludes to directions about "holy war" found in Deuteronomy 20, which lays down certain grounds for exempting individuals from military service. Of the four categories of exemption, three are relevant here: the one who has "built a new house but not dedicated it" (v. 5), the one who has "planted a vineyard but not yet enjoyed its fruit" (v. 6), and the one who has "become engaged to a woman but not yet married her" (v. 7). The significance of these categories of exemption becomes clearer in light of the curses listed in Deuteronomy 28:

> You shall become engaged to a woman,
> but another man shall lie with her.
> You shall build a house,
> but not live in it.
> You shall plant a vineyard,
> but not enjoy its fruit. (Deut 28:30)

The deprivation of these activities—marrying, building a house, planting vineyards—is a curse. Conversely, their enjoyment is the realization of blessings associated with living in the promised land. In Jer 29:5–7 activities usually associated with life in the promised land are now mandated for the community in exile. The effect of the letter's directives is to change the perception of Babylon. It is now something other than an alien place, in which life must be simply endured.

The reference to building a house refers to another tradition about life in the promised land. The expression "to build a house" most frequently appears in texts associated with the building of the temple. However, it also occurs at a key place in the patriarchal narratives. After his meeting with Esau, Jacob goes to Succoth and settles there: "Jacob journeyed to Succoth, and built himself a house and made booths for his cattle" (Gen 33:17). This is the first instance in the patriarchal narratives in which any form of settlement is indicated. Jacob's actions mark the shift from the patriarchal journeys to settlement in the promised land. The commands to multiply and not decrease are also alluded to in the patriarchal traditions, except that now the promises of many descendants made to Abraham (Gen 16:10; 17:2, 20; 22:17), Isaac (26:4, 24), and Jacob (28:3; 35:11) are to be realized not in the land of Israel but in Babylon.

Perhaps the most startling feature of Jeremiah's letter is the directive to pray for the welfare of Babylon: "Seek the welfare of the city . . . pray on its behalf" (v. 7). The word "welfare" translates the Hebrew *šālôm* so that a reference to the *šālôm* of the city would surely have allusions to the city of *šālôm* from which they had been exiled—Jerusalem. Prayer for the welfare of Jerusalem, as exhorted by Ps 122:6, now becomes praying for the welfare of the enemy city.

There are also cultic overtones to the directive to pray for Babylon, as the use of the verbs "seek" and "pray" indicate. In fact the letter begins with a reference to the full cultic name of YHWH: "Thus says the LORD of hosts, the God of Israel." The use of such cultic language indicates a belief that YHWH's power extends to foreign lands and is not in any way subordinate to the Babylonian deities. At the same time it borders on the blasphemous. As a foreign land, Babylon is unclean, yet the use of cultic language in vv. 4 and 7 has the effect of placing it on a par with the holy city of Jerusalem. Moreover, there is a terrible irony in the command to pray on behalf of Babylon, because earlier in the book (7:16; 14:11) Jeremiah is forbidden to pray, that is, to exercise the prophetic ministry of intercession, for those in Judah. The letter goes even further. Jerusalem itself is threatened with further destruction, "sword, famine, and pestilence" (29:17)—and the city of "peace" is now Babylon!

How are we to understand the function of these verses, with their radical advice? Why give directives to regard life in Babylon as if it is life in the promised land? Some scholars have seen the letter as an example of *Realpolitik*. This may well be true when reading the letter in its historical context. However, as part of a book that came to its final form over a long period, the letter takes on a further meaning. When read in the postexilic period, long after the demise of the Babylonian

Empire, the directives in the letter provide a way for the community to interpret its existence back in Judah as still a form of exile.

2A. *Babylon in the Book of Jeremiah*

The book of Jeremiah's portrayal of Babylon is distinctive and multi-layered. Within the book there are two different views of Babylon. Jeremiah 50–51 reflects what might be called a conventional understanding of Babylon: that is, the proud empire that, having oppressed Judah, then suffers retribution at the hand of YHWH. This perspective is also found in the Isaian oracles against Babylon (chaps. 13–14). In the prophetic traditions the demise of Babylon is an occasion of triumphant joy (e.g., Isaiah 12–14) and deliverance from Babylon a new exodus (Isa 43:14–21; 48:20–21). The conventional view is also found in Psalm 137, with its outpouring of anger against Babylon. Jerusalem is remembered with longing and affection (vv. 4–6), while Babylon is portrayed as the tormentor (v. 3) and destroyer (v. 8). Perhaps the most negative portrayal of Babylon is found in the book of Revelation: "Babylon, the great, mother of whores and of earth's abominations" (Rev 7:5). Although it functions as a cipher for Rome in Revelation, such a function would not be possible unless Babylon signified par excellence the evil empire.

In contrast, the book of Jeremiah contains a second and much more positive picture of Babylon, represented especially by its interest in the metonymic figure of King Nebuchadnezzar.

2B. *Nebuchadnezzar—YHWH's Partner*

The figure of Nebuchadnezzar first appears in Jer 21:1–10. The setting of these verses is Jerusalem, not long before its capture in 587. Zedekiah sends representatives to ask Jeremiah to intercede with YHWH on behalf of the city (v. 2). His hope is that Jerusalem will be freed from the Babylonian siege, just as it was in 701 from that of the Assyrians. On that occasion the prophet Isaiah assured King Hezekiah that the city would not fall (2 Kings 18–19; Isaiah 36–37). However Jeremiah's response (vv. 4–10) makes clear that there will be no repeat of the previous miraculous deliverance. It presents two alternatives: to surrender to Nebuchadnezzar and live, or to remain in the city and die (v. 9).

Nebuchadnezzar is presented as YHWH's partner in the siege. In vv. 4–6 the verbs that refer to acts of war have YHWH as their subjects. The siege is first of all YHWH's attack on Jerusalem, as vv. 5–6 show: "I myself will fight against you . . . and I will strike down the inhabitants of this city." In v. 7 the focus shifts to Nebuchadnezzar. YHWH will give the city into the hand of the Babylonian king. He is now the agent of destruction. Where in v. 6 YHWH is the subject of the verb "strike," in v. 7 it is Nebuchadnezzar: "He shall strike them down with the edge of the sword; he shall not pity them, or spare them, or have compassion."

In v. 7 there is a difference in the readings of the MT and the LXX, and this highlights the MT's particular interest in Nebuchadnezzar. The MT of v. 7 has Nebuchadnezzar as the subject of the verbs "pity" (*rḥm*), "spare" (*ḥûs*), and "have compassion" (*ḥml*). However, the LXX of v. 7 reads: "I will not pity them, nor will I have compassion on them." The significant difference between the LXX and the MT here is that in the former the subject of the verbs "pity" and "have compassion" is YHWH, not Nebuchadnezzar. This difference is important, because the two verbs are found together only once in the whole book (13:14), and in that instance their subject is YHWH. The LXX has retained the reading of 13:14 in 22:7, but the MT has changed the subject from YHWH to Nebuchadnezzar. In the MT, dispositions associated with YHWH (13:14) are now associated with Nebuchadnezzar. The effect of this is to closely unite the purposes of YHWH and those of the Babylonian king. Where the narrative of Jerusalem's deliverance in 701 showed a unity between the hopes of Hezekiah and the purposes of YHWH, the perspective of Jer 21:1–10 is different. Zedekiah is no Hezekiah, and Nebuchadnezzar is certainly no Sennacherib.

2C. *Nebuchadnezzar, YHWH's Servant and Subordinate*

The elevated status of Nebuchadnezzar is also shown in Jeremiah 25. The chapter is situated at a critical point in the book. It marks the place in the book at which the MT and the LXX differ radically. In the LXX 25:14 marks the beginning of the Oracles against the Nations. In the MT these come much later in the book. The end of chap. 25 concludes the first part of the book in the MT's arrangement.

Jeremiah 25 MT contains two references to Nebuchadnezzar, neither of which are found in the LXX. The first is a reference to the year of his reign (v. 1); the second is his designation as "my servant" (v. 9). Jeremiah 25 is set in the year 605, which the text identifies as the fourth year of Jehoiakim's reign and the first of Nebuchadnezzar's. The function of the regnal citation of Nebuchadnezzar is to signify that Judah is now as much under the power of the Babylonian ruler as under that of its own king. The reference in Jer 25:1 to Nebuchadnezzar also foreshadows his appearance in v. 9 as the agent of YHWH's judgment against Judah and the surrounding nations.

According to 25:9 MT, YHWH calls Nebuchadnezzar "my servant." It is a startling designation because those described elsewhere in the Old Testament by YHWH as "my servant" are Moses (Num 12:7; Josh 1:2, 7), David (1 Sam 22:8; 2 Sam 3:18; 1 Kgs 11:32, 34), and Isaiah (Isa 20:3). The Babylonian king, as the *only foreigner* in the Old Testament designated by YHWH as "my servant," is in elite company! (cf. Isa 44:28). Moreover, the term "the Servant of the Lord" is used of Joshua (Josh 24:29), who carried out YHWH's war against the inhabitants of Canaan. Nebuchadnezzar now appears as an antitype of Joshua, conducting YHWH's war not only against the people of Judah and Jerusalem but also against the surrounding nations (Jer 25:9–11).

At the same time, Nebuchadnezzar and therefore Babylon are always subordinate to YHWH. In v. 9 the Babylonian king appears as a somewhat passive figure. It is YHWH who summons the armies of the north and YHWH who does the fighting: "I am going to send for all the tribes of the north . . . I will bring them against this land . . . I will utterly destroy them" (25:9). The time of Babylonian domination is also not unlimited, and Babylon too will undergo its own subjugation to unnamed nations (vv. 13–14 MT).

The figure of Babylon also appears in 25:26. The verse concludes the section of the chapter that uses the symbol of a cup of wine to describe YHWH's judgment on all of the world's nations (vv. 15–26). Jeremiah is given a cup of wine from which all the nations must drink. The cup is to be given first to Jerusalem and the cities of Judah and then to all the nations. The text gives an extensive list of nations and groups (vv. 18–26), which embraces "all the kingdoms of the world that are on the face of the earth" (v. 26). The climax of the judgment happens when the king of Babylon drinks (v. 26). Again, as in vv. 1–14, Babylon must submit.

In Jeremiah 25 MT, Babylon is both the agent of YHWH's judgment and the subject of it. While enjoying a special status via the figure of Nebuchadnezzar, Babylon is still completely subordinate to the God who has power over all the nations.

2D. *Nebuchadnezzar, a Mythical New Adam*

The high standing of Babylon is also strikingly represented in Jeremiah 27 MT, again by the figure of Nebuchadnezzar. Portrayed in language that has a mythical dimension, he is more than a historical figure. The portrait of his power is more than an exercise in *Realpolitik*.

Jeremiah 27 MT is set in the reign of Zedekiah, some time after the first deportation of exiles to Babylon in 597 B.C.E. Ambassadors from various countries around Judah were meeting with Zedekiah to plan some form of rebellion against the Babylonians. Jeremiah is commanded by YHWH to appear before the ambassadors wearing an ox yoke on his neck, to symbolize that YHWH required the submission of both Judah and its neighbors to Babylon (vv. 2–3).

The prophetic message that interprets the symbolism of the yoke contains another extraordinary portrait of Nebuchadnezzar:

> It is I
> who by my great power and my outstretched arm
> have made the earth,
> with the people and animals that are on the earth,
> and I give it to whomever I please.
> Now I have given all these lands
> into the hand of King Nebuchadnezzar of Babylon,
> my servant,
> and I have given him
> even the wild animals of the field to serve him.
> All the nations shall serve him
> and his son and his grandson,
> until the time of his own land comes;
> then many nations and great kings
> shall make him their slave. (vv. 5–7)

The language of this passage alludes to a number of Israel's sacred traditions. The use of such language goes beyond what would be required to portray Nebuchadnezzar simply as YHWH's agent in the destruction of Jerusalem.

The mythic dimension in the text's portrait of the figure of Nebuchadnezzar comes in part from the use of the expressions associated with Israel's sacred traditions. The expressions "great power" and "outstretched arm" originate in the exodus traditions (Deut 9:29; 2 Kgs 17:36). The expression "to whomever I please," also used of Nebuchadnezzar, is more literally translated "to whomever is right in my eyes." It is important in this context because it is reminiscent of a formula used in the Deuteronomistic History to evaluate the reign of the various kings of Judah and Israel—that a certain king "did what was right in the eyes of the Lord." Kings to whom this favorable judgment was applied include David (1 Kgs 15:5), Hezekiah (2 Kgs 18:3), and Josiah (22:2). Perhaps the most notable failure in this regard is Solomon (1 Kgs 11:33, 38). The designation of Nebuchadnezzar as someone who is "right in my eyes" places him again in exclusive company.

According to Jer 27:5–7, Yhwh will also give unspecified lands to
him. This alludes to the patriarchal promises, promises of land to Israel's ancestors. While the usual formula in the patriarchal texts refers
to the giving of the land (singular), Gen 26:3, 5 does speak of the gift
of lands. In addition, Nebuchadnezzar is also given the earth with its
human and animal inhabitants (Jer 27:5). In v. 6 the text explicitly indicates that even wild animals are to be under his control. This is significant because the yoke is used in 27:11 as a symbol of the submission of
the nations to Nebuchadnezzar, a submission demanded by Yhwh. If,
as v. 6 indicates, unyoked wild animals are subject to his control, how
much more are those who are yoked. Behind the imagery of vv. 5–6
stands the creation tradition of Genesis 2, according to which (the
original) Adam is given authority over all of the created world. Nebuchadnezzar is a new Adam.

As in Jeremiah 25, Nebuchadnezzar's role is presented in chap. 27 as
subordinate to Yhwh. The repetition of "I have given" in vv. 5–6 shows
this. Moreover, Babylonian domination is also clearly limited: "All the
nations shall serve him and his son and his grandson" (v. 7). The precise
meaning of this verse is not clear, however, and we will return to it later.

The distinctive understanding of Nebuchadnezzar and consequently
of Babylon is primarily theological and metaphorical. If we were to
adopt an understanding of Nebuchadnezzar that was purely historical,
it would be very difficult to explain why he is described in such evocative language. The use of language from the sacred traditions of Israel's
beginnings—the creation and the exodus—would surely have been extremely offensive and served no useful rhetorical purpose.

The book of Jeremiah portrays Nebuchadnezzar, and hence Babylon, as entities in the present and not just as historical figures from the
past. As continuing entities they signify that the events of exile that began in 587 have not yet come to a conclusion. Their positive portrayal
blurs the clear-cut distinction between Babylon and Judah and under-
mines the conventional understanding of Babylon and Judah as polar
opposites—Babylon as alien and Judah as home. As Jeremiah's letter to
the exiles showed, living in Babylon can be like living in the homeland.
As the community's experience in the land after the restoration was to
show, living in Judah can also be like living in exile.

3. The Exile as Unended in Jeremiah (MT)

Up to this point we have identified two elements in the book of Jeremiah that contributed to the idea of an unended exile. One was the

prophet's letter, which dismantled the conventional view of Babylon as the alien and hostile "other." The other was the mythical construction of the figure of Nebuchadnezzar in Jeremiah 25 and 27. Now an examination of the shape of the MT of Jeremiah shows that the idea of an unended exile is reflected in the very structure of the book.

The idea is represented in the book's superscription (1:1–3) and its conclusion (chap. 52). Verses 1–3 contain chronological material that situates Jeremiah's ministry in a 40-year period, from 627 ("the thirteenth year of Josiah") down to 587 ("the exile of Jerusalem"). What is interesting about this information is that the book contains material dated later than 587. If we also take into consideration the fact that the number 40 often has symbolic significance, we are left with the possibility that the chronological information in vv. 1–3 also has a theological significance. Verses 1–3 identify 587 as a cut-off point: at its beginning the book takes us up to the fall of Jerusalem and the beginning of exile. It is also significant that its concluding chapter starts with the events of 587 and concludes with the release of Jehoiachin in 560. The book has an exilic frame. Its contents are circumscribed by the exile, which has not yet ended. Its juxtaposition of promises of judgment and salvation also reflect the book's portrayal of an exile as yet unended. The book of Jeremiah contains sudden switches from doom to salvation and vice versa. The vision of a return of the earth to the state of primal chaos (4:23–26) is then mitigated by v. 27b: "The whole land shall be a desolation; yet I will not make a full end." Similarly in the middle of material about death and expulsion from the land (chaps. 16–17) there is an *ex abrupto* appearance of a promise of a new exodus (16:14–15). This happens also at the macro level in the book, where large blocks of salvation material are circumscribed by promises of judgment. Chapters 29–33 consist nearly exclusively of promises of restoration and return to the land. However they are embedded in a section of the book (chaps. 26–36) that concludes with a proclamation that the divine judgment is inevitable (36:27–31). Near the end of the book in its Hebrew form, the oracles against the nations (chaps. 46–51) are immediately followed by another narrative of Jerusalem's fall in 587.

By way of contrast we may note the structure of the book of Ezekiel. It begins with proclamations of judgment (chaps. 1–24), followed by the oracles against the nations (chaps. 24–32), and promises of salvation and restoration (chaps. 33–48). Instead of a juxtaposition of salvation and judgment material we have here a smoother progression from judgment to an implied salvation for Judah (represented by the oracles against the nations) and then to explicit promises of restoration and return to the land. The conclusion of the book of Ezekiel is also quite different. Instead of the juxtaposition of the oracles against the nations and the narrative about the events of 587, we find a long and sustained description of the future glory of Jerusalem and the new temple (chaps. 40–48).

Where the final form of books such as Isaiah and Ezekiel reflects a redactional process in which proclamations of judgment are followed by announcements of salvation, the book of Jeremiah does not reflect this. The promises of restoration are more circumscribed, and the juxtaposition of judgment and salvation creates a tension in the text about what the future will bring.

While the book of Jeremiah saw the exile as not yet ended, it did not see it as unending. In its portrait of Babylon, the period of its domination is always limited. In 25:9 MT, the length of Judah's subjugation is 70 years. In 27:7 the rule of Nebuchadnezzar is said to be three generations, "until the time of his own nation comes." In 29:10 the end of the 70-year Babylonian domination is identified also as the end of Judah's exile. It was the term "70 years" in the Jeremian prophecies that provided the springboard for reflection in the postexilic community about the end of the exile.

4. When Will the Exile End?

The belief in an unended exile emerged over a period of time. At first, in the early postexilic period, it was believed that the exile had ended with the establishment of the Persian Empire. This is the view reflected in 2 Chr 36:20–21, which linked the rise of Cyrus to the 70-year predictions of Jeremiah: "In the first year of King Cyrus of Persia, in fulfillment of the word of the LORD spoken by Jeremiah . . ." (v. 21). Similarly the books of Ezra–Nehemiah, which describe the reconstitution of the community in Judah after the return, see the rise of Cyrus as the fulfillment of a Jeremian prophecy (1:1).

However, the realities of life in the postexilic community gave rise to a sense of disillusionment when the wonderful vision of the restoration, particularly as expressed in Isaiah 40–55, was not realized. The community was deeply divided over a number of issues, as Isaiah 56–66 reveals. Besides, although the temple was rebuilt early in the process, its building was not without problems. Recollections of the greater splendor of the preexilic temple would also not have helped. As a result, the failure of the vision of the restoration shifted the community's focus to the future, in which the great vision of the homecoming would come about. Life in the present was still life in exile.

There are a number of expressions of this belief. One is found in the book of Tobit. A second- or third-century composition, its setting is eighth-century Nineveh after the destruction of the Northern Kingdom. While Tobit is portrayed as an Israelite exile (1:3–4), the restoration to which he looks is that of Jerusalem: "After this they all will return from their exile, and will rebuild Jerusalem in splendor" (14:5). In accord with the twin Deuteronomic themes of divine retribution and subsequent mercy, the book of Tobit portrays the exile as the result of the nation's sin, and the promised restoration as an act of YHWH's grace. According to the fictive world of Tobit 14, the return to the land and the rebuilding of Jerusalem and its temple lay at some point in the indefinite future.

A similar understanding of the exile is found in the book of Baruch. According to its superscription, it contains the words of Baruch, the scribe of the prophet Jeremiah. Whereas the setting of the book is the beginning of the Babylonian exile, it was composed at a much later date, somewhere between 150 B.C.E. and 60 C.E. It situates the community in exile (2:14), and its interpretation of the situation is also informed by the Deuteronomic tradition: "See, we are today in exile where you have scattered us . . . for all the iniquities of our ancestors who forsook the LORD our God" (3:8). Bar 2:21 specifically resumes the Jeremian theme that submission to Babylon will insure continued possession of the land. The book describes the future in language similar to the book of Deuteronomy. The hope of an end to exile is equated with the promises in Deuteronomy of the gift of land. The language of Deut 1:8; 6:10; and 34:4 is reflected in Bar 2:34: "I will bring them again into the land which I swore to give to their fathers, to Abraham and to Isaac and to Jacob."

A somewhat different view of the unended exile is found in the book of Daniel. It agrees with the view in the books of Tobit and Baruch that the reason for the exile is the people's sin. However, its apocalyptic theology produces a different understanding of the end of the exile. The book of Daniel, although composed in the Maccabean period, is set in Babylon during the reign of Nebuchadnezzar (1:1). Daniel 9 takes up the meaning of Jeremiah's prophecy that "the devastation of Jerusalem" must last 70 years (9:2). The reference is to Jer 25:11–12, according to which the land of Judah will be devastated and its people subjugated to Babylon for 70 years.

The seer's questioning (Dan 9:2) is followed by a prayer on behalf of the people (vv. 9–19) and a revelation from Gabriel (vv. 20–27). The prayer anticipates Gabriel's explanation about why the exile is not yet ended: "While I was speaking, and was praying and confessing my sin and the sin of my people Israel . . ." (v. 20). It is the sin of both past and present generations that is responsible for the nation's continuing exile. The language and content of the prayer are another link between Daniel 9 and the book of Jeremiah. The language of the prayer is conventionalized and reflects elements of Deuteronomistic theology that are also found in the book of Jeremiah.

In Dan 9:20–27 the length of the exile is revealed as "70 weeks" or 70 sabbath cycles (9:24). According to Lev 25:1–7 a sabbath cycle is 7 years, and so the "70 weeks" of Dan 9:24 are interpreted as 490 years. As foreshadowed in the prayer of Daniel, the ending of the exile is associated with the cessation of "transgression" and "sin" (v. 24), terms that embrace both the sin of the Jewish people and events such as the desecration of the temple by Antiochus Epiphanes and his Jewish sympathizers. The period of "70 weeks" begins "from the time the word went out to restore and rebuild Jerusalem." The meaning of the expression is ambiguous, and does not provide any clear fixed point that might be used to determine the end of the exile.

In contrast to the view of 2 Chr 36:20–21, the end of the exile in Daniel 9 is shrouded in mystery. The end is not associated with a return to the land in the same way that it is in Tobit and Baruch. In Daniel 9 the return to the land and the rebuilding of the city are a prelude to the coming of a new age whose advent is shrouded in mystery. In this respect the book of Daniel represents a further "de-historicizing" of the idea of exile.

The disillusionment about life in the land after the restoration gives rise in later writings to further negative judgments on the postexilic period. Dan 9:25 reflects this negative view by its description of the period after the return as a "troubled time." More extreme judgments on the history of the postexilic community are found in other literature, such as that of Qumran. The *Damascus Document* claims that the members of the Qumran community are the ones who will return and repossess the land. Implied in such an understanding is a repudiation of the history of the postexilic community. True postexilic history begins with the Qumran community.

5. Conclusion

The postexilic community was in the paradoxical situation of living in the promised land while at the same time understanding itself as still in exile. Their situation is well expressed in the words of William Blake:

"Whether this is Jerusalem or Babylon, we know not." The imagery of exile and homecoming is central both to Judaism and Christianity. Both are powerful images for these religions in their interpretation of the paradox of human existence in which we stand between promise and fulfillment. In such a situation, the book of Jeremiah is a rich resource. While it sees the exile as finite, it recognizes it as yet unended. A hope for the future is offered, a hope that is real and not glib.[1]

---

1. The themes in this essay are treated in my longer and more technical work, *Friend or Foe? The Figure of Babylon in the Book of Jeremiah MT* (Biblical Interpretation 40; Leiden: Brill, 1999).

Divine Reliability and the Conceptual Coherence of the Book of Consolation (*Jeremiah 30–31*)

BOB BECKING
Utrecht University

1. Introduction

In its canonical shape, the book of Jeremiah is presented as a unity. Traditionally the book was read and interpreted as a collection of authentic Jeremian material stemming from different periods of the life of the prophet. However, the rise of modernism in the nineteenth century inspired a different approach to the text of Jeremiah. A major feature of this new historically oriented approach was the search for "primary sources." A primary source was understood as the oldest written document relating a past event. Biblical scholars were expected to search for sources either in archives or by reconstruction, for many ancient sources (such as the Bible) were seen as "secondary" and were therefore judged to be late documents, covered by the dust of tradition, which obscured historical truth. Accordingly, biblical scholars saw themselves as historians trying to ascertain "what really happened" (much like secular historians engaged in the reconstruction of primary sources hidden in documents) rather than as interpreters of texts.

In regard to the book of Jeremiah, this approach has led to fragmentation of the text into various sources. The main architects of this approach, which flourished a century ago, were the German scholar Bernard Duhm and his Scandinavian colleague Sigmund Mowinckel. They claimed that the book of Jeremiah was composed from four different sources:

Author's note: This essay was translated by the editor. For a full analysis of these two chapters, see my *Between Fear and Freedom: Essays on the Interpretation of Jeremiah xxx–xxxi* (Oudtestamentische Studiën 52; Leiden: Brill, 2004).

A. Oracles and reports by the prophet in the first-person singular
B. Reports concerning the prophet written in the third-person singular (the so-called Baruch biography)
C. Prose sermons, Deuteronomistically redacted, and
D. Prophecies of hope.

Duhm, Mowinckel, and others who followed them, considered source A the most authentic part of the book of Jeremiah, presumably originating from the prophet himself. Accordingly, they relied on the A material to construct their view of the prophet. Source B was also accepted as a primary source, informing the reader about the fate of the prophet. Since it showed many traces of a later redaction, C was not considered a primary source. The adjective "Deuteronomistic" (often associated with this source) refers to the world view of Deuteronomy and that of the larger historical work, from Deuteronomy to 2 Kings, which Martin Noth labeled the Deuteronomistic History.

There are many similarities in language and ideology between the prose sermons in Jeremiah (for example Jeremiah 7) and theologically oriented historiography. Thus, the putative "authentic" parts of the book, sources A and B, provided a picture of a prophet of doom. Jeremiah 30–31, the main body of source D, contains mostly oracles of hope and liberation, which led to the assumption that these chapters, often called the Book of Consolation, are a later intrusion. Because of words and phrases in common with Deutero-Isaiah (Isaiah 40ff.), the author of the Book of Consolation has often been thought of as belonging in Deutero-Isaian circles.

William Holladay has developed a redaction-critical alternative. Since many words and phrases in the Book of Consolation have parallels in the book of Jeremiah, he assumed the existence of a primary document, which he labeled "The Early Recension to the North." This text, he claimed, contained seven poetic strophes expressing hope for the remnant of Northern Israelites exiled in Assyria by Tiglath-Pileser III and Sargon II and would be dated early in the career of Jeremiah. This material was supposed to have been reused and augmented by the prophet just before the fall of Jerusalem in 587 B.C.E. With three extensions (Jer 3:10–11; 30:15–16; and 31:7–9) and some reworking, Jeremiah applied the earlier message to the people of Judah. This new text Holladay labels the "Recension to the South." During and after the exile this text was expanded with unauthentic material of various provenances, reapplying the prophetic hope to a new generation.

Obviously, this approach does not consider the text of Jeremiah 30–31 as a coherent unit or as an integral part of the book of Jeremiah. On the other hand, Barbara Bozak,[1] applying a "new critical" method, reads these chapters as a unit. She discusses the poetic quality of the text by identifying various literary features such as alliteration, repetition of vowels, and consonants.

The Book of Consolation is to be read as a message of divine salvation for the people of Israel in exile. This salvation is described as a process of continuity and discontinuity: divine favor will be continued, while despair and oppression will end. Bozak has given an impressive interpretation of Jeremiah 30–31. By concentrating on the text as it stands, she has liberated the reader of the Book of Consolation from a preoccupation with sources. Her work reflects a basic change in attitude toward the text; it is no longer seen as material for historical reconstruction, but is construed as a mirror of words containing a message for its readers.

However, there are certain points in Bozak's work which must be critiqued, chiefly the question of the composition of Jeremiah 30–31 and its major theme.

2. Macrostructure of Jeremiah 30–31

First, I must make a few remarks on the structure of Jeremiah 30–31 as a whole. Bozak has tried to show that Jeremiah 30–31 is a clearly structured unit. Her view may be illustrated by the following outline:

30:1–4	Prose Introduction
30:5–11	Poem I—masculine audience
30:12–17	Poem II—feminine audience
30:18–31:1	Poem III—masculine audience
31:2–6	Poem IV—feminine audience
31:7–14	Poem V—masculine audience
31:15–22	Poem VI—feminine audience
31:23–34	Prose Conclusion—Part I
31:35–40	Prose Conclusion—Part II

---

1. B. Bozak, *Life "Anew": A Literary-Theological Study of Jeremiah 30–31* (Analecta Biblica 122; Rome: Pontifical Biblical Institute, 1991).

Bozak's view is mainly based on a distinction between prose and poetry. This is problematic, however, since we have no clear definitions of prose and poetry in classical Hebrew. On the other hand, from a syntactical point of view a distinction may be made in classical Hebrew between narrative and discursive texts. A narrative text is explicitly relating a story and is characterized by the well-known chain of "imperfect" (*wayyiqtol*) forms. A text may be classified as discursive when it:

1. provides background information to a narrative
2. contains direct or indirect speech, or
3. is of a more reflective character.

Granted, some passages in Jeremiah 30–31 appear to be more poetic than others, but there are no textual units that can clearly be characterized as narrative.

When describing the composition of Jeremiah 30–31, we should pay attention to *macro-syntactical indicators* in the text, specifically, the prophetic formulas with which various units are introduced. This produces the following scheme:

30:1–3	Introduction
30:4	Envelope 1: Prophetic introduction
30:5–11	Prophecy, introduced by: "Thus says YHWH"
30:12–17	Prophecy, introduced by: "Thus says YHWH"
30:18–24	Prophecy, introduced by: "Thus says YHWH"
31:2–6	Prophecy, introduced by: "Thus says YHWH"
31:7–14	Prophecy, introduced by: "Thus says YHWH"
31:15–22	Prophecy, introduced by: "Thus says YHWH"
31:23–25	Prophecy, introduced by: "Thus says YHWH"
31:26	Envelope 2: Remarks on the dream-character of the prophecies
31:27–30	Prophecy introduced by: "See, the days are coming"
31:31–37	Prophecy introduced by: "See, the days are coming"
31:38–40	Prophecy introduced by: "See, the days are coming"

This outline clearly differs in detail from the one proposed by Bozak. Particularly noteworthy are the contents and the position of 31:26. The remark on the awakening of the prophet functions to qualify the textual unit Jer 30:1–31:26 as verbalization of a dream. This notion, I think, is related to the complex introduction in 30:1–4. Before considering this, we may observe that seven textual units are introduced in Jeremiah 30–31 by the formula "thus says YHWH," while three are prefaced by "see, the days are coming."

Both formulas are attested in 30:1–3, which is composed as follows:

30:1—formula describing the happening of the revelation
30:2—summons to the prophet introduced by the formula "thus says YHWH"
30:3—motivation for the summons in the preceding verse using the "see the days are coming" formula

A few remarks need to be made on these elements. Verse 1 most likely goes back to the editor who gave Jeremiah 30–31 its place in the architecture of the book. The formula "thus says YHWH" in v. 2 introduces a summons to write down "all the words that I have spoken to you." This commission may be related to the remark in 31:26 referred to above. Verse 2 may thus offer an interpretation of 31:26. It qualifies the dream-vision as an authentic word of God. Because of the preceding "for," v. 3 is to be interpreted as the motivation of the commission in v. 2. Meanwhile, the words in v. 3 function as an indication of the kernel of the textual units in Jeremiah 30–31: YHWH will change the fate of Israel and Judah. Verse 4 is thus to be seen as a transition to the textual units that follow. The relation between 30:2–3 and the other parts of chaps. 30–31 suggest that these three verses form an integral part of the Book of Consolation.

I construe 30:1–3 as the general introduction to chaps. 30–31. Jer 30:4 and 31:2b are to be seen as an envelope holding the first seven sub-cantos that are thus presented as being based on a divine word transmitted in a dream.

Two units will be analyzed in this paper, one introduced by "thus says YHWH" (30:12–17) and one by the formula "see the days are coming" (31:31–37). In discussing the first unit, 30:12–17, I will argue against the view that proposes a literary-critical or redaction-historical subdivision of this unit. The second unit, 31:31–37, will be discussed in two parts. First, 31:31–34 will be read, using a variety of methods. Next, 31:35–37 will be interpreted from a text-critical point of view. In all readings, literary integrity is assumed and may be seen as exemplary for readings of the other units in the Book of Consolation.

3. Jeremiah 30:12–17

3.1. Translation

12	a	For thus says YHWH:
	b	"Incurable is your fracture.
	c	Unhealable is your wound.
13	a	There is none
	b	who procures you justice.
	c	For a suppurating wound there are medicines.
	d	For you there is no healing with new flesh.
14	a	All your lovers have forgotten you.
	b	They do not ask for you.
	c	Indeed, with the blow of an enemy I have struck you
	d	with the chastisement of a ruthless one,
	e	because of the abundance of your iniquity,
	f	because your sins are numerous.
15	a	Why do you cry for your fracture?
	b	Is your pain incurable?
	c	Because of the abundance of your iniquity,
	d	because your sins are numerous,
	e	I have done this to you.
16	a	All your devourers will be devoured, however.
	b	All your adversaries shall go into captivity in their entirety.
	c	Your plunderers shall become plunder.
	d	All your despoilers I will make spoil.
17	a	For I shall let healing rise over you.
	b	For your wounds I will heal,
	c	oracle of YHWH,
	d	for they have called you, Zion, the banished,
	e	the one none asks for."

3.2. Literary Unity and Conceptual Coherence

Should these verses be considered a unit, or is a literary or redaction-critical subdivision necessary? Although there are some unsolved problems, it is assumed here as a working hypothesis that the arguments favoring literary unity are more convincing than those pleading for a complex genesis of the textual units.

A preliminary hypothesis on the conceptual coherence of Jer 30:12–17 will now be presented. By "conceptual coherence" I mean that the parts of a text may, in spite of their differences in form or literary genre and despite some inconsistency on the level of a first reading, be interpreted as a coherent model, expressing a single idea or a coherent set of ideas.

My view of the unity of Jer 30:12–17 is based on:

1. the observations by Holladay that vv. 12–15 as well as vv. 16–17 contain authentic Jeremian phraseology, and
2. the lucidity of the text-internal chronology.

The textual unit models a God who changes: Yhwh in the "past" struck Zion/Judah/Jerusalem with an incurable fracture, but who would heal that wound in the "future"? To bolster this point, I will make my hypothesis more explicit by

1. discussing some extrabiblical material
2. discussing the linguistic status of *lākēn* ("however," v. 16a), and
3. referring to a parallel model of God in other textual units in the Book of Consolation.

3.3. Motif and Model: Incurable Fracture, Divine Superior Force

3.3.1. Hillers's Hypothesis

Derek Hillers has referred to parallels of the "incurable fracture" motif in curses occurring in Neo-Assyrian vassal treaties and loyalty oaths. He has concluded that this motif is related to covenant theology and that 30:12–17 should therefore be interpreted as the description of a situation caused by the execution of a curse.

This is an attractive and interesting view. There are, however, three problems:

1. Hillers does not deal with the Mesopotamian material in a systematic way.
2. He surmises that the motif only occurs in Mesopotamian texts in the framework of treaty curses.
3. He does not convincingly argue that, when a motif occurs in two texts and one of these texts can be classified as belonging to a well-defined genre, the other text should therefore belong to the same genre.

There is no room here to discuss the extant Mesopotamian material, but I hope to show that the motif under consideration is also attested in texts that cannot be classified as vassal treaties or loyalty oaths.

At first view, Hillers seems to be correct. There are several passages in the Neo-Assyrian vassal treaties and loyalty oaths in which "illness" is

presented as the outcome of a divine curse because of the disloyalty of
the vassal. One of the curses in the vassal treaties of Esarhaddon reads:

> May Anu, king of the gods, let disease, exhaustion, malaria,
> sleeplessness, worries and ill health rain upon all your houses.

In the Gula curse of the same textual corpus, a comparable discomfort
will befall a disloyal vassal:

> May Gula, the great physician, put sickness and weariness [in your hearts]
> and an unhealing wound in your body. Bathe in [blood and pus] as if in
> water!

3.3.2. Preliminary Conclusion

The infliction of an incurable wound by a deity, or instrumentally by
a human being, is an image that has been used in the ancient Near East
at different times and in various contexts. The image is to be seen as the
expression of *divine superior force*. Within these texts, a human being is
punished with an incurable wound for crossing a border that should
not have been crossed. This border was marked by law, tabu, custom,
or the like and was part of the social code. The deity, as guarantor of
the social order, was seen as empowered to restore order. Within this
model, a vassal relationship or a covenant concept may or may not function. Both treaty and covenant may be seen as written expressions of
the social code and the divine guarantee. In other words, Hillers is pre-
senting a restricted interpretation of the material. Unless other indicators are found, the divine imagery in Jer 30:12–17 need not be related
to the concept of covenant. The motifs of the "incurable fracture" and
the "unhealing wound" may be seen as related to divine superior force.

3.4. The Linguistics of *lākēn* ("however")

A key role in the interpretation of 30:12–17 is played by the particle
lākēn (NRSV: "therefore"; in this paper: "however," v. 16a) which is normally construed as an indicator for literary-critical division. Brueggemann interprets *lākēn* as an anaphoric character. Bozak, however,
interprets *lākēn* adversatively. In short, there is a problem.

The Hebrew word *lākēn* is a complex adverb constructed from the
preposition /l/ and the pronominal particle /kēn/. A distinction has to
be made between the "ordinary" preposition / l/ with a wide variance of
meaning, and the emphatic /l/. Constructed with the ordinary preposition /l/, *lākēn* means "therefore, for, hence," and could be used in a
causal clause. Constructed with emphatic /l/, *lākēn* may have a variety of

meanings, such as "indeed, however, thus" (e.g., 1 Sam 28:2; Jer 2:33; Mic 2:5). This implies that an adversative translation of *lākēn* in Jer 30:15 has a legitimate basis in grammar, which would render a literary-critical or redaction-historical subdivision unnecessary. The adversative character of *lākēn* underscores the change in God's action.

3.5. Conclusion: A Twofold Change

Jer 30:12–17 is a text about change. Two transformations are implied:

1. Transformation I looks to the *past* and expounds the sum of all those events that led to the situation of a bitterly wounded and inconsolably hurt people.
2. Transformation II looks to the *future* and may be described as the hoped-for process that would end this situation.

I suspect that a comparable set of transformations is present or implied in all the other textual units of the Book of Consolation (contra Bozak, who only mentions Transformation II). Moreover, it should be noted that the shift from Transformation I to Transformation II expresses the change in God from "punishment" to "mercy." Both positions may be interpreted as based on divine superior force.

4. Jeremiah 31:31–34

The second text to be discussed here is the well-known unit on the "New Covenant," 31:31–34. Does this text also illustrate divine change-ability?

4.1. Translation

31　a　See, the days are coming
　　b　—oracle of YHWH—
　　c　that I will conclude with the house of Israel and with the house of Judah a new covenant,
32　a　not like the covenant
　　b　that I concluded with their fathers on the day
　　c　that I took them by the hand
　　d　to let them go out of the land of Egypt,
　　e　my covenant that they have broken,
　　f　although I have been master over them
　　g　—oracle of YHWH—.
33　a　For this is the covenant
　　b　that I will conclude with the house of Israel after these days

c   —oracle of YHWH—:
d   "I will put my law within them
e   and on their heart I shall write it,
f   in order that I shall be a God to them
g   and they shall be to me a people."
34   a   Then they shall no longer teach, a man his friend and a man
his brother:
b   "Know YHWH!"
c   for they shall all know me,
d   from the smallest one to the greatest one among them
e   —oracle of YHWH—.
f   Yes, I will forgive their iniquity
g   and remember their sins no longer.

4.2. Stylistic Remarks

Bozak has made various observations on the stylistic features of Jer 31:31–34. Some additional comments may be made on contrasts within the textual unit:

1. The "new covenant" is contrasted to the old (32a).
2. The breaking of the covenant by the people of Israel (32e) is contrasted to God's liberation in the exodus out of Egypt on one hand (32cd) and by God being master on the other hand (32f).
3. It should be noted that 32e and 32f have a parallel construction, namely, pronoun, verb, object:

   32e   "They have broken the covenant."
   32f   "I am master over them."

4. "Knowing God" (or: the knowledge of God) will no longer be taught (34ab). The adverbial construction "no longer" occurs several times in the book of Jeremiah and especially in the Book of Consolation to indicate discontinuity. All these contrasts can be related to a text-internal chronology. Within the textual unit a distinction is made between "then," "now," and "later."

4.3. YHWH and His People

Within this textual unit two main actors are portrayed, namely, YHWH and his people. YHWH is construed as a singular actor, remaining the same person throughout the internal chronology. "The people" are seen as a plural subject. In reading the textual unit, we see that an identification has been made. The persons who are "now" teaching each other to know God are identified with their ancestors. The portrait of these two actors as supplied to us by the narrator and through his perspective will now be given in detail.

*Y*HWH
   "Then":
         concluded a covenant (32b)
         took the people by the hand (32c)
         took them out of Egypt (32d)
         was master over them (32f)
   "Now":
         promises a new covenant (31a)
         is master over them (32f)
   "Later":
         will conclude a new covenant (31a)
         put his law within them (33d)
         will write the covenant on their hearts (33e)
         will be God for the people (33f)
         will forgive their iniquity (34f)
         will no longer remember their sin (34g)
The People
   "Then":
         stood in a covenantal relationship with YHWH (32b)
         broke the covenantal relationship (32e)
         sinned against YHWH (34fg)
   "Now":
         still breaking the covenantal relationship (32e)
         teaching each other to know YHWH (34b)
   "Later":
         shall be a people for YHWH (31a)
         shall no longer teach each other to know YHWH (34ab)
         will all know YHWH (33e).

4.4. Sin and No More Sanction: A Conceptual Analysis

A few observations may be made here on a more conceptual level. As in Jer 30:12–17, two Transformations are implied here. Transformation I looks back to the past and can be depicted as the sum of changes that led to or were part of the exile out of the promised land. Transformation II looks forward and can be depicted as the hoped-for process that will have the return to the promised land as its outcome.

In Jer 31:31–34 both Transformations are theologically qualified. As in some other units of the Book of Consolation, Transformation I is related to the theme of "guilt." Words from this semantic field are used in 32e (to break), 34f (iniquity), and 34g (sin). Unlike the other textual units in Jeremiah 30–31, the theme of guilt is here related to the idea of an ancient covenant relationship between Yhwh and the people. Transformation II is seen in other textual units as a divine exploit on behalf of the people. As a new element—"new" in contradiction to the other textual units in Jeremiah 30–31—the relationship between Yhwh and the people that is expected to be established in the "later" period is described by the concept of a new covenant. This new covenant relationship is only partly contrary to the "old" covenant relationship. The main difference is its increased enthusiasm. The covenant relationship will no longer be something external but will be internalized at the center of one's personality. The view that Jer 31:31–34 expects "a new creation" of the human partners in covenant does not appear to be based on the immediate context within the Book of Consolation, for there is no reference to a change in the physical or psychological nature of humankind. Even the textual unit Jer 31:35–37, in which direct reference is made to the idea of creation, does not speak of a new creation at all. Rather, the adjective "new" refers to the covenant and not to humankind in Jer 31:33. Moreover, a semantic analysis of Hebrew "new" shows that the noun modified usually has the connotation of "renewed" rather than "totally new." Finally, 31:34fg says that as an outcome of, or within the framework of, the new covenant relationship, iniquity will be forgiven and sins will be remembered no longer. In my view, these two clauses express the newness of the "new covenant" relationship; beyond the earlier covenant relationship, remission of sin is introduced.

Summarizing, the events described in Transformation I are the result of divine punishment provoked by the sins of "the people." The historical realities of exile, ruination, and despair are thus interpreted as punishment for sin. *Here too, Yhwh is seen as acting with divine superior force.* Transformation II, however, shows that there is no longer punishment for human (mis)conduct.

5. Divine Reliability

The analysis of Jer 30:12–17 and 31:31–34 has shown that both textual units may be interpreted as literarily and conceptually coherent texts. However, in order to define the coherence of both units discussed, "divine changeability" has been assumed. Yнwн was interpreted to be a God who changed his mind. In an earlier phase, his punishment brought about an incurable fracture. Later he is presented as healing the wounds of his people and forgiving their sins. These two sides of God are not only implied by the two texts discussed but are also found in other units of the Book of Consolation, within the existential uncertainty caused by the destruction of Jerusalem and the exile of most Judahite citizens. It seems as though the author of the Book of Consolation is offering a model of an arbitrary God, who sometimes punishes and at other times comforts. Such a model does not help a despairing people to cope.

It should be remarked, however, that the two sets of divine acts, some related to "punishment" and some related to "consolation," are not conflated in the Book of Consolation. Rather, they are distributed in time. The first category is attributed to the past, the second to the future. This is, however, only a partial solution of the problem, since it leaves open the possibility of future acts of God in which he would arbitrarily punish his people. This possibility would be a partial annihilation of the offered consolation because it would leave the people of God with uncertainty concerning their future. In the section directly following Jer 31:31–34, a few remarks are made about the reliability of God. This section will now be discussed.

5.1. Jeremiah 31:35–37: Text and Translation

As in many other places in the book of Jeremiah, differences between the Old Greek version of the book of Jeremiah and the Masoretic Text are apparent in the Book of Consolation. Since there are some intriguing variants between Jer 31:35–37 MT and its Old Greek rendition, both texts will be given in translation:

MT Jer 31:35–37	LXX Jer 38:35–37
	"Even if the
	heaven is
	elevated into
	the heights, says the Lord,
	and if the bottom
	of the earth is lowered
	downward, I shall
	not reject the people of Israel."

35 Thus says YHWH   Thus says the Lord,
    —who gives the sun   —he who gives the sun
    as a light by day,   as a light for the day,
    and who adjusts the moon and   the moon and the stars
    the stars as a light for the night,   as a light for the night,
    who stirs up the sea,   who bawls against the sea,
    so that its waves roar,   so that its waves roar,

    YHWH of hosts is his name—:   Lord almighty is his name—:
36 "If these institutions will totter   "If these laws will cease
    before my face   before my face
    —oracle of YHWH—   —says the Lord—
    then the offspring of Israel too   then the offspring of Israel
    will cease being a nation   would cease being a nation
    before my face,   before my face,
    during all the days."   during all the days."

37 Thus says YHWH:
    "If the heavens above
    could be measured,
    and the foundations of the earth
    below
    could be fathomed,
    then I would reject
    the whole of the offspring of Israel,
    for all that they have done
    —oracle of YHWH."

With regard to text-critical matters, two problems are evident:

1. the differing order and
2. the textual deviations

The following comments will only deal with the first problem.

5.1.1. The Differing Order

There are at least two ways to explain the difference in order. The traditional approach to text-critical problems sees one text as the original (Vorlage) of the other. With regard to the MT and LXX of Jeremiah, both the order in the MT and in the Old Greek version have been regarded as authentic. In regard to the difference in order, it appears likely that two diverging collections of material related to the prophet Jeremiah circulated independently. Consequently, the question of the superiority of one version over the other is a literary-critical and redaction-critical concern, the answer to which depends on one's overall view regarding the genesis of the book of Jeremiah. The two versions of this smaller textual unit should be interpreted separately.

On the form-critical level the two versions have some elements in common and some that differ. In both versions the unit is composed of three textual elements, though differently constructed. In the Old Greek version the unit is organized in concentric symmetry. In this textual unit the hymnic depiction of the Lord as the guarantor of the regularity of the forces of nature functions as the central motivation for the oracle of salvation: that he guarantees the endurance of the people of Israel.

In the Hebrew (Masoretic) version virtually the same material is organized climactically. In this version the hymnic depiction of YHWH is the inducement for two sentences that are construed in a syntactically parallel way. Jer 31:36 expresses negatively that Israel will not cease to exist as the people of God. In the same way v. 37 states that Israel will not be rejected by YHWH. "Rejection" should be interpreted as the stronger and more theologically charged expression of God's abandoning of the covenant. Consequently, v. 37 should be regarded as an extended parallel of v. 36.

5.1.2. Conclusions

A theological conclusion may be drawn about the textual history of the unit under consideration: the rearrangement of the subject matter in the textual unit together with some textual deviations do not lead to a divergent meaning. However, the same motivation for the endurance of the new covenant is expressed in two differently modeled textual units. This somewhat tentative remark on Jer 31:35–37 (MT) leads to the conclusion that, within the composition of the Book of Consolation, in both versions, the motif of God as creator functions as an ultimate motivation for the promise of the new covenant. In both versions, though phrased differently, the firmness of God's creation and the reliability of the laws of the created order together underscore the trustworthiness of the promises of YHWH. The observation of the reliability of reality, experienced in the stability of the cycles of sun and moon and in the immutability of the stars, suggests a metaphor of divine reliability.

6. The Conceptual Coherence of Jeremiah 30–31

6.1. Jeremiah 31:31–37: Reliability and Relationship

Within the textual organization of the Book of Consolation, Jer 31:31–37 should be interpreted as a unit. This implies that the theme of divine reliability functions as a motivation for the promise of a new covenant: YHWH will stand as guarantor of the new relationship. As a syntactical analysis of 31:31–34 shows, the so-called relationship formula "I will be a God to them and they shall be to me a people" will be written "on their heart" (33fg). Both themes, reliability and relationship, may be related to the two Transformations mentioned above. They function as indicators that both sets of events are not brought about arbitrarily. The punishment was not based on divine arbitrariness. The fall of both Samaria and Jerusalem was due to the accumulation of sin and disobedience by the people of Israel and Judah. His graceful turn to the people is also not an accident, as if YHWH acted in a haphazard way. He reacted to the deeds and doings of mankind. He was bound and even limited by his relationship to Israel; in all of this he acted in a reliable way.

6.2. Jeremiah 30–31: New Hope

The Book of Consolation is in my view an exilic or perhaps early postexilic text. This implies that the textual units may be read within the framework of the existential uncertainty caused by the exile. Within that framework Transformation II functions as a symbol of hope: even after the exile YHWH would not leave his people. This theme of new hope was not only implied in the two units discussed but also in the other units of the Book of Consolation, as will be shown. To illustrate this motif, the text may be outlined as follows:

- The return to the land and the ownership of it are promised (30:1–3).
- The yoke of the oppressor will be broken (30:5–11).
- To the oppressors will befall the fate of the oppressed, and the incurable wound will be healed (30:12–17).
- The people will be as numerous as before, under a new leader (30:18–24).
- Rest and divine love are promised (31:2–6).
- The remnant of Israel will be gathered from the ends of the earth (31:7–14). Consolation and deepened divine love are offered to "Rachel" and Ephraim. The people will return to the land (31:15–22).
- There will be divine blessing and fertility in the land (31:23–25).
- There will no longer be decay and destruction; YHWH will build and plant; people will live and be personally responsible for their deeds (31:27–30).

- A new covenant relationship is offered; the reliability of reality functions as a metaphor for the divine reliability (31:31–37).
- A newly structured Jerusalem is promised as a city with ramparts (31:38–40).

These promises, which may be summarized in the words "there is hope for your future" (31:16), are all based on the conviction that YHWH is reliable. In the historical context in which a fundamental change would take place (or had already taken place) the Book of Consolation offers concrete words of divine hope on the most elementary level of life: a land to live in, fertile soil, and no oppressors. This reliable promise of a renewed relationship would certainly help people to cope with the reality they faced.

6.3. The Book of Jeremiah?

The remarks made above illustrate the conceptual coherence of the Book of Consolation. It has been suggested that chaps. 30–31 may be read as an integral whole and that there is no need for literary-critical or redaction-historical subdivisions. The question whether these two chapters are an integral part of the book of Jeremiah or an alien corpus is not easily answered and is moreover beyond the scope of this paper. A few remarks on the topic may be made here by way of conclusion.

(1) The book of Jeremiah presents itself to the reader as *a single text*. This implies that at least at one moment in the genesis of the book a redactor, editor, or author construed that book, including chaps. 30–31, as a coherent and meaningful whole.

(2) A computer concordance can easily supply a list of words and idioms common to Jeremiah 30–31 and the rest of the book of Jeremiah. Such a list might hint at common authorship. A warning must be offered, however. Probably half of the list of common words would consist of words and idioms that might be classified as "standard Hebrew," the common language of the exilic era. Moreover, the list would also contain some words with a broad semantic spectrum that are used with different meanings in the book of Jeremiah. Finally, for argument's sake, the list should be balanced by a checklist containing all words and idioms occurring in the Book of Consolation but not elsewhere in Jeremiah.

(3) A more fruitful approach would be to analyze the theological concepts and ideas in various units in the book of Jeremiah. I hope that my reading of Jeremiah 30–31 has offered the reader an example of a way that such an ancient text may be approached.

Citations from the Book of Jeremiah in the New Testament

J. W. Mazurel

Amsterdam, The Netherlands

The purpose of this essay is to study the way in which words from the book of Jeremiah are cited in the New Testament. According to the concordances, Jeremiah is named only twice in citations, in Matt 2:17 and 27:9 (though the latter quotation does not appear in the book of Jeremiah). On the other hand, additional citations from the book of Jeremiah are found in the New Testament where the name of the prophet is not indicated. Seven texts are cited in the index of Nestle-Aland's Greek New Testament that go back to the book of Jeremiah: Matt 2:18; 21:13 and parallel verses; 1 Cor 1:31; 2:9; 2 Cor 6:17; Heb 8:8–12; and 10:16–17. The first five passages will be discussed here.

1. Matthew 2:18

In the overture to his gospel, Matthew in 2:13–18 narrates the reaction to Jesus' appearance in Bethlehem in Judea: magi came to Jerusalem to worship him, asking: "Where is the king of the Jews who has been born?" Their question came to the attention of King Herod, which resulted in mass confusion in Jerusalem. After consulting with the high priests and scribes, Herod called in the magi; he sent them on to Bethlehem, where they saw the child and worshiped him. However, they ignored Herod's request to inform him after they had found the child, and so they did not return to him. When Herod realized that he had been fooled by the magi, he became enraged. This is how his true intention was revealed: he did not want to worship but to get rid of the child. He had all children aged two years and younger in Bethlehem and the surrounding area killed.

Editor's note: This essay was translated by the editor from an article entitled "Citaten uit het boek Jeremia in het Nieuwe Testament," *Amsterdamse Cahiers voor Exegese en Bijbelse Theologie* 16 (1997) 126–39.

Matthew closes his narrative with a "fulfillment citation," which relates to the actions described above. After the introductory formula, "Then was fulfilled what was spoken by Jeremiah the prophet, when he said . . ." (2:17), Matthew cites Jer 31:15:

> A voice is heard in Ramah,
> lamentation and bitter weeping:
> Rachel is weeping for her children;
> she refuses to be comforted for her children,
> because they are not.

Did Matthew allow this citation to function in a manner consistent with the intention of the author? To answer this question, the MT of Jer 31:15 must be considered. The immediate context of this verse is Jer 31:15–17:

> 16 Thus says YHWH:
>   Keep your voice from weeping,
>   and your eyes from tears,
>   for there is reward for your labor
>   —saying of YHWH.
> 17 There is hope for your future,
>   —saying of YHWH,
>   sons will return to their land.

Jer 31:15–17 is related closely to 31:18–20, which fully highlights Ephraim. This connection is evident particularly because of the central location of the verb "to hear" in both parts and because of the comforting promise with which both conclude. Moreover, the combination "to be comforted" and "to return" (vv. 15–17) uses the same verbs as the combination "(make) return" and "repent" (vv. 18–19).

The segment Jer 31:3–22 constitutes the broader context of Jer 31:15. It concentrates exclusively on Israel, the former Northern Kingdom, which is also called Ephraim and sometimes Jacob.

I deduce from the foregoing that Jer 31:15–17 deals with Israel/Ephraim. The role of Rachel supports this view. The author of the book of Jeremiah highlights her in 31:15 as a symbolic figure, as "mother" of Ephraim. The repeated expression "her sons" removes any doubt about this. These sons are the object of her lamentation. She weeps for them constantly. Just as Jacob refused to be comforted about the loss of his son Joseph (Gen 37:34ff.), Rachel refused to be comforted because "her sons are not." It appears from the call to Rachel to cease her loud weeping (Jer 31:16, motivated by a "saying of YHWH") that the sons she laments are to be found in the land of the enemy. Thus, Rachel's weeping is a "prophetic verbalization of the lament over the exile." The sons she mourns are the inhabitants of the former kingdom of Israel/Ephraim, which were exiled at the time of Shalmaneser V and Sargon II.

Those who deny that Jer 31:15–17 deals with Israel/Ephraim refer to the place where Rachel's let her voice be heard: in *ramah*. The common opinion is that the town of Ramah was intended. It appears from Jer 40:1 that Ramah was a staging area from which exiles from Jerusalem and Judah were taken to Babylon. If *ramah* would indeed indicate the place Ramah, then Jer 31:15–17 refers to the departure of Judahite exiles in 587 B.C.

But in the Old Testament the place Ramah is called *ha-ramah*; it always has the article, except in Jer 31:15 and Neh 11:33. In my view *ramah* in Jer 31:15 therefore refers to a high place where a human voice might be heard, where weeping and lamenting was done (see Jer 3:21; 9:18; 22:20). Neither do I find the argument convincing that *ramah* refers to the place Ramah because 1 Sam 10:2 refers to Rachel's grave in Zelzah, which is supposed to be located near Ramah. However, there is also the repeated assertion that Rachel's grave was near Bethlehem (Gen 35:16–20; 48:7). Quite possibly *ramah* was understood as referring to the place Ramah because of its function as a staging area for exiles to Babylon. This understanding might have come about when the different, separate prophecies in Jeremiah 30 and 31 were joined, namely, the prophecies referring to Israel/Ephraim, those dealing with Judah only and those dealing with Israel as a whole.

When Matthew named the place Ramah in the citation from Jer 31:15, he established a contact with the Judahites who were taken to Babylon. With the murder of the children at Bethlehem, he would have thought primarily of Rachel because of her grave, which was located in the vicinity. Moreover, Matthew wished to let the children's murder point to the death of Jesus, the Son of David, who was born in Bethlehem.

From the introductory formula in 2:17, it appears that Matthew understood the words of Jer 31:15 as a prophecy. By seeing the children's murder in Bethlehem as a fulfillment of it, he gave this prophecy an interpretation. He saw the description of the lament over Israel's removal into exile as an announcement, a prophetic preview of the mourning about the murder that took place in his own time. The question whether Matthew let the citation from Jer 31:15 function in a manner agreeing with the author's intention must therefore be answered in the affirmative.

2. *Matthew 21:13, Mark 11:17, and Luke 19:46*

In the New Testament, the formula "it is written" regularly introduces a citation of one or more unnamed prophets. Two citations, one of the prophet Isaiah and one of the prophet Jeremiah, are introduced thus in Mark 11:15–17 and in the parallel passages, Matt 21:12–13 and Luke 19:45–46. These short literary units, which only differ in details, describe what Jesus did when he entered the sanctuary in Jerusalem: he took action against the sellers and buyers in the Court of the Gentiles, as he used to do against demons and unclean spirits; he threw them out, because they kept themselves busy with profaning practices: the money changers transgressed the first commandment (Exod 20:3) because they brought Roman money with the image of the deified emperor into the temple. Quite likely the sellers of pigeons committed fraud by selling weak and sick animals that did not qualify for the sacrificial service (cf. Mal 1:14). For the money changers and the sellers of pigeons, Jesus' action was a catastrophe. He clarified the motivation for his action by quoting Isa 56:7: "My house shall be called a house of prayer for all peoples," adding, "But you have made it a den of robbers," an expression that was borrowed from Jer 7:11 (the only place where it occurs).

To discover the original context of this expression we need to refer to the MT of Jer 7:1–5. YHWH commissioned the prophet to go to the gate of his house and there to call on those entering to improve their ways and their doings. They needed to stop their atrocities, in the false confidence that the temple would guarantee YHWH's presence and protection at all times. Did they think they could steal, kill, and commit adultery, swear and lie, go after other gods, and then appear before the face of YHWH? Did they think they were delivered so that they might perform all these atrocities? YHWH asked the Judahites the rhetorical question whether his house had become a den of robbers in their eyes, a haven of refuge for the practitioners of these horrors. Because of everything they had done and were still doing, YHWH would make his house share the fate of the sanctuary in Shiloh and the Judahites share the fate of the Northern Kingdom. The fate of Shiloh was destruction; that of Israel/Ephraim, ruin and exile of the people. We learn that YHWH did this because of the evil the people had done. The disaster that YHWH had announced to the Judahites was clear: he would have enemies destroy his sanctuary and the city of Jerusalem and take the inhabitants in exile (Jer 7:12–15).

The preceding suggests the question whether the evangelists have adopted the customary rabbinical way of citation. The rabbis did not only refer to the scriptural word or verse, but often intended, sometimes exclusively, its context. Was this also the intention of the evangelists? Did they wish to refer hearers or readers to the entire context when they used the expression "den of robbers"?—and particularly with the announcement of disaster in Jer 7:13–15? More citations would need to be investigated to see whether this conclusion might be drawn. However, a saying of Jesus concerning the destruction of the temple as reported by the evangelists (see Matt 24:2; Mark 13:2; Luke 21:5–6) appears to argue for this conclusion.

3. 1 Corinthians 1:31

The pericope 1 Cor 1:26–31 ends with a citation from Jer 9:23[English 9:24]. Paul prefaces this passage with a discourse on the opposite pairs "wisdom of God/wisdom of the world" and "wisdom/folly." He argues that God made foolish the wisdom of the world, which does not know him, judging the preaching of the crucified Christ as foolishness. However, for the called and for those who have been delivered, Jesus the crucified is the power of God and the wisdom of God. Paul closes his discourse with the words: "For the folly of God is wiser than man, and the weakness of God is stronger than man." Subsequently, in 1:26–31 he clarifies the meaning for the called in Corinth—a congregation counting not many wise, mighty, and noble—that what is folly in the eyes of the world is chosen by God; thus he also chooses those who have nothing to boast of and who are nothing. On the other hand, he shames the wise and the strong; those who are something he brings to naught so that none can boast before God to be something by themselves. But, Paul admonishes the Corinthians, you may boast of what you are through him: "You are (called) in Christ Jesus, whom God made our wisdom, righteousness, sanctification, and redemption." To emphasize "through him," he adds the citation from Jer 9:23[English 9:24]: "as it is written, Let him who boasts, boast of the Lord."

For the context of these words, here is the MT of Jer 9:22–23[English 23–24] in translation:

> Thus says YHWH:
> Let not the wise man boast in his wisdom,
> let not the mighty man boast in his might,
> let not the rich man glory in his riches,
> but let him who boasts boast in this,

> that he understands and knows me,
> that I am YHWH,
> who does steadfast love, justice, and righteousness
> on the earth,
> for in these things I delight,
> —saying of YHWH.

In these verses the author claims that taking pride in one's possession of wisdom, power, or riches cannot be justified. Those who wish to boast, let them boast that they have insight and know YHWH as the one who shows covenant faithfulness and justice and does righteousness on the earth.

Verse 23b leaves unclear wherein YHWH finds delight: does he in "these things," that is, in the doing of covenant faithfulness, justice, and righteousness on earth, or does he rather take pleasure in "these"—in those who know him? Likely both may be intended here.

The citation in 1 Cor 1:31 may not be viewed apart from its context. A comparison of both texts shows that the apostle has borrowed the material for his discourse from Jer 9:22–23. The wise and powerful referred to there serve as a model for the wise and the strong in 1 Cor 1:27–28 and the rich for those who are something.

Paul claims that the wise and the strong will be shamed by God and that those who are something will be brought to naught. He does not give any reason for this. However, it appears from the words "so that no flesh might boast before the Lord" that the wise, the strong, and those who are something are boasting. Neither does Paul mention the content of their boasting, but we may guess that they base it on their wisdom and power.

In 1 Cor 1:30–31 Paul gives the essence of Jer 9:23[English 9:24]. He changes the order of the parts of the sentence. In Jer 9:23 the boasting about knowing YHWH stands first; thereafter, YHWH shows himself in doing covenant faithfulness, justice, and righteousness on earth. For Paul, these have become enfleshed in Christ Jesus, "whom God made our wisdom (!), our righteousness (!), our sanctification, and redemption." The fact that he had learned to know God thus (i.e., by his deeds) is the reason that he does not begin with the words "Let him who boasts, boast of the Lord" but ends with them. 1 Cor 1:27–31 makes clear the way that rabbinical literature handled citations.

4. 1 Corinthians 2:9

Paul writes in 1 Cor 2:6–9 that he speaks wisdom among the faithful, the "perfect." This is not the wisdom of the world and of its rulers but wisdom that is a mystery, the hidden wisdom of God. This wisdom is Christ (1:24) the crucified, whom God before all time destined to be the glory of the faithful. According to Paul, the following words apply to the wisdom of God:

> What no eye has seen
> nor ear heard
> nor the heart of man conceived,
> all that God has prepared
> for those who love him. (1 Cor 2:9)

This quotation is not found in the Old Testament or in extracanonical Jewish writings. It does occur a few times in the Apostolic Fathers. Often a connection with Isa 64:3[English 64:4] is made. The words "nor the heart of man conceived" are separated. They are regarded as a citation from Jer 3:16. The question is whether this view is correct. Does it find support in the context of these words? In search for an answer, we cite Jer 3:16–17:

> in those days . . .
> they shall no more say:
> "The ark of the covenant of the Lord!"
> It shall not come to mind,
> or be remembered,
> or missed;
> it shall not be made again.
> At that time Jerusalem shall be called
> "the throne of YHWH."

These words suggest that a new situation will occur in which the ark, which stands for the temple in Jerusalem, has disappeared for good. It will have become superfluous because the presence of YHWH will no longer be tied to the ark.

The question is whether Paul makes a connection between the superfluity of the temple and the crucified Christ who is God's wisdom. This does not appear to be the case; the words "it shall (not) come to mind," rather, refer to an expression common to both testaments. It is used for the arising of thoughts and considerations in the heart of man (2 Kgs 12:5[English v. 4]; Isa 65:17; Jer 3:16; 51:50; Ezek 38:10; Acts 7:23) and also in the heart of YHWH (Jer 7:31; 19:5; 32:35; 44:21).

The expression "it shall not come to mind" (1 Cor 2:9) is not a literal translation of Jer 3:16. This does not preclude Paul from having thought of this verse when he used the expression "nor the heart of man conceived." It supplements the expressions of "not seeing of the eye and not hearing of the ear" in the citation. It is suggested here that the succession of verbs in Jer 3:16 with the repeated denial was a model for Paul for the writing of 1 Cor 2:9.

5. 2 Corinthians 6:17

Paul warns the Christians in Corinth in 2 Cor 6:14–17 against the infiltration of paganism. In various ways he impresses on them that believers are not to compromise with unbelievers; there is no room for idols in the temple of God, says Paul, "for we are the temple of the living God." As proof he introduces a collection of citations that open with the formula "as God has said." The first citation is Lev 26:11a, 12, which contains the promise:

> I will walk among you,
> and I will be your God,
> and you shall be my people.

Paul applies this promise, given to Israel, to the Christian congregation and lets them act as God's people. He follows this with another citation:

> Therefore come out from them
> and separate yourself,
> says the Lord,
> do not touch the unclean. . . .

This entire situation, in which only the sequence of the parts of the verse has been altered, is derived from Isa 52:11. It calls the exiles to leave pagan and therefore unclean Babylon. Those who on the way back had to carry the holy vessels that had been robbed from the temple needed to purify themselves. Paul applied these words to the Corinthians: as the people of God, they needed to separate themselves from the pagans and their idols in order not to pollute themselves. He gave a moral-religious interpretation to the cultic words of Isa 52:11.

Only the words "come out from them" (2 Cor 6:17) were derived from Jer 51:45. In this verse the exiles are invited to leave Babylon in order to save their lives from the burning anger of YHWH. This verse, which is lacking in the LXX, does not mention a command not to touch the unclean or to cleanse themselves.

Summary and Conclusion

The manner in which the citation of Jer 31:15 functions in the story of the children's murder (Matt 2:16–18) shows that the entire context of the situation needs to be heard. In the Synoptic Gospels, the words of Jer 7:11, especially the entire context of Jer 7:13–15, presuppose familiarity by the hearers. With the Apostle Paul, the context of a citation also plays an important role: Jer 9:23 furnishes the materials for his discourse in 1 Cor 1:27–31; the structure of Jer 3:16 was probably a model for the citation in 1 Cor 2:9. In 2 Cor 6:17 Paul may have cited a part of Jer 51:45, although this is not apparent from the context.

Based on this investigation, the following conclusion may be drawn: in the Synoptics and the Pauline letters, citations that are introduced with reference to the Scriptures must not be considered separately from their context. Indeed, it seems highly likely that the respective writers intended that their citations be understood in this manner.

Bibliography

Ackroyd, P. R.
  1968   *Exile and Restoration: A Study of Hebrew Thought of the Sixth Century B.C.* London: SCM.

Baumgartner, W.
  1988   *Jeremiah's Poems of Lament.* Translated by E. E. Orton. Sheffield: Almond.

Becking, B.
  1989   "I Will Break His Yoke from off Your Neck": Remarks on Jeremiah xxx 4–11. Pp. 63–76 in *New Avenues in the Study of the Old Testament,* ed. A. S. van der Woude. Oudtestamentische Studiën 25. Leiden: Brill.

Bellis, A. O.
  1994   *The Structure and Composition of Jeremiah 50:2–51:58.* New York: Edwin Mellen.

Blank. S. H.
  1977   *Prophetic Thought: Essays and Addresses.* Cincinnati: Hebrew Union College Press.

Blenkinsopp, Joseph
  1983   *A History of Prophecy in Israel: From the Settlement to the Hellenistic Period.* Philadelphia: Westminster.

Bozak. B.
  1991   *Life "Anew": A Literary-Theological Study of Jeremiah 30–31.* Analecta Biblica 122. Rome: Pontifical Biblical Institute.

Bright, John
  1977   *Covenant and Promise.* London: SCM.
  1965   *Jeremiah: Introduction, Translation, and Notes.* Anchor Bible 21. Garden City, N.Y.: Doubleday.

Brueggemann, Walter
  1986   *Hopeful Imagination: Prophetic Voices in Exile.* Philadelphia: Fortress.
  1994   *A Social Reading of the Old Testament: Prophetic Approaches to Israel's Communal Life,* ed. Patrick D. Miller. Philadelphia: Fortress.
  1997   *Theology of the Old Testament: Testimony, Dispute, Advocacy.* Minneapolis: Fortress.
  1985   The Uncared For Now Cared For: A Methodological Consideration. *Journal of Biblical Literature* 104: 419–28.
  1988   *To Pluck Up, To Tear Down: A Commentary on Jeremiah 1–25.* Grand Rapids, Mich.: Eerdmans.
  1991   *To Build, To Plant: A Commentary on Jeremiah 26–52.* Grand Rapids, Mich.: Eerdmans.
  1998   *A Commentary on Jeremiah: Exile and Homecoming.* Grand Rapids, Mich.: Eerdmans.

Buber, Martin
  1949   *The Prophetic Faith.* New York: Macmillan.

Budde, C.
1878 Über die Capitel 50 und 51 des Buches Jeremias. *Jahrbücher für Deutsche Theologie* 23: 428–70, 529–62.

Carroll, Robert P.
1986 *Jeremiah: A Commentary.* Old Testament Library. Philadelphia: Westminster.
1979 *When Prophecy Failed: Reactions and Responses to Failure in the Old Testament Prophetic Traditions.* London: SCM.

Childs, B. S.
1979 *Introduction to the Old Testament as Scripture.* Philadelphia: Fortress.

Christensen, D. L.
1975 *Transformations of the War Oracle in Old Testament Prophecy.* Harvard Dissertations in Religion 3. Missoula, Montana: Scholars Press.

Clements, R. E.
1988 *Jeremiah: A Biblical Commentary for Teaching and Preaching.* Atlanta: John Knox.
1996 Jeremiah: Prophet of Hope. Pp. 123–41 in *Old Testament Prophecy: From Oracles to Canon.* Louisville: Westminster John Knox.
1977 Patterns in the Prophetic Canon. Pp. 42–55 in *Canon and Authority,* ed. G. W. Coats and B. O. Long. Philadelphia: Fortress.

Diamond, A. R.
1987 *The Confessions of Jeremiah in Context: Scenes of Prophetic Drama.* Journal for the Study of the Old Testament Supplement Series 45. Sheffield: JSOT Press.

Gottwald, Norman K.
1964 *All the Kingdoms of the Earth: Israelite Prophecy and International Relations in the Ancient Near East.* New York: Harper & Row.

Heschel, A. J.,
1962 *The Prophets.* 2 vols. New York: Harper & Row.

Hill, John
1999 *Friend or Foe? The Figure of Babylon in the Book of Jeremiah MT.* Leiden: Brill.

Hillers, D. R.
1964 *Treaty-Curses and the Old Testament Prophets.* Biblica Orientalia 16. Rome: Pontifical Biblical Institute.

Holladay, William L.
1986 *Jeremiah 1: A Commentary on the Book of the Prophet Jeremiah, Chapters 1–25.* Philadelphia: Fortress.
1989 *Jeremiah 2: A Commentary on the Book of the Prophet Jeremiah, Chapters 26–52.* Minneapolis: Fortress.

Janzen, J. Gerald
1973 *Studies in the Text of Jeremiah.* Cambridge: Harvard University Press.

Jong, D. de
1978 *De volken bij Jeremia.* Kampen.

Keown, Gerald L.; Scalise, Pamela J.; and Smothers, Thomas G.
1995 *Jeremiah 26–52.* Word Biblical Commentary 27. Dallas: Word.

Kessler, Martin
1968   Jeremiah 26–45 Reconsidered. *Journal of Near Eastern Studies* 27: 81–88.
1994   *Voices from Amsterdam: A Modern Tradition of Reading Biblical Narrative.* Atlanta: Scholars Press.
2003   *Battle of the Gods: The God of Israel versus Marduk of Babylon.* Studia Semitica Neerlandica 42. Assen, The Netherlands: Van Gorcum
Klein, Ralph W.
1979   *Israel in Exile: A Theological Interpretation.* Philadelphia: Fortress.
Lemke, Werner E.
1966   Nebuchadrezzar, My Servant. *Catholic Biblical Quarterly* 28: 45–50.
Levinson, J. D.
1993   *The Hebrew Bible and Historical Criticism: Jews and Christians in Biblical Studies.* Louisville: Westminster John Knox.
Long, B. O.
1981   Social Dimensions of Prophetic Conflict. *Semeia* 21: 31–53.
Lundbom, Jack
1999   *Jeremiah 1–20.* Anchor Bible 21A. New York: Doubleday.
2004a   *Jeremiah 21–36.* Anchor Bible 21B. New York: Doubleday.
2004b   *Jeremiah 37–52.* Anchor Bible 21C. New York: Doubleday.
McKane, William
1986   *A Critical and Exegetical Commentary on Jeremiah*: Vol. I. International Critical Commentary. Edinburgh: T. & T. Clark.
1996   *A Critical and Exegetical Commentary on Jeremiah: Vol. II.* International Critical Commentary. Edinburgh, T. & T. Clark.
Miskotte, K. H.
1967   *When the Gods Are Silent,* trans. J. W. Doberstein. New York: Harper & Row.
Nicholson, E. W.
1970   *Preaching to the Exiles: A Study of the Prose Tradition in the Book of Jeremiah.* Oxford: Blackwell.
O'Connor, K. M.
1988   *The Confessions of Jeremiah: Their Interpretation and Role in Chapters 1–25.* Society of Biblical Literature Dissertation Series 94. Atlanta: Scholars Press.
Overholt, Thomas W.
1968   King Nebuchadnezzar in the Jeremiah Tradition. *Catholic Biblical Quarterly* 30: 39–48.
1970   *The Threat of Falsehood: A Study in the Theology of the Book of Jeremiah.* Studies in Biblical Theology 2nd series 16. Naperville, Ill.: Allenson.
Perdue, Leo G., and Kovacs, Brian W. (eds.)
1984   *A Prophet to the Nations: Essays in Jeremiah Studies.* Winona Lake, Ind.: Eisenbrauns.
Pohlmann, Karl-Friedrich
1978   *Studien zum Jeremiabuch.* Forschungen zur Religion und Literatur des Alten und Neuen Testaments 118. Göttingen: Vandenhoeck & Ruprecht.

Polk, T.
  1984 *The Prophetic Persona: Jeremiah and the Language of the Self.* Journal for
        the Study of the Old Testament Supplement Series 32. Sheffield: Shef-
        field Academic Press.
Rad, Gerhard von
  1965 *Old Testament Theology: Vol. II.* New York: Harper & Row.
  1983 "The Confessions of Jeremiah." Pp. 88–99 in *Theodicy in the Old Testa-
        ment*, ed. J. L. Crenshaw. Issues in Religion and Theology 4. Philadel-
        phia: Fortress / London: SPCK.
Raitt, Thomas M.
  1977 *A Theology of Exile: Judgment/Deliverance in Jeremiah and Ezekiel.* Phila-
        delphia: Fortress.
Rowley, H. H.
  1963 *Men of God: Studies in Old Testament History and Prophecy.* London:
        Thomas Nelson.
Rudolph, W.
  1968 *Jeremia.* 3rd ed. Handbuch zum Alten Testament 1/12. Tübingen:
        Mohr.
Seitz, C. R.
  1989 The Prophet Moses and the Canonical Shape of Jeremiah. *Zeitschrift
        für die alttestamentliche Wissenschaft* 101: 1–15.
Seitz, C. R. (ed.)
  1988 *Reading and Preaching the Book of Isaiah.* Philadelphia: Fortress.
Skinner, John
  1948 *Prophecy and Religion: Studies in the Life of Jeremiah.* Cambridge: Cam-
        bridge University Press.
Smith, Daniel L.
  1989 *The Religion of the Landless: The Social Context of the Babylonian Exile.*
        Bloomington: Meyer-Stone.
Soderlund, Sven
  1985 *The Greek Text of Jeremiah: A Revised Hypothesis.* Journal for the Study of
        the Old Testament Supplement Series 47. Sheffield: JSOT Press.
Stulman, Louis
  1999 The Prose Sermons as Hermeneutical Guide to Jeremiah 1–25: The
        Deconstruction of Judah's Symbolic World. Pp. 34–63 in *Troubling
        Jeremiah*, ed. A. R. Pete Diamond, Kathleen M. O'Connor, and Louis
        Stulman. Journal for the Study of the Old Testament Supplement Se-
        ries 260. Sheffield: Sheffield Academic Press.
Thompson, J. A.
  1980 *The Book of Jeremiah.* Grand Rapids, Mich.: Eerdmans.
Unterman, Jeremiah
  1987 *From Repentance to Redemption: Jeremiah's Thought in Transition.* Journal
        for the Study of the Old Testament Supplement Series 54. Sheffield:
        Sheffield Academic Press.
Wright, N. T.
  1982 *The New Testament and the People of God.* Christian Origins and the
        Question of God 1. London: SPCK.

Index of Authors

195

Index of Scripture

Old Testament

New Testament

Apocrypha